FRAMING THE MARGINS   THE SOCI
AL LOGIC OF POSTMODERN CULTURE

HARPER, PHILLIP BRIAN

FRAMING THE MARGINS

FRAMING
THE
MARGINS

The Social Logic

of Postmodern

Culture

Phillip Brian Harper

New York   Oxford

OXFORD UNIVERSITY PRESS

1994

Oxford University Press

Oxford   New York   Toronto
Delhi   Bombay   Calcutta   Madras   Karachi
Kuala Lumpur   Singapore   Hong Kong   Tokyo
Nairobi   Dar es Salaam   Cape Town
Melbourne   Auckland   Madrid

and associated companies in
Berlin   Ibadan

Published by Oxford University Press, Inc.,
200 Madison Avenue, New York, New York 10016

Library of Congress Cataloging-in-Publication Data
Harper, Phillip Brian.
Framing the margins : the social logic of postmodern culture / Phillip Brian Harper.
p. cm.   Includes bibliographical references and index.
ISBN 0-19-508238-9
ISBN 0-19-508239-7 (pbk.)
1. American literature—20th century—History and criticism.
2. Postmodernism (Literature)—United States.
3. Literature and society—United States.
4. Social problems in literature.
I. Title.   PS228.P68H37   1994
810.9'1—dc20   93-1055

1   2   3   4   5   6   7   8   9

Printed in the United States of America
on acid-free paper

For Thom, **as always**

and for my parents, **at last**

ACKNOWLEDGMENTS

I am very fortunate to have benefited from the help and support of a number of people during the writing of this book, foremost among whom are the teachers who supervised the work through its early stages. Molly Hite, Henry Louis Gates, Jr., Mark Seltzer, and Sandra Siegel formed a most helpful dissertation advisory committee whose contributions were carefully balanced between warm encouragement and healthy skepticism. The late Walter Slatoff urged me to trust my intuition that there was, indeed, some relation to be articulated among the various works that I treat in the book, and so helped immensely in the shaping of my project. Walter Cohen first introduced me to the key theoretical concepts that I engage in this study, and that continue to be a focus for my critical work. Jonathan Culler read significant portions of the manuscript and offered invaluable advice regarding revision. Dorothy Mermin and Laura Brown provided crucial moral support and professional guidance, without which my work would never have come to fruition in any form. A host of additional friends and colleagues from the extended Cornell community either read and commented on various parts of the manuscript, discussed with me the general issues addressed therein, or both; these include John Ackerman, Phillip Barrish, Lauren Berlant, Suvir Kaul, Jeff Nunokawa, and, especially, Rosemary Kegl, with whom I feel a particular affinity and whose critical sensibility closely approximates my own.

The larger community of scholars and critics has also afforded me some key supporters, including Houston Baker, who generously and extensively advised me on some of the earliest portions of the manuscript and continues to encourage me in my work, and Henry Abelove, who has offered me crucial practical guidance. The Brandeis University English department provided a wonderfully congenial atmosphere in which to work, and while there I enjoyed the particular support of

Susan Staves, Eugene Goodheart, Michael T. Gilmore, John Burt, Mary Campbell, William Flesch, Helena Michie, Paul Morrison, and Rosemarie Thomson. Continued encouragement and professional advice has been forthcoming from my colleagues at Harvard, particularly Philip Fisher, Barbara Johnson, Kwame Anthony Appiah, and Henry Finder.

The formulation of the ideas presented in this volume benefited greatly from presentations and discussions at the second Summer Institute for the Study of the Avant-Gardes at Harvard University, in which I participated in 1989. I am grateful to Institute directors Susan Suleiman and Alice Jardine for giving me the opportunity to take advantage of this resource, to my fellow participants in the institute, who offered keen critical insights about the issues we addressed, and to the National Endowment for the Humanities for funding my enrollment in the program. A portion of the book was written while I was on a Ford Foundation Minority Postdoctoral Fellowship in 1990 and 1991, for which support I am very appreciative. Marjorie Garber and the staff of Harvard's Center for Literary and Cultural Studies—Rebecca Monroe Hankins and Herrick Wales—were exceedingly helpful in providing me with material resources and institutional support during the tenure of this fellowship.

A portion of Chapter 4 was presented at a 1989 MLA special session on New Historicism, and I am indebted to my co-panelists, Lee Heller, Emory Elliott, and Eric Sundquist, for their useful responses to the material. A shorter version of Chapter 5 appeared in *Black American Literature Forum* 23:4 (Winter 1989).

I am most grateful to the people who assisted me in getting the book in final form, including the staff at Oxford University Press, especially my editor, Elizabeth Maguire, and her assistant, Susan Chang. My readers for the press, Jonathan Arac and Andrew Ross, offered extremely helpful suggestions for revision and refinement. Tim Blackburn generously consulted on matters of design, and Brett Bourbon and Eve Raimon proofread the book with startling efficiency. Production costs were covered in part by the Rollins/Robinson funds of the Harvard English department.

It probably goes without saying that the people I name here have helped me not just by offering specific advice at discrete moments, but by constituting a generally supportive community in which I could pursue my undertaking. Most central in that community is Thom Freedman, whose wit and warmth have sustained me over the past twelve years, and with whom I am privileged to enjoy a most companionate partnership; I thank him above all others.

CONTENTS

FRAMING THE MARGINS

INTRODUCTION

The Postmodern, the Marginal,

and the Minor

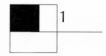

Postmodernism and the Decentered Subject

This book takes as a primary object of interrogation current theories on the nature of postmodernism as both social phenomenon and cultural praxis. Since at least the early 1980s, commentators from a wide range of disciplines have identified the postmodern condition with a heightened consciousness about the problematic nature of human subjectivity. To characterize it very roughly, postmodernist theory suggests that our sense of the individual human psyche as an integrated whole is a necessary misconception, and that various technological, economic, and philosophical developments of the late twentieth century demonstrate to us the psyche's fundamentally incoherent and fragmentary, or "decentered," nature. This decenteredness is manifested in the cultural realm through a number of signal effects and practices; in particular, characteristic fiction of the postmodern era thematizes psychic decenteredness in both its narrative structures and its depiction of the human subject.

It is this latter claim about postmodern fiction's presentation of a decentered subject that comprises the immediate object of my inquiry here. My interest lies not in disputing the validity of this characterization—indeed, I find it generally convincing—but rather in correlating this aspect of postmodernist fiction with comparable effects in other fictional modes. For if postmodernist fiction foregrounds subjective fragmentation, a similar decenteredness can be identified in U.S. novels written prior to the postmodern era, in which it derives specifically from the socially marginalized and politically disenfranchised status of the populations treated in the works. To the extent that such populations have experienced psychic decenteredness long prior to its generalization throughout the culture during the late twentieth century, one might say that the postmodern era's preoccupation with fragmented subjectivity represents the "recentering" of the culture's focus on issues that have always concerned marginalized constituencies.

And yet, as will become clear shortly, my main objective is not to make an original claim for the ways that fictions of social marginality prefigure postmodern decenteredness. Indeed, the approximation of postmodern subjective fragmentation to the decentered condition of marginalized groups has already constituted a basic tenet among many theorists of social and cultural difference for the last several years. For instance, in her 1990 volume *Yearning,* bell hooks writes that "[t]he overall impact of postmodernism is that many other groups now share with black folks a sense of deep alienation, despair, uncertainty, loss of a sense of grounding even if it is not informed by shared circumstance."[1] My aim with this book is to substantiate such claims as hooks makes about socially marginalized groups' anticipatory experience of postmodern "uncertainty," but also—and more importantly—to suggest that marginalized groups' experience of decenteredness is itself a largely unacknowledged factor in the "general" postmodern condition.

This condition has, of course, already been the subject of a large body of theoretical work, and while it is neither necessary nor practicable here to provide a complete redaction of the extant materials, it will be very useful to consider briefly a few of the founding essays in the current debate. Such a review will provide us with a sense of how the politics of postmodernism has been conceived so far; indicate the degree to which the notion of subjective decenteredness is implicated in that conception, even when it does not constitute a dominant term in the discussion; and substantiate my claim that the experiences of socially marginalized groups implicitly inform the "general" postmodern condition without being accounted for in theorizations of it.

In her wide-ranging study on *The Politics of Postmodernism,* Linda Hutcheon claims that "[t]he debate about postmodernity . . . seems to have begun with the exchange on the topic of modernity between Jürgen Habermas and Jean-François Lyotard"—an exchange that, as Hutcheon suggests, was quickly complicated by the subsequent commentary of Fredric Jameson.[2] Given the originary status that has been granted to these three theorists' work on the postmodern condition, their formulations provide us with a good place to begin an investigation of the terrain onto which most considerations of the phenomenon have ventured.

As Hutcheon suggests, an examination of these formative theorizations of postmodernity inevitably leads us to questions about the nature of modernity, since it is largely the problematic of the distinction between the two that animates the critical forays of our theorists, particularly Habermas. In his essay "Modernity versus Postmodernity"—which was delivered as a lecture in both Frankfurt (1980) and New York (1981) before being published in the United States in 1981 (under the title cited above) and again in 1983 (as "Modernity—An Incomplete Project")—Habermas characterizes modernity as a motivated undertaking based in the Enlightenment impulse to provide for "the rational organization of everyday social life."[3] This rational organization would follow from the establishment of effective communicative interaction among the three spheres of "objective science, universal morality and law, and autonomous art," which, in the context of early modernity, had been developed as specialized realms "according to their inner logic" (9). By the twentieth century, however, progress toward the modernist objective had been preempted by the conception of science, morality, and art as not merely *differentiated* but *autonomous* spheres, cut off from "the hermeneutics of everyday communication" (9). This disengagement not only renders the specialized realms of activity ineffectual in the promotion of social progress but actually implicates them in the detrimental effects of a "reified everyday praxis" (11). Habermas identifies as *postmodern* the acquiescence to or embracement of the disengaged autonomy that characterizes the specialized realms of human activity in the contemporary era. That disengagement itself manifests as decenteredness in that, if there is no effective interplay among the different spheres of activity, then neither can there be any centralized "legitimating" narrative that comprises them all; but insofar as social progress for Habermas depends on just such a (modernistic) synthesizing vision, postmodernist decenteredness presents itself to him as a fundamentally conservative phenomenon to be vigorously resisted.

In pointed opposition to Habermas, Jean-François Lyotard rejects the idea of effective, "transparent" communication among the various spheres of human activity, considering it as based on a conception of "consensus" that is both false and dangerous in its tendency toward totalization.[4] For a means through which to preempt the misguided "desire for a return of terror" (82) that he sees evidenced in the Habermasian call for communal norms, Lyotard looks specifically to avant-garde art, which effectively disrupts "the solace of good forms" that lulls consumers into a collective nostalgia for an unattainable unity (81). This disruption is effected through the avant-garde's continually reminding us of the fundamental gap that potentially characterizes our cognitive experience—a gap that Lyotard suggests is best theorized by Immanuel Kant in his description of the sublime. Paraphrasing Kant, Lyotard asserts that the "sentiment" of the sublime

> takes place . . . when the imagination fails to present an object which might, if only in principle, come to match a concept. . . . We can conceive the infinitely great, the infinitely powerful, but every presentation of an object destined to "make visible" this absolute greatness or power appears to us painfully inadequate. Those are Ideas of which no presentation is possible. . . . They can be said to be unpresentable. (78)

The effect of avant-garde art, then, is to recall for us, through "the questions [it] hurl[s] at the rules of image and narration" (79) the gap between the conceivable and the presentable that founds the experience of the sublime—or, as Lyotard puts it, "to present the fact that the unpresentable exists" (78)—thus awakening us to the falseness of the notion of effective "correspondence" that must found any principle of "universal consensus" (77). Such art, proclaims Lyotard, "I shall call modern" (78), which raises the question of what constitutes the *post*-modern in his schema.

   The place and function of Lyotard's postmodernism become clear once we recognize that, given the conditions for the reception of art in the late-twentieth-century context, he is compelled to reckon with the rapid metamorphosis of modernist innovation into static convention. Tracing the quick succession of new visual-artistic strategies that emerged during the first half of the century—from Cézanne to Picasso and Braque to Duchamp to Buren—Lyotard remarks that "[a]ll that has been received, if only yesterday . . . , must be suspected. . . . In an amazing acceleration, the generations precipitate themselves" (79). Thus, the salutarily jarring effect of any given modernist strategy, having been mitigated by its inevitable conventionalization and general acceptance, must be continually renewed by dint of an impulse that has already assimilated the proper function of modernism itself. This impulse continually to renew the modernist "shock" constitutes the postmodern, in Lyotard's conception, so that, as he puts it, the postmodern "is undoubtedly a part of the modern. . . . A work can become modern only if it is first postmodern. Postmodernism thus understood is not modernism at its end but in the nascent state, and this state is constant" (79). Evidently, Lyotard stakes a great deal on the ability of work in the cultural realm to awaken us to the realities of the sociopolitical realm since, in his view, the postmodern "avant-gardes are perpetually flushing out artifices of presentation which make it possible [wrong-fully] to subordinate thought to the gaze" (79), thus freeing our intellectual capacity for critical engagement with hard political facts.

While this conception of postmodernism salvages it as a politically progressive practice, it also obviously privileges it as a specifically *cultural* activity. As Fredric Jameson puts it in his foreword to *The Post-modern Condition*, Lyotard's "commitment to cultural and formal innovation still valorizes culture and its powers in much the same spirit in which the Western avant-garde has done so since the fin de siècle" (xvi). Commenting further on this aspect of Lyotard's theory, Jameson indicates the direction of his own thought regarding postmodernism, as he suggests that Lyotard's

> assimilation of postmodernism to [the] older conception of high mod-ernism and its negative, critical, or revolutionary vocation deproble-matizes a far more interesting and complex situation, which is part of the dilemma posed by "late capitalism" (or consumer or postin-dustrial society, etc.) in those other areas of science and technology, production, social change, and the like. (xvi–xvii)

In his own highly influential consideration of postmodern culture, Jameson links it specifically to the conditions of late capitalism in the United States, asserting both that "aesthetic production today has become integrated into commodity production generally" and that "this whole global, yet American, postmodern culture is the internal and superstructural expression of a whole new wave of American military and economic domination throughout the world."[5] Consequently, for Jameson postmodernism is neither merely a social–philosophical attitude nor simply a culturo-aesthetic strategy, either of which would be voluntaristically applauded or condemned; rather, it is a fundamental datum of our existence under late-twentieth-century capitalism, functioning as a "cultural dominant" that manifests itself in many, though not all, cultural productions of the period.

That manifestation most characteristically inheres in what Jameson calls a "new kind of flatness or depthlessness, a new kind of superficiality in the most literal sense" (60), which marks signal works of the era, and which is betokened by an evident "waning of affect" (61) in cultural productions of the time. This affective diminution in turn suggests postmodernism's rendering of a "fundamental mutation . . . in the disposition of the subject" (60), which Jameson traces through two particular distinctive features of postmodern culture: the reconceptual-ization of the historical past as merely raw material for pastiche rather than a meaningful referent in relation to which we would seek to understand our own moment, and "the breakdown of the [linguistic] signifying chain" (71) such that the referential qualities of language are eclipsed by its status as a collection of "pure material Signifiers" (72) that indicate no deeper "reality." The failure of history and language to function any longer as referential phenomena signals the inability of the human subject to orient itself in relation to the objective world, and particularly in relation to the multinational network of late capitalism, which Jameson suggests functions as the contemporary apotheosis of the Kantian sublime.

The final sections of Jameson's essay consider the possibility of a politically contestatory art in the era of postmodernism, given the lack of "critical distance" that now characterizes the relation of culture to the socioeconomic realm due to the former's thorough permeation by the logic of the marketplace (85). Jameson's ultimate proposal is that postmodern art might in a sense actually achieve its political edge through that logic, by providing consumers with conceptual models, or "cognitive maps," of the new socioeconomic terrain that we must daily negotiate—indicating to us our position with respect to the multinational–capitalist world order so that we might mount a resistance to it out of an appropriately heightened political consciousness (89–92).

Whatever their differences, Habermas, Lyotard, and Jameson all recognize fragmented or decentered experience as a constituent of the postmodern condition. Habermas's idea that postmodernity consists in the ramified nature of human activity such that it can no longer be comprised in an overarching metanarrative is an acknowledgment of its decentered quality, as I have already suggested. Lyotard, in theorizing the postmodern as approximating the experience of the Kantian sublime—which is itself founded on a sort of cognitive gap, the difference between our ability to conceive of certain ideas and our inability to represent them—specifies subjective disjunction and fragmentation as key factors in the postmodern condition. And Jameson's sense that the contemporary period is characterized by the absence of a referential standard in relation to which the individual human subject might orient itself implies a sort of dispersal of that subject among the various "superficial" signifiers that now alone constitute objective reality. Indeed, in distinguishing the effects of the postmodern condition from those of modernism, Jameson specifically notes that, in the shift from the earlier to the later epoch, "the alienation of the subject is displaced by the fragmentation of the subject" (63).

Framing the Margins

That fragmentation, furthermore, is considered by all three commentators to be profoundly politically significant, representing, for Habermas, a fundamentally conservative development in contemporary social life, for Lyotard, a progressive strategy of demystification, and, for Jameson, the expression of late capitalist logic. However differently they might interpret the political meaning of subjective fragmentation, though, all our theorists conceive of that meaning in terms of macrolevel social and economic structures, leaving aside considerations of more contingent political phenomena, in particular those having to do with the social identities of the various subjects who manifest fragmentation in the postmodern context. This omission makes for some notable lacunae in the theoretical work, as we can see by considering more closely one aspect of Jameson's exposition.

As an objective emblem for the psychic disorientation he claims characterizes postmodern subjectivity, Jameson posits the "postmodern hyperspace" of contemporary building design, which he considers as a "mutation in built space itself" that the human collectivity—itself not yet equipped to negotiate this new terrain—must confront according to apparently random contingencies: "My implication is that *we ourselves,* the human subjects *who happen into this space,* have not kept pace with that evolution" (80; my emphasis). Thus, through his use of the collective pronoun and his suggestion of the chance nature of the encounter with postmodern architectural structures, does Jameson indicate the *general* quality of the human experience with contemporary hyperspace.

For the sake of illustration, Jameson becomes more specific, identifying John Portman's *Bonaventure* Hotel in Los Angeles as an exemplar of this architecture that, in the repudiation of spatial perspective effected by its monstrous symmetry, vast interiors, and confusing network of elevators and escalators, "transcend[s] the capacities of the individual human body to locate itself, to organize its immediate surroundings perceptually, and cognitively to map its position in a mappable external world" (83). In order to impress upon us the extremely disconcerting effect of this hotel on those who enter it, Jameson takes us on a sort of verbal tour of the complex, the presentation of which quickly alerts us to inherent problems with the generalizing rhetoric with which he had characterized the hyperspace experience:

> The entryways of the *Bonaventur[e]* are as it were lateral and rather backdoor affairs: the gardens in the back admit you to the sixth floor of the towers, and even there you must walk down one flight to find the elevator by which you gain access to the lobby. Meanwhile, what

9

The Postmodern, the Marginal, and the Minor

one is still tempted to think of as the front entry, on Figueroa, admits
you, baggage and all, onto the second-storey shopping balcony, from
which you must take an escalator down to the main registration desk.
(81)

Even this short excerpt from Jameson's description is enough to illustrate one of its most interesting rhetorical features: As a means of providing us with a sense of immediate experience, it is characterized by
a colloquial usage of the second-person pronoun, the supposed generic reference of which—emphasized by the "slip" to the pronominal
"one" at the beginning of the second sentence—is completely belied
by certain activities and attributes ascribed to the hypothetical "you"
under consideration. That is to say that the "you" whom Jameson has
in mind is no generalized entity, but rather one armed with "baggage
and all" who clearly seeks to check in at the hotel's "main registration
desk"—a "you," in other words, who has sufficient means to travel to
and stay in a hotel such as the *Bonaventure* in the first place.

Evidently, then, there is a class politics operative among those who
"happen into" the *Bonaventure* complex, which is not at all to say that
only people of means enter into the space. There are, after all, scores
of employees who toil there daily, ministering to the needs of the hotel
guests or the customers in the adjacent stores. Jameson's tour, however, posits our experience of the space specifically in terms of the
moneyed consumer, thereby putting a particular spin on his analysis
of the hyperspace experience. It isn't completely inappropriate that
Jameson should take this approach; part of his point, after all, is that
the culture of late capitalism has developed along a specifically *consumerist* logic. Nonetheless, the category of labor still does obtain in
the late-twentieth-century service economy, and the experiences of labor should not, I think, be assimilated to those of the consumer where
a clear distinction can be drawn between the two.

This is not to suggest that the service workers in the *Bonaventure* do
not suffer the same architecturally induced disorientation as the paying
visitors to the complex, but rather that the significance of that disorientation is different for the two constituencies; if, for instance, as Jameson notes, "it has been obvious, since the very opening of the hotel in
1977, that nobody could ever find any of [the] stores" in the complex
(83), this accrues to the mere inconvenience of the patrons, while it
actually impedes the staff in performing the tasks on which it depends
for its livelihood. It seems to me that it is the specific import of different
constituencies' fragmented experience in the postmodern context that
has been elided in most general theoretical considerations of postmod-

ernism, which don't take into account social identity as a pertinent micro-level political contingency.

This gap in the theorization of the postmodern can be discerned as well in one of Jameson's more general propositions regarding the "de-centered subject," which appears in a parenthetical consideration of the various ways of accounting for the emergence of such a subjectiv-ity in the postmodern context:

> (Of the two possible formulations of this notion—the historicist one, that a once-existing centred subject, in the period of classical capi-talism and the nuclear family, has today in the world of organiza-tional bureaucracy dissolved; and the more radical poststructuralist position for which such a subject never existed in the first place but constituted something like an ideological mirage—I obviously incline towards the former; the latter must in any case take into account something like a "reality of the appearance.") (63)

It appears logical enough to juxtapose the atemporal quality of the poststructuralist position against the contextual specificity dictated by the historicist one, but when we consider the case of a number of socially marginalized and politically disenfranchised groups in the United States, it becomes clear that a sort of timelessness is actually inscribed within the historicist analysis: Granting the historicist claim for "a once-existing centred subject," it must also be acknowledged that, for cer-tain groups in the United States—people of African descent, for in-stance—the historical status of such a subjectivity is precisely that of *never having existed,* due to the historical distribution of the power to conceive of oneself as a centered, whole entity. Jameson's positing of the historicist perspective as fundamentally opposed to a conception of the centered subject as never having existed indicates a deep fault in the theory of the postmodern subject, an oblivion into which the experiences of marginalized populations have been cast, effectively untheorized.[6]

Clearly then, though I say above that I find "generally convincing" the notion that postmodernism is characterized by the presentation of a decentered human subjectivity, I am not convinced that most theo-retical or critical accounts adequately engage certain key sociopolitical factors in that decenteredness. It is also clear, too, that to expound on those factors—as I seek to do in this study—is necessarily to revise the received idea of what constitutes the subjective fragmentation that characterizes the postmodern era. Rather than conceiving that frag-mentation as deriving solely from the various technological, economic, and philosophical developments that I cite above as reorienting our idea of human subjectivity in the late twentieth century, I would like to suggest that postmodern decenteredness may actually be a function of the increasing implication in the "general" culture of what are usually thought of as socially marginal or "minority" experiences. This means that my work here is characterized by, on the one hand, an acceptance of some of the terms and concepts that already have currency in the discourse on postmodernism, and, on the other hand, the introduction of concerns that will actually constitute a challenge to our understanding of those terms and concepts, thereby transforming them even as I apply them in my analysis. Such is the ineluctable logic of my undertaking, indicating the necessarily dialectical nature of postmodern critique. I proceed in my own version of that critique by examining fictional representations of the experiences of marginalized groups alongside postmodernist depictions of fragmented subjectivity in order to explicate a relation between the two, thus both broadening our conception of the political significance of the postmodern condition and making more specific our discussion of it. Before I embark on the close readings that constitute the major portion of my study, however, it is necessary to clarify the meanings—unstable as they will undoubtedly prove to be—of two terms on which it largely depends.

Social Marginality and Minor Literature

If the term "social marginality"—which I have used very freely in the foregoing pages—is highly problematic, this is chiefly because it is well-nigh oxymoronic: On the one hand, the idea of "marginality" depends on the notion of a fixed "center" in relation to which it derives its meaning; on the other hand, it is precisely one of the lessons of postmodernity—promulgated in the teachings of poststructuralist theory—that the disposition of various subjects in a social entity is anything but fixed. It is clear, however, despite what we know "theoretically," that certain individuals have less access than others to political power in contemporary U.S. society, based on the configuration of their "identities" and other factors that mark them socially. The question is how to reconcile the simplifying designation for this phenomenon, "social marginality" (which, despite its problems and largely because of its wide currency, is extremely useful), with the complicated and unstable nature of lived power relations in the context under question. In his

introduction to *Out There: Marginalization and Contemporary Culture,*
Russell Ferguson articulates the problem this way:

> When we say marginal, we must always ask, marginal to what? But
> this question is difficult to answer. The place from which power is
> exercised is often a hidden place. When we try to pin it down, the
> center always seems to be somewhere else. Yet we know that this
> phantom center, elusive as it is, exerts a real, undeniable power over
> the whole social framework of our culture, and over the ways that
> we think about it. Audre Lorde calls this center the mythical norm,
> defined as "white, thin, male, young, heterosexual, Christian and fi-
> nancially secure."[7]

While the "mythical" (that is to say, socially constructed) nature of this
norm is undeniable, its hegemony—or what we might call "political
centeredness"—is demonstrated by the fact that, nonetheless, persons
who deviate from any one of the characteristics that it comprises are
apt to be relatively less politically empowered than those (however few
they may be) who conform to all of them, whatever *psychic* decenteredness these latter might experience in the postmodern era. At the
same time, there are bound to be power differentials among the "de-
viants" themselves, which derive from the variedness of their relations
to the characteristics of the "norm," and which alter with changes in
social context, as Marcia Tucker suggests when she says that "through
shifts in position, any given group can be ignored, trivialized, rendered
invisible and unheard, perceived as inconsequential, de-authorized,
'other,' or threatening, while others are valorized."[8]

Thus, given the complicated nature of the disposition of power in
our society, my use of the term "social marginality" throughout this
study evokes two different but related phenomena: (1) the formation
and function of constituencies whose deviation from the practically
centered "mythical norm"—particularly in terms of race, gender, or
sexual orientation—renders them relatively powerless in many social
contexts; and (2) the "shifts in position" whereby even more contingent factors are implicated in the production of power differentials;
that of "social class" is of particular interest for me here. While the
difference between these ways of accounting for social marginality ultimately has little effect on my analysis of the phenomenon and its
relation to postmodernism, it does have ramifications for the ways we
identify the politics of marginality as operative in the literature under
consideration.

To the degree that any work of fiction is realistic—and even the

The Postmodern, the Marginal, and the Minor

stylistic innovations of postmodernism, like those of modernism before it, do not necessarily dissociate it from all the effects of realist "reflection"—to that degree it engages the complexities of social relations as they are lived in the world beyond it. Thus we can see recapitulated in such literature the inequities that characterize the society we inhabit, not because these constitute the primary subject matter of the fiction but because we bring to the work a knowledge of the significance of certain social configurations based on our own lived experience of them. Consequently, for example, any female character depicted in a fictional work can potentially be construed as a marginalized entity based on what we know about women's relative powerlessness in society, regardless of her position as represented in the fiction. This would undoubtedly be the primary way of interpreting a work of literature as engaging the politics of social marginality.

At the same time, a work of fiction presents its own world, potentially characterized by its own principles of social differentiation that may not exactly correspond to those by which we live. Thus it is possible for a novel to manifest a politics of marginality based on the social identities and contingent positional shifts that characterize the fictive world, with the terms of those phenomena deriving specifically within that world. Such a manifestation, while less obviously reflective of our own political "reality," is no less implicated in the phenomenon I am examining than those based in our experiential sense of "real-life" social stratification. Indeed, the very existence of such fictively produced examples of social marginality usefully suggests the degree to which social power differentials, *in general,* are discursively constituted. Thus, in addition to analyzing how different works of fiction represent the experiences of constituencies whom we know to be socially marginalized in lived reality due to their deviation from the mythical norm, I also find it useful to consider as social marginalization the process whereby certain groups in the world of a given fictional work are rendered less powerful than others.

Thus I employ a sort of dual strategy by which to read the politics of social marginality as operative in the works I examine. As might be expected, these two methods of reading are often utilized in tandem in an attempt to account for the extremely complex ways that literature engages the sociopolitical contexts in which it is produced and interpreted. Yet the objective is always the same: to identify as clearly as possible the various types of social marginality that are thematized in the works under consideration and that constitute, I argue, if not the

recognized *subject matter* of postmodern fiction, certainly the informing *social text* of postmodernist practice.

Having formulated a method for delineating a literary work's engagement with the politics of marginality, it remains to determine an
appropriate literary-critical category in reference to which such engagement can be most productively analyzed and understood. For
postmodernist fiction—the genre in relation to which I want to consider what we might call "literature of marginality"—there has already
been established a clear direction for critical inquiry, based on the
widespread notion that the principal subject matter of postmodernist
literature is in fact the decenteredness of the postmodern experience
itself. This idea was suggested as early as 1973, when Gerald Graff
posited the "dissolution of ego-boundaries" as a primary function of
postmodernist art.[9] Over the ensuing decade, this notion was codified
as a defining tenet in the theory of postmodern literature, culminating
in Ihab Hassan's famous and problematic 1982 list of the "Differences" between modernism and postmodernism (the latter thematizes
"deconstruction" rather than "totalization," "absence" rather than
"presence," "silence" rather than "logos," and "dispersal" rather than
"centering"),[10] and allowing for the establishment of a veritable canon
of postmodernist authors, to which I allude further in chapter 6. Thus
the terms for discussion of postmodernist fiction are fairly well set. As
for fiction that depicts the experiences of marginalized populations, I
have found it useful to consider such work in relation to a concept of
"minor" literature that it would now be helpful to explicate somewhat.

By far the most extensive recent consideration of "minor literature"
as a critical category deployed in the construction of U.S. literary history is Louis Renza's *"A White Heron" and the Question of Minor
Literature.* Comprising a sustained analysis of a short story by Sarah
Orne Jewett, Renza's book represents an attempt

> to focus on minor literature *as* a question, . . . momentarily suspend-
> ing canonical judgments, [so as to] give an account of 'A White Heron'
> . . . as . . . striving to elude [prevailing canonical] criteria in order
> to retain its "dull little life" or minor literary value.[11]

Thus Renza is concerned to elaborate for apparently willfully "minor"
works a mode of critical recognition that does not implicate them in
variously ascribed aspirations to the status of the literarily "major." As
a preparation for this undertaking, he reviews the critical tools prof-
fered by previous considerations of the function of "minor literature,"

but finds all of the projects he examines to manifest "tendencies to impose paradigms reflecting literary and/or ideological ambitions of their own" (xxix). Moreover, it becomes clear that, along with the anxious pretensions to literary significance that undergird them (in the case of work by Leslie Fiedler, Northrop Frye, Harold Bloom, and Roland Barthes) or the ideological agendas that inform them (as with the Marxist positions of Jameson or Terry Eagleton, and the "anti-Oedipal" ones of Gilles Deleuze and Félix Guattari), these theoretical expositions of minor literature manifest not a motivated reckoning with lesser works on their own terms but, on the contrary, an irreducible need to consider them precisely in relation to the canon of major literature whose criteria Renza suggests the minor works strive to evade in the first place. As Renza puts it,

> [t]he critical wish to regard minor literature from a non-canonical perspective collides with criticism's . . . "power" relation to such literature. . . .
> In short, by definition and simply in its attempting to define minor literature as a datum of literary experience, criticism is condemned to interpret it in canonical terms. (39)

The only way to avoid this doom is for criticism of minor literature to undermine purposefully its own foundation in canonical criteria, thereby assuming the same "minor" condition as its critical object. Renza sees this as a matter of necessity:

> Clearly, then, what we need to imagine is a minor criticism of minor literature. Such a criticism would have to (self-)deconstruct its canonical tendencies in interpreting minor literary texts. . . .
> In short, a minor criticism of minor literature entails the critical intention to deny canonicity unselfconsciously. (41)

And yet, to deny canonicity effectively in the way that Renza proposes would necessarily entail opting for some alternative condition essentially unimplicated in the demands of the canonical. This is an impossible undertaking to the degree that the alternative to which Renza aspires—motivated minorness—derives precisely in relation to the canonically major. Renza himself gestures toward this fact when he notes that "'minor literature' serves as a conservative justification for an established if variable concept of 'major literature' " (3), but while this formulation addresses the interdependency of "minor" and "major" literatures at the functional level, it does not reckon with the degree to which the two categories are actually *constituted* through that very interdependency. As Abdul JanMohamed and David Lloyd put it in their theorization of "minority discourse" (in which they implicitly critique Renza by their unacknowledged appropriation of his phrase), " '[b]ecoming minor' is not a question of essence . . . but a question of position: a subject-position that in the final analysis can be defined only in 'political' terms." [12]

According to this view, not only does Renza's project of apprehending minor literature in purposefully minor terms become invalidated, since it seeks to deny the positional logic by which the minor is defined in the first place, but those commentators whose ideological concerns Renza sees as precluding the sound theorization of minor literature become key to our understanding of it. JanMohamed and Lloyd themselves specifically invoke Deleuze and Guattari (9–10), and insofar as these latter are interested, as I am, in understanding the significance of "minority praxis" (Renza, 35), they seem to offer the most useful terms through which to consider minor literature's sociopolitical significance.

In their book *Kafka: Toward a Minor Literature,* Deleuze and Guattari assert that "[t]he three characteristics of minor literature are the deterritorialization of language, the connection of the individual to a political immediacy, and the collective assemblage of enunciation." [13] They then immediately go on: "We might as well say that minor no longer designates specific literatures but the revolutionary conditions for every literature within the heart of what is called great (or established) literature" (18). It is clear from this elucidation of minor literature's revolutionary character—as well as from their references specifically to "*a* minor literature"—that Deleuze and Guattari are interested in theorizing the status of a body of literature that is already recognizable as performing a particular political function in relation to "majority" culture. They do not engage works whose minorness seems to consist, first of all, in their lack of any alignment with similarly nonmajor productions, but more precisely in their repudiation of any motivated relation to the criteria of majority culture. Renza is thus accurate when he says that

> [t]he Deleuzian privileging of a politicized, rhetorically inverted minor literature . . . thus excludes a minor literature which does not show it can "hate all literature by masters." Without any question, Deleuze and Guattari's antioedipal schema would lead us to devalue further what we could term a bourgeois or oedipean brand of minor literature. (36)

As is undoubtedly evidenced in the foregoing discussion, however, I am not interested in theorizing minor literature, *per se*, or in accounting comprehensively for every condition of literary minorness; rather, I want to consider the function of minor literature as a critical category through and in which the sociopolitical import of various literary works has historically been contained. Consequently, the critical fate of "bourgeois or oedipean" minor literature does not particularly concern me here. What the approach of Deleuze and Guattari does allow, conversely, is for me to consider as functionally aligned literary works whose politically contestatory nature already seems clear to me—in other words, to consider as *similarly minor* works whose minorness, according to bourgeois critical assessments, had been seen as deriving from *diverse* conditions.

Aside from specific aesthetic judgments, the validity of whose grounding is extremely difficult to assess (though they are not any the less powerful for all that difficulty), any number of general factors might accrue to a given literary work's designation as "minor." For instance, a work might be subject to depreciation based on quantitative criteria: It is itself too short (though it may be "aesthetically excellent") to warrant designation as a major work; or it has been produced by an author whose complete oeuvre is slim and who has personally, therefore, been deemed of minor importance to the tradition. Alternatively, qualitative factors may conspire to a work's designation as minor: It manifests an experimental style that has not issued in any significant development in literary practice generally, or it belongs to a genre that is itself considered to be a lesser mode of literary expression (satire, for instance). All of the works I consider in this study as thematizing experiences of social marginality could be characterized by at least one of the foregoing charges. And yet, the sheer variety of the works' manifestation of these factors, along with their complicated relation to other criteria of literary judgment, militates against the works' collective positioning in a stable category of "minor literature," according to the terms of bourgeois criticism.

It is possible, for instance, that a work that is considered minor owing to its status as its author's solitary production is—based on its accession to other standard criteria such as "breadth and depth of vision"—accorded recognition as a major work for the purpose of inclusion in the syllabus of a college survey course. Such discrepancies would lead to argument about my designation as "minor" some of the works I examine in this book. Any objections to that designation necessarily fall away, however, when we adduce the definition of minor literature posited by Deleuze and Guattari. If, as I claim, the works that constitute my primary objects of study here all thematize the collective experiences of populations whose political disenfranchisement has resulted in the radically imperfect discursive constitution of their subjectivities, then they necessarily meet the criteria of linguistic deterritorialization, political immediacy, and collective enunciation that found the category of minor literature according to Deleuze and Guattari. Thus, "minor literature" becomes a useful and meaningful designation for a body of works whose only similarity—over against their disparate stylistic strategies and narrative concerns—is their engagement with various types of social marginality.

Modernist Alienation/Postmodern Fragmentation

The categories of social marginality that I treat here are the standard ones for contemporary cultural criticism, reflecting political disenfranchisement due to class status, gender, sexual orientation, and racial identification, and various permutations thereof. Each of the next four chapters focuses on a particular social identity as it is treated by a given author or pair of authors, in order to make clear the specific means through which subjective decenteredness obtains in each case. Almost all of the works I address were produced in the period from 1930 to 1960, predating the heyday of postmodernist culture and thus indicating the degree to which the subjective fragmentation of social marginality diverges from that of postmodernism, even when it apparently approximates and coincides with it.

At the same time, it is not by pure chance that such approximation and coincidence should be manifested, insofar as (1) the works I examine can all be considered as sort of second-wave exemplars of literary modernism, which was established as a predominant cultural force in the decades just preceding 1930, and (2) postmodernism is widely recognized as not merely a critique but also a logical development of key modernist interests, not the least of which had to do with the questionable coherency of the human subject. The degree to which the continuity between modernism and postmodernism is generally acknowledged may be indicated by an allusion to it in M. H. Abrams's standard reference work, A Glossary of Literary Terms, where Abrams characterizes postmodernism as involving both "diverse attempts to break away from modernist forms" and also "a continuation, carried to an extreme, of the countertraditional experiments of modernism." [14]

But it isn't just in stylistic "experimentation" that postmodernism continues the undertaking inaugurated in modernist culture; rather, the very social–philosophical commentary that we can discern in postmodern praxis is operative as well, if often only implicitly, in much of the modernist enterprise.

To see how this is so, let us turn to another standard literary guidebook for its account of "The Name and Nature of Modernism." In their introduction to *Modernism: 1890–1930,* one of the Pelican Guides to European Literature, editors Malcolm Bradbury and James McFarlane offer two different explanations of the modernist impulse. On the one hand, they indicate, modernism is associated "with the coming of a new era of high aesthetic self-consciousness and non-representationalism, in which art turns from realism and humanistic representation towards style, technique, and spatial form in pursuit of a deeper penetration of life." [15] This seems a fair characterization of what is generally recognized as modernism's aestheticist tendency, whereby it sought to produce, as Bradbury and McFarlane put it, "an order in art independent of or else transcending the humanistic, the material, the *real*" (25), for which it would substitute a more appealing—because more harmonious—aesthetic rendering. In Bradbury's and McFarlane's summation of this view, "[t]he world, reality, is discontinuous till art comes along . . . ; but within art all becomes vital, discontinuous, yes, but within an aesthetic system of positioning" (25).

On the other hand, Bradbury and McFarlane also present the alternative view that modernism

> responds [in the sense of *corresponding*] to the scenario of our chaos.
> . . . It is the literature of technology. It is the art consequent on the
> dis-establishing of communal reality and . . . traditional notions of
> the wholeness of individual character, on the linguistic chaos that
> ensues when public notions of language have been discredited and
> when all realities have become subjective fictions. (27)

The references here to the disintegration of communal reality and of human character, and to the breakdown of effective linguistic referentiality, strikingly resemble the characterizations of the *post*modern condition offered by Habermas, Lyotard, and Jameson, and thus suggest the degree to which postmodern thematizations of subjective fragmentation are actually traceable to a fundamental modernist concern.

To say, however, that modernism and postmodernism share certain philosophical concerns is not to say that they represent identical enterprises. Indeed, what distinguishes modernism is precisely the fact that, as Bradbury and McFarlane indicate, it comprises two varying modes of relating to the "chaos" that constitutes contemporary social and historical "reality": aestheticist repudiation of it, on the one hand, and consequentialist correspondence to it on the other. While it may well be that the current tendency in critical considerations of modernism is to elevate the former mode over the latter (think of the relatively greater canonical status accorded *The Waste Land* or *Ulysses,* with their, respectively, thematic and formal appeals to classical order, in comparison to the more marginal position granted to the dis-integrative linguistic play of *Finnegan's Wake* or Gertrude Stein's post-"Melanctha" work), a full characterization of the modernist undertaking must inevitably recognize as one of its primary constituent factors the mutual implication and continuing interrelation of the two modes throughout the modernist period. Indeed, if formalist aestheticism appears to us as the dominant tendency of "high modernism" as it is currently apprehended, then it must be acknowledged as well that this aestheticism derives its significance from its status as a reaction against the apparent meaninglessness and absurdity of contemporary life, which was seen as *reflected* in the modernist works that thematized chaos and contingency. In other words, the dis-integrated, fragmentary nature of modern human existence is always a subtext of high modernist aestheticism, which is also precisely a defensive hedge against the former. Conversely, modernist explorations of discontinuity and disorder always function in the context of aestheticist endeavors that counterbalance them and keep them in check.

Given this view of the matter, it becomes possible to see how postmodernism can constitute both a break from and a continuation of the modernist undertaking. Postmodernism breaks with the formalist aestheticism that functioned to suppress modernism's full playing-out of the ramifications of experiential disjuncture, and, thus unencumbered, it continues the exploration of that disjuncture, which was always implicit in modernist practice. Indeed, it is through this unrestrained exploration that postmodernism accedes to what I have identified as one of its prime characteristics, the thematization of subjective *fragmentation,* over against the more modernist concern of subjective *alienation,* a distinction invoked by Jameson that we would do well to clarify a bit here.

Though we can discern in much of modernist literature an interest in questioning the "wholeness of individual character," as Bradbury and McFarlane put it, that questioning is not, I think, identical to the predominant expression of human subjectivity as fundamentally and

The Postmodern, the Marginal, and the Minor

irreducibly fragmented, which characterizes postmodernist work. Rather, in the context of modernism, the apprehension of the individual human subject as a disintegrated entity occurs as a merely collateral effect of inquiry into the more pressing disjuncture that obtains among different human subjects or between human subjects and the entities that constitute the objective world. It is possible to think of this latter disjuncture as a function of the limits of language, whereby the inadequacy of that medium to apprehend the essences of the things to which it refers both underscores and reinstates the irremediable gap between thinking, speaking subject, and the objects of thought or speech. The consequent and continual realization that these objects are unavoidably Other in relation to ourselves—and we in relation to them—issues in the sense of alienation that I take to characterize the modernist mood.

Take, for instance, Virginia Woolf's *Mrs. Dalloway* (1925), wherein the title character's primary existential dilemma is summed up in a short passage that presents her ruminating on the sight of her elderly neighbor in the house opposite, whom she watches from her own window. Reflecting on the contemptible inadequacy of human strategies for communion (her daughter has just gone out with the evangelically inclined Doris Kilman; her old friend Peter Walsh has recently announced to her that he is "in love"), Clarissa Dalloway thinks to herself,

> Why creeds and prayers and mackintoshes? when . . . that's the miracle, that's the mystery; that old lady, she meant, whom she could see going from chest of drawers to dressing table. She could still see her. And the supreme mystery which Kilman might say she had solved, or Peter might say he had solved, but Clarissa didn't believe either of them had the ghost of an idea of solving, was simply this: here was one room; there another. Did religion solve that, or love?[16]

It is precisely the difference between "here" and "there"—the irreparable distance between two rooms and the people in them—that founds the alienation to which I refer above as the defining feature of modernist culture. And yet, the fact that Clarissa Dalloway sees no "solution" to this alienation does not mean that she has no idea as to why it obtains; indeed, as Peter Walsh recalls in reminiscing about their youth, "Clarissa had a theory in those days— . . . it was to explain the feeling they had of dissatisfaction; not knowing people; not being known" (152). And according to that theory, this lack of communion that founds subjective alienation is itself founded in turn on a subjective dispersal that greatly resembles postmodern fragmentation:

It was unsatisfactory, they agreed, how little one knew people. But she said, sitting on the bus going up Shaftesbury Avenue, she felt herself everywhere; not "here, here, here"; and she tapped the back of the seat; but everywhere. She waved her hand, going up Shaftesbury Avenue. She was all that. So that to know her, or any one, one must seek out the people who completed them; even the places. (152–53)

And Clarissa continues to hold to this notion even as an older woman, as she wonders to herself in the opening pages of the novel,

> did it matter that she must inevitably cease completely; all this must go on without her; did she resent it; or did it not become consoling to believe that death ended absolutely? but that somehow in the streets of London, on the ebb and flow of things, here, there, she survived, Peter survived, lived in each other, she being part, she was positive, of the trees at home; of the house there, ugly, rambling all to bits and pieces as it was; part of people she had never met; being laid out like a mist between the people she knew best, who lifted her on their branches as she had seen the trees lift the mist, but it spread ever so far, her life, herself. (9)

Notably, the "here, there" motif that in Clarissa's ruminations about her neighbor suggests the fundamental distance between different human subjects indicates in this passage the disjunctive condition of the individual self, its status as a dispersed and "decentered" entity. So, an inquiry into the *alienated* condition of the human subject—represented in Clarissa's explanation of why it should be difficult for people to know one another—leads inevitably to a sense of the *fragmented* condition of the human subject, the signal characteristic of postmodernist culture.

And yet, Woolf's presentation of such a decentered subject by no means qualifies her novel as a postmodernist venture. The reason for this is largely, as I have already suggested, a matter of emphasis. Subjective fragmentation tends to be a relatively minor concern in modernist literature, presented, as in *Mrs. Dalloway,* as merely a secondary effect of inquiry into the more primary problem of subjective alienation. But it is also a matter of *how* that emphasis is achieved—specifically, *Mrs. Dalloway* thematizes the aestheticist hedge against experiential fragmentation that I have identified as a key strategy of modernist practice. Dispersed as she may feel herself to be, Clarissa nonetheless manages literally to compose herself into a harmonious unity for the sake of her social function, inspecting herself in her mirror as she does so:

> She pursed her lips when she looked in the glass. It was to give her face point. That was her self—pointed; dartlike; definite. That was her self when some effort, some call on her to be her self, drew the parts together, she alone knew how different, how incompatible and composed so for the world only into one centre, one diamond, one woman who sat in her drawing-room and made a meeting-point, a radiancy no doubt in some dull lives, a refuge for the lonely to come to . . . (37)

Thus, through the dissemblance of the subject's actual disunity beneath an artfully constructed image of composure, the interrogation of the self's dispersed status is foreclosed and the problem of subjective coherency is subordinated to the problem of intersubjective communion: The novel is distinguished as an inquiry into modern alienation as opposed to postmodern fragmentation.

Insofar as they conceive of subjective alienation as an effect of subjective fragmentation—as does Clarissa Dalloway herself—and insofar as they foreground subjective fragmentation as itself the product of specific social conditions and a problem to be worked through—as *Mrs. Dalloway* does not—the works I examine in chapters 2 through 5 seem to me to occupy the cusp between the modernist and postmodernist enterprises, and thus to constitute prime material for an inquiry into the social problematics that subtend contemporary postmodernist practice. I proceed in that inquiry according to the outline that I sketch here.

In chapter 2, drawing implicitly on Pierre Bourdieu's notions of "cultural capital" and "educational capital" as factors in the constitution of class status, I examine the collected novels of Nathanael West to point out their consistent depiction of a social class whose disenfranchisement is figured as its inaptitude at linguistic expression. In their attempt to remedy this fault, West's characters who are members of this class often undertake picaresque journeys in search of "the real," which eludes whatever linguistic formulations they can muster. In the course of these journeys, West's characters expose the falsity of any claims for the ability of language to capture the essences it is taken to represent, and thus explode the epistemological stability that grounds conventional notions of centered, coherent human subjectivity. This "explosion" is often figured in West's texts as the literal dismemberment of the disenfranchised hero of the story, which can be taken as a metaphor for the (postmodernistic) dismantling of humanist subjectivity that the works thematize, and that they depict as the direct result of a class-oriented *ressentiment* that motivates the characters' actions. Thus, my chapter on West demonstrates how one form of social marginality (based in class) provides a context in which the fragmentary nature of the human subject is both effected and exposed; but it also, through its revision of the concept of class, initiates an interrogation of the nature of "the political" that continues in my subsequent chapters on the representation of racial, sexual, and gender difference.

In chapter 3, I treat the works of Anaïs Nin and Djuna Barnes, who, like Nathanael West, depict human subjects as fragmented entities. Unlike West, however, who seems to intend to represent this fragmentation as afflicting all humankind but unwittingly suggests its limitation to a more restricted "mankind," Nin and Barnes depict a psychic fragmentation that is unique to women and actually constituted in femininity itself. Nin's "continuous novel," *Cities of the Interior,* elaborately demonstrates the fragmentation of women's subjectivity in patriarchy, and even suggests a remedy for women's psychic incompletion in the construction of a sort of "structural unity" among the collectivity of female subjects. Nin retreats from the depiction of such a collectivity, however, due to a misconstrual of its homosocial nature as a homoerotic one, and to a homophobic resistance to the latter. Barnes, on the other hand, while forthrightly representing lesbian attachments in her novel *Nightwood,* nevertheless conceives of those attachments themselves as most vividly exposing the incompleteness of the female subject. This is due to her inability to conceive of homoerotic relations as associated with a potent homosocial factor that might be effectively marshaled in feminist political strategy. In examining these authors' failure to posit an explicit feminist politics, as well as their representations of the feminine psyche, chapter 3 demonstrates not only the approximation of postmodernist fragmentation to the feminine condition but also the operation in lived reality of patriarchal forces that necessitate the suppression of the texts' feminist message into a "political unconscious" that implicitly informs the novels. Thus the ineffectivity of the feminine subject that is figured in Nin's and Barnes's texts is evident as well in the ineffectual silence that is imposed upon the authors themselves in the social and historical contexts in which they write. In its engagement with these contexts, the chapter on Nin and Barnes anticipates the more explicit historical analysis that follows in chapter 4.

If we are interested in theorizing the variety and specificity of different groups' experiences in the U.S. social context, then we must not only show up as false the "universal" experience of the white heterosexual male with some disposable income, we must also be sure not to present as generic any of the other experiences to which we appeal in our analysis, such as that of the white middle-class woman. In chapter 4, I examine one instance of bourgeois feminist theory that posits as applicable to all women a particular experience of motherhood, upon which it then bases various claims about the feminine psyche generally. In order to expose as invalid the assumptions that underlie this universalizing tendency, I provide a reading of Gwendolyn Brooks's poem "A Bronzeville Mother Loiters in Mississippi. Meanwhile, a Mississippi Mother Burns Bacon," which demonstrates a disparity in black and white women's experiences of motherhood. Subsequent to thus demonstrating the specificity of black women's experiences, I examine Brooks's 1953 novel *Maud Martha* in conjunction with primary historical sources to clarify the nature of black women's oppression in the 1940s United States. That oppression is symptomatically indicated in black women's imposed silence in the face of their predicament—a silence that both indicates their subjective ineffectivity and, in its literary representation in Brooks's novel, suggests the condition of the postmodern subject as Ihab Hassan, among others, has conceived it. Moreover, when this silence is broken and the black woman articulates her demands, those demands are recuperated into the economy of capitalism, and the black woman is inscribed in the system as a consumer, ready-made to conform to the postmodern logic of late-twentieth-century society as Jameson has outlined it in his theoretical essay. Thus, the specific experiences of black women that Brooks depicts actually provide us with a means to understand the general workings of late capitalist society, itself generally considered as constitutive of the postmodern subject.

In chapter 5, I read Ralph Ellison's *Invisible Man* in light of one of the most influential contemporary strategies for theorizing postmodern subjectivity, namely Lacanian psychoanalysis, which demonstrates the fundamental incoherence of the human psyche and the linguistic manipulations through which its apparent unity is constituted. By presenting a narrative motif that recalls Lacan's "mirror stage," *Invisible Man* provides a context in which we can consider the effects of social and historical factors on this self-constitutive process as it operates for blacks. Ellison's protagonist, who is prevented by his social position as a black youth from constituting an effective self, locates the problem specifically in the black community, which he sees as a threat to his individual personality. He attempts to escape this threat by distinguishing himself from the community through singular aesthetic production—his ability to deliver rousing oratory—which he exercises through the "Brotherhood," the novel's version of the Communist party. As he becomes aware of the Brotherhood's cooptation of his efforts, however, the protagonist begins to realize that the black community represents not a *threat* to his individual subjectivity, as he had thought, but rather the only means by which he can effectively exercise it in the context of a racist U.S. society. Once he realizes this, his oratory regains the force it once had, as he reconceives it not as his own individual production but as a communal improvisation to which any member of the group might subscribe. The inclusive nature of this aesthetic production is the source of its moral and political power, but it also represents a danger to the community itself, as anyone who can master its codes can appropriate it for uses not necessarily beneficial to the group. This seems to me to suggest the functional status of marginalized populations in contemporary postmodern culture, which often simulates the experiences of disempowered groups while simultaneously eliding their social and political significance, a point that I elaborate in my final chapters.

I begin chapter 6 with a review of short works by three recognized practitioners of postmodernist fiction: the short story collection *Unspeakable Practices, Unnatural Acts,* by Donald Barthelme, *The Universal Baseball Association, Inc., J. Henry Waugh, Prop.,* by Robert Coover, and *The Crying of Lot 49,* by Thomas Pynchon. My objective is not to provide an exhaustive poetics of postmodern literary practice but rather to identify in these texts some of the key features of postmodern fiction in order to correlate them with similar effects in the literature of social marginality. Barthelme's stories illustrate both the fragmented nature of contemporary life and the highly uncertain status of the human subject as it reckons with that fragmentation. Coover's book addresses human beings' attempts to impose order upon a chaotic universe through the creation of fictions that imbue it with meaning, and the danger of forgetting the fictive nature of these constructs and thus becoming trapped in the very mythologies we have created. Pynchon's novel thematizes the overwhelming ambiguity of contemporary life and of the signs through which it is constituted at the same time as it presents a motivated resistance to the world's chaos in the form of an underground society whose true nature itself seems ultimately undecidable; the result is an effective representation of the random quality of the contemporary human condition. Implicit in these works (and rendered explicit in much of the criticism on them) is the notion that the psychic disorientation they depict is the result of rapid technological development in the twentieth century and associated revisions in our conception of the human subject. I do not seek to negate these claims, especially since many postmodernist works derive considerable power from their status as commentary on such developments. Nonetheless, I do want to show that similar instances of psychic disorientation are represented in other contemporary literary works, in which they derive not from general developments in technology or even in the economic structure but from fundamental social relations in which difference figures as a major factor. Thus, in the final section of the chapter I propose that Maxine Hong Kingston's *Woman Warrior* be considered as a prime example of such work. Kingston's book is extremely useful for illustrating my point because, as the *autobiographical* narrative of a Chinese-American woman marginalized in the United States due to her racial and ethnic identity and in both Chinese and North American cultures because she is female, it clearly grounds the psychic experiences it depicts in the lived reality of a "minority" subject. And those experiences are strikingly similar to the effects represented in the works by Barthelme, Coover, and Pynchon: In response to the highly ambiguous and disorienting account of her and her family's life provided by her mother, the protagonist of Kingston's book constructs elaborate narratives through which she forges her sense of self, all the while commenting metanarrativistically on the "talk-story" process by which this is accomplished. The result is the representation of a postmodernistic human subject whose existence is highly unstable and contingent upon the various narrative motifs that at any moment are deployed to ground her personality; that representation derives, in this case, specifically from the narrative treatment of social difference and marginality.

Finally, in a short coda at the end of the book, I consider how the subjective disorientation entailed by social marginality is implicated in dominant conceptions of the generalized postmodern condition, with the potential consequence that its specific sociopolitical import is obscured in discourse in and about contemporary culture. This analysis centers on a recent major studio film—*The Commitments,* by Alan Parker—that I think exemplifies mass cultural appropriation of the effects of social marginality, and in contradistinction to which I argue for a more politically aware—and thus more effectively socially committed—cultural practice.

My primary contention, of course, is that social marginality's production of fragmented subjectivity has not been fully addressed or appreciated in the most influential theoretical work on postmodernism. In focusing on it in this study, I am not proposing that social marginality displace other phenomena as the originary factor in the development of the postmodern subject. I am, however, suggesting that what "minority" subjects often experience as their primary source of disorientation—the social effects of their difference in contexts where it is construed as negative—will complicate their experience of what has heretofore been conceived as the "general" disorientation characteristic of the postmodern condition. Moreover, insofar as that general condition simulates the experiences of disenfranchised groups, these groups do not represent the margins of contemporary cultural life in the United States, but rather are thoroughly implicated in even its most "generic" manifestations. Thus a full understanding of the condition of social marginality is essential to any viable theory of postmodern subjectivity and its manifestations in contemporary culture, and this book represents a small step toward the achievement of that objective.

SIGNIFICATION, MOVEMENT, AND RESISTANCE IN THE NOVELS OF NATHANAEL WEST

2

Moving Violation

> **It is against the rules and regulations of the New Jersey Turnpike Authority to drive in the wrong direction on the New Jersey Turnpike.**
> Laurie Anderson, "New Jersey Turnpike," *United States*, part I[1]

> **You're driving . . .**
> **And you took a turn back there**
> **and you're not sure now that it was the right turn,**
> **but you took the turn anyway**
> **and you just keep going in this direction.**
> **Eventually . . . you look out**
> **and you realize**
> **you have absolutely no idea where you are.**
> **So you get out at the next gas station and you say:**
> **Hello. Excuse me. Can you tell me where I am?**
> Laurie Anderson, "Say Hello," *United States*, part I

In dramatizing for his reader the automobile accident in which Nathanael West was killed, biographer Jay Martin writes that, at the moment of the tragedy, West "saw, dreamily, a sign that read *Stop*. But he did not stop."[2] What is notable about this formulation is not the conjecture that is posited as fact—that, indeed, "he saw . . . a sign"— but, much more simply, the terse conjunction of what we do know to be two incontrovertible facts: that, at the intersection of Routes 80 and 111, just north of the California–Mexico border, there was a sign that read "Stop"; and that, when Nathanael West approached that sign in his station wagon on December 22, 1940, he did not stop. The traffic laws required West to stop, and he did not stop, and the deaths of both West and his wife, Eileen McKenney West, were the irremediable consequence of that violation.

As Martin notes, "[f]ew people were surprised, though many were shocked, at the news" of West's accident (7); for,

> [c]haracteristically, West drove over the speed limit; he drove on the inside of mountain curves; he once made a U-turn across six lanes of rush-hour traffic on Ventura Boulevard; before dawn, at Los Banos, in central California, West crossed over the center line on a curve, broke the car axle on a 4 × 4 guard post, and ran it down into a shallow irrigation ditch—the tales are numerous. (8)

West himself admitted that he'd been in countless accidents since he began driving at age thirteen; "And," Martin quotes him as saying, "I've no doubt that's the way I'm going to go" (8).

West's fatal accident, seemingly foreseen by the writer himself, does not merely affirm the accuracy of his speculation; more subtly, it seems to culminate the vision that informs West's fiction itself. Not that life imitates art—though this is a tempting conclusion—at least not in the sense of repetition, the uncanny approximation by history of the "facts" of fictional narrative; rather, in the circumstances of West's death, we can discern a structural similarity to the phenomena of social marginality and personal resistance so often depicted in the novels. An examination of these depictions will lead to a better understanding of West's writings as commentary on the general nature of sociopolitical struggle in the twentieth-century United States. To begin, we must remind ourselves of the two simple facts at the center of West's fatal accident: The sign said "Stop"; he did not stop.

How to Say Things with Words

If you can't talk about it, point to it.
Laurie Anderson, "If You Can't Talk About It, Point to It" (for Ludwig Wittgenstein and Reverend Ike), *United States*, part 2

We can begin to understand West's conception of the nature of social marginality by examining a long excerpt from his first novel, *The Dream Life of Balso Snell* (1931). In it, Balso, the itinerant hero, quotes Picasso as saying, "[T]here are no feet in nature." His travel guide asks that Balso "[p]lease explain [his] interpretation of the Spanish master's dictum":

> "Well the point is . . . " Balso began. But before he could finish the guide started again. "If you are willing to acknowledge the existence

Resistance in the Novels of Nathanael West

of points," he said, "then the statement that there are no feet in nature puts you in an untenable position. It depends for its very meaning on the fact that there are no points. Picasso, by making this assertion, has placed himself on the side of monism in the eternal wrangle between the advocates of the Singular and those of the Plural. As James puts it, 'Does reality exist distributively or collectively—in the shape of *eaches, everys, anys, eithers,* or only in the shape of an *all* or *whole?*' If reality is singular then there are no feet in nature, if plural, a great many. If the world is one [everything part of the same thing—called by Picasso nature] then nothing either begins or ends. Only when things take the shape of *eaches, everys, anys, eithers* [have ends] do they have feet. Feet are attached to ends, by definition. Moreover, if everything is one, and has neither ends nor beginnings, then everything is a circle. A circle has neither a beginning nor an end. A circle has no feet. If we believe that nature is a circle, then we must also believe that there are no feet in nature. . . ."

"Cézanne said, 'Everything tends toward the globular.' " . . .

"Cézanne?" the guide said. . . . "Cézanne is right. . . ."[3]

This last declaration represents wishful thinking on the part of the guide, however, insofar as sentiments expressed by other characters in the novel indicate that they, like all of us socialized in Western epistemologies, inhabit a world that is essentially dualistic: split into the categories of subject and object, human consciousness and exterior "reality." How "to know the Real," as they put it, is the overriding concern of the characters in *The Dream Life of Balso Snell.* Those whom Balso meets on his travels seem obsessed with the problem. The biographer Mary McGeeney notes "[our] great difficulty in discovering the Real" (35). The protean John Gilson laments his personal inability to achieve true knowledge: "I can know nothing; . . . I must devote my whole life to the pursuit of a shadow" (16); and he pines, "If I could only discover the Real. A Real that I could know with my senses" (14). It is the reference to "knowledge" itself that indicates the characters' existence in an order that is anything but "globular." This latter term indicates an all-inclusive whole, complete and perfect in itself, with no origin or termination, no "feet." Such a version of reality would allow for no gap, no split, no rupture, no duality along which human consciousness, on the one side, and exterior reality, on the other, might be classed. There would be no space across which the former would strive to "know" the latter—the idea of knowledge itself depending upon such a gap—but rather an uninterrupted oneness of subject and object that would preclude both the necessity and the possibility of those concepts. "To know the Real" would not be a problem in the

Framing the Margins

globular configuration Balso Snell's guide identifies with "reality." Insofar as the other characters Balso meets conceive of it as a problem, the world they inhabit does not "tend toward" but rather diverges from the globular, and the degree of this divergence corresponds to the extent of what we might call the "decenteredness" that characterizes the relation of human consciousness to objective reality.

Now, in order to cure this decenteredness, it is necessary to suture the gap between subject and object, to re-fuse human consciousness with a reality that is apparently "exterior" to it. This can be attempted in either of two ways: by moving, as it were, from the "here" of the mind to the "there" of nature, or by bringing the "there" "here." The first mode explains the impulse to travel that motivates many of West's characters (which I examine later); the second accounts for the use of language as a potential bridge between subject and object, and constitutes, as well, the basis for the establishment of a social hierarchy in the world of West's novels.

One commentator has said that in *Balso Snell* "West introduced his readers to the eccentric, the mystic, the pervert, the crippled, and the disillusioned who were to be credibly presented as major players in his later novels."[4] And we do see them later, notably in *Miss Lonelyhearts* (1933)—in which they are "the same people as those who write to Miss Lonelyhearts for help" (*Miss Lonelyhearts,* 94)—and in *The Day of the Locust* (1939), where they are the ones who have "come to California to die" (*The Day of the Locust, passim*). Balso himself notes another peculiarity in the first novel, however: the fact that, during his journey, he is accosted "solely by writers in search of an audience," which he himself must constitute (37). The writer/audience dichotomy that Balso invokes suggests that West's "eccentric" characters must not be considered as an undifferentiated mass, but rather as inhabitants of one or the other of two realms in a binary social structure. By identifying in this binarism the basis for a distinction between the casts of characters in two different West novels, we can better understand the nature of the dichotomy within the single set of disoriented personages presented in each novel.

At one point in *Miss Lonelyhearts,* the title character, writer of an advice column for a daily metropolitan newspaper, imagines those who write to him as attempting to contact him from a far-away desert,

> [a] desert . . . not of sand, but of rust and body dirt, surrounded by a back-yard fence on which are posters describing the events of the day. . . . Inside the fence Desperate, Broken-hearted, Disillusioned-with-tubercular-husband and the rest were gravely forming the letters

Resistance in the Novels of Nathanael West

MISS LONELYHEARTS out of white-washed clam shells, as if decorating the lawn of a rural depot. (96–97)

And later:

> He . . . turned again to the imagined desert where Desperate, Broken-hearted and the others were still building his name. They had run out of sea shells and were using faded photographs, soiled fans, timetables, playing cards, broken toys, imitation jewelry—junk that memory had made precious, far more precious than anything the sea might yield. (98)

The shift from Miss Lonelyhearts's first vision to his second is significant in that it attends to the change in his correspondents' mode of communication. Having run out of seashells with which to construct the letters of Miss Lonelyhearts's name, they turn from nature to products of industrial manufacture in order to frame their message. The bits of "junk" they use, however, are "far more precious than anything the sea might yield" in that each has been invested with a unique significance by its owner, now a member of this wretched band in the desert. Each of these newer elements in the alphabetical construction has a specific meaning beyond its function in the assemblage. This distinguishes them from the seashells, whose relatively low value for the correspondents indicates their lack of any alternative reference, except for the insignificant world of nature, to which no one of them has any unique claim. From the moment the mementos become incorporated in the name construction, then, the latter becomes a special type of composition, embodying both the meaning of the letters it spells out— Miss Lonelyhearts's name—but also the alternative significance of each souvenir. This new construction is the inverse of the Apollinairean calligram.

The inverse, because the form of "concrete poetry" associated with the French modernist Guillaume Apollinaire derives its dual significance from the "literal" meaning of the words that constitute it and from the shape or picture formed by the arrangement of those words in print. In the construction of the words *Miss Lonelyhearts* in West's novel, the words themselves govern the placement of the elements, the concrete objects, that constitute the former. Nevertheless, the threefold function of the calligram remains the same in the Westian conception as it is in the Apollinairean form; that function has been outlined by Michel Foucault: "to augment the alphabet, to repeat something without the aid of rhetoric, to trap things in a double cipher."[5] The calligram's function of intensifying expression points up what is characteristic of Miss Lonelyhearts's correspondents—that they do succeed at self-expression to some degree; indeed, we might say that they even improve upon the Apollinairean method in that, while the traditional calligram strives to double meaning, conjoining that of the words and that of the picture; West's characters incrementally increase the significance of their construction with each meaningful memento they add to it. The characters' cleverness at signification sets them apart from the people "who come to California to die" in *The Day of the Locust*. The latter are profoundly devoid of any expressive ability. This is illustrated in the demise of Homer Simpson, the displaced midwesterner whose acquaintance is made by West's protagonist, Tod Hackett. Homer meets a violent end in a frenzied crowd of fellow sojourners. Tod sees him "rise above the mass for a moment," in a final instant of inarticulateness; he is "shoved against the sky, his jaw hanging *as though he wanted to scream but couldn't*" (*The Day of the Locust*, 415; my emphasis). On the other hand, those who write to Miss Lonelyhearts, engaged though they are in a desperate search for meaning, appear to have achieved some portion of their goal in that they themselves can signify, though *what* they signify is highly ambiguous, as we will see.

Miss Lonelyhearts's correspondents do not express themselves in a vacuum; they write, of course, to Miss Lonelyhearts. In this way, the distinction between them and the hapless Californians is recapitulated within *Miss Lonelyhearts* itself. For though Miss Lonelyhearts's readers write, they do so in order to be written *to*. A letter to Miss Lonelyhearts begs for a response, in anticipation of which his correspondents themselves become the inarticulate audience for his proclamation: "When he did speak," Miss Lonelyhearts thinks at one point, "it would have to be in the form of a message" (127). Thus, the lot of characters West represents to us—"the eccentric, the mystic, the pervert, the crippled, and the disillusioned"—that group is divided, within a single novel, into those who seek a message and those who will deliver it, those who listen and those who speak. Members of the former category, Miss Lonelyhearts realizes, make "profoundly humble pleas for moral and spiritual advice" (106), or, as the lame Peter Doyle puts it in his letter to the columnist, they want to know "what is the whole stinking business for" (125). They hope that Miss Lonelyhearts (or, in *The Day of the Locust*, those in the movie industry or the various California gurus) has captured an essence, a reality that can in turn be conveyed to them, a means to order that they themselves can grasp.

Miss Lonelyhearts's readers expect some illuminating verbal communiqué, a cipher through which they might touch the Real. They themselves deploy intricate methods as they try to apprehend reality, insofar as their version of the calligram attempts not merely "to trap things in a double cipher," as Foucault says of Apollinaire's form, but rather to contain things triply, quadruply, and so on, in the multiplicity of significant artifacts that make up their alphabetically signifying construction. And yet, the dual meaning of the operative word in the English translation of Foucault's study hints at the futility of attempting to capture reality through any verbal signification: A "cipher" is both a particular type of code in which meaning is embodied and "zero," "naught," a nonentity or absence. Foucault allows us to see that at the center of the verbal component of the calligram's double trap there sits, ironically, an absence, implicitly commented upon in the Magritte painting Foucault examines in his book. Put simply, at the moment we focus on, for example, the pipelike pattern described by the arrangement of a group of letters—THIS IS A PIPE—on a page, we necessarily fail to discern the literal message conveyed by the alphabetic constituents of the picture; there is no "caption," no verbal confirmation that this is indeed a pipe. Conversely, when we read the letters, they cease to shape the pipe for us, since in reading we can only attend to the inscription as it presents itself as verbal communication, not as pictorial representation. And, of course, at this point the demonstrative "this" becomes highly problematic, for it can now refer only to itself, or, at most, the whole group of letters, but not to anything that is or even clearly represents a pipe. As Foucault says, "Nowhere is there a pipe" (29); the Real, emphatically pointed to by words at their most simply indicative, nevertheless cannot be apprehended by them, and the seemingly double security of the calligram breaks down. Insofar as it obliquely "points" to something other than itself, to something we call for the sake of convenience "the Real," and that constitutes the object of its function, we might say that language, *per se*, is "decentered."

To see this more clearly, we need only look at a calligram by Apollinaire himself; it is one that Foucault uses to illustrate his essay, and its title is "L'Oeillet," which translates as "The Carnation" (see Foucault, plate 8). The poem is arranged in print to approximate the shape of a flower, and the English version of the text reads as follows:

> May this carnation tell you the law of odors which has not yet been announced and which one day will come to rule in our minds far more precisely and more subtly than the sounds which guide us
> I prefer your nose to all your organs O my love. It is the throne of future knowledge[6]

For the nose to be "the throne of future knowledge," a fundamental barrier between intellection and sensation will have to have been eradicated, a barrier that manifests itself as language insofar as language is the means by which we "know" anything. And yet this barrier is simultaneously the bridge by which we join subject and object, a bridge that Apollinaire (like West's John Gilson, who seeks, as he puts it, "a Real that I could *know with my senses*" [my emphasis]) wants to burn in favor of a more direct sensory experience. The irony of Apollinaire's manifesto, of course, is that it is embodied in the "double cipher" of the calligram, whose two modes of "trapping" objective reality (pictorial imaging and linguistic representation) not only are mutually exclusive, as Foucault demonstrates, but in this case serve to discredit their own claim on the Real, since they conjoin only to refer the reader elsewhere—away from both visual and auditory linguistic signification and even from "this [pictorially represented] carnation" to another that can appeal to the sense of smell, new touchstone of objective reality. Even the augmented language of the calligram is, in its *re*ferral, only a mechanism of Derridean *de*ferral, pointing toward and yet obliquely situated with respect to the object it represents.

We can see the Apollinairean wish to escape the mediating nature of language recapitulated (in a disguised fashion) in *Balso Snell*, in which Mary McGeeney relates the life of one Perkins, "a great, if peculiar, genius." His predominant peculiarity she relates thus:

> "At an age when most men's features are regular, before his personality had been able to elevate any one portion of his physiognomy over the rest, Perkins' face was dominated by his nose. . . .
>
> ". . . Nature had concentrated in his sense of smell all the abilities usually distributed among the five senses. . . .
>
> "[He was thus] forced to interpret the whole external world through conclusions reached by the sense of smell alone[.] . . ."

Miss McGeeney enjoins Balso to "imagine . . . how horrible was the predicament of this sensitive and sensuous man" (*Balso Snell*, 33–35), and so it is; but the horror, for West's characters, seems to inhere in the necessity to "interpret" what one senses at all, since this intellectual operation inevitably mediates the direct *rapprochement* of subject and object. Apollinaire's point, after all, is that the supremacy of the sense of smell would allow for the *immediate* experience of reality, which is precisely what Miss McGeeney and the others whom Balso meets wish to achieve for themselves.

Resistance in the Novels of Nathanael West

Despite the increasingly evident impossibility of uniting human subject and external object through language, the task is conceived as a noble one by most of West's characters; those who, like Miss Lonelyhearts, are perceived to be successful at it are conferred with a high degree of respect by the less able characters, and with a social status consonant with their apparent abilities. On the other hand, those who neglect the task or, worse, deny its necessity risk being completely discounted from the community of rational beings, relegated to the extreme margins of the Westian social structure.[7] This is the fate that befalls characters from West's two most famous works.

The women with whom Miss Lonelyhearts and Tod Hackett attempt romantic relations are strikingly similar in one respect, summed up in the description of Tod's reaction to being with Faye Greener, with whom he is infatuated:

> The sensation he felt was like that he got when holding an egg in his hand. Not that she was fragile or even seemed fragile. It wasn't that. It was her completeness, her egglike self-sufficiency, that made him want to crush her. (*The Day of the Locust,* 320)

The metaphor here is apt. It recalls Yeats's "Among School Children," in which "two natures blent / Into a sphere . . . / Or else . . . / Into the yolk and white of the one shell."[8] The spherical completeness that characterizes the union of two souls in Yeats's poem is analogous to the "globular" oneness for which West's characters strive and that would obliterate the distressing subject/object duality. The attainment of such completeness is itself the achievement of self-sufficiency, beyond the shell of which rages chaos and a constant threat to the fragile equilibrium represented in the ovicular entity. At the same time, this self-sufficiency is suspect, for two reasons: First, it is established through a voluntaristic gesture that simultaneously excludes a portion of "reality"; second, because of both its exclusiveness and, ironically, its disallowance of fissure, it precludes the possibility of meaning. Miss Lonelyhearts harbors these objections with respect to his fiancée, Betty:

> She had often made him feel that when she straightened his tie, she straightened much more. And he had once thought that if her world were larger, were *the* world, she might order it as finally as the objects on her dressing table. . . .
>   . . . It was Betty, however, that he criticized. Her world was not the world and could never include the readers of his column. *Her sureness was based on the power to limit experience arbitrarily.*

> *Moreover, his confusion was significant, while her order was not.* (*Miss Lonelyhearts,* 79; my emphasis)

So, the egg metaphor itself gives away the fault of Faye's and Betty's brand of self-sufficiency: Reality of a genuinely globular nature would in fact have no need of a shell, for there would be nothing outside it to *keep* out, nothing it didn't include; the shell around Faye's and Betty's world is the demarcation of an arbitrary limit they themselves impose on reality, a limit that globular reality itself would neither need nor allow.

Further, Miss Lonelyhearts notes that the order that characterizes Betty's self-sufficiency is not "significant." In the unity of "knowing" subject and "known" object, this would be literally true, in that it is only across the gap between subject and object that signs become necessary. At the same time, Miss Lonelyhearts's criticism implies a lack of meaning in Betty's world that is evident, as well, in Faye's, where ironically there is a radical discontinuity between signifier and signified: "The strange thing about her gestures and expressions was that they didn't really illustrate what she was saying. They were almost pure" (*The Day of the Locust,* 387). That purity consists in Faye's disassociation from the eternal struggle of signification to embody "reality." She sets herself apart from that horror, builds a shell between it and herself, in the same way that Betty arbitrarily limits her experience. In the view of Miss Lonelyhearts and Tod, at least, Betty and Faye are outside the significant order of human existence, within which everyone else valiantly wages the battle for meaning; in their egglike self-sufficiency, they really occupy the margins of worthwhile human endeavor.[9]

Such a view, however, which posits Faye and Betty as extraneous to the chaotic struggle for meaning, must itself conceive of that chaos as a unity, delimited at some point, for otherwise there could be no exteriority to it that Faye and Betty would inhabit. This unity cannot be an individualistic unity, like that of Betty or Faye, complete for each human subject; rather it must be a structural unity, existent in the relation of subject to object, of different subjects and objects to each other, governed by specific laws, beyond the scope of which must lie "the marginal."

To see whether such a conception of the nature of marginality is tenable, let us return to biography—not that of West himself, but that of his forebears, the Wallensteins and Weinsteins of nineteenth-century Russia. According to Jay Martin, these two families lived in Lithuania during a time when Jews were "[s]corned [in Russia] as an unwelcome inheritance from Old Poland" (13). Martin describes some of the historical occurrences that impinged upon Jews living in the province during the last two centuries:

> . . . [A]s early as 1791 several million Jews were loosely confined by Catherine II within a Pale of Settlement in western Russia, chiefly to forward the policy of Russification. . . . [About seventy years later,] Alexander II . . . issued a rescript allowing Jewish artisans and members of professions to settle outside the Pale. . . . (13)

It was during the approximately twenty-year period of the easing of restrictions on Jews that West's maternal ancestors, the Wallensteins, made their fortune in the contracting and construction business; members of the Weinstein family, West's father Max among them, were employees of the Wallensteins' firm. During this time, the province was under the heavy cultural and political influence of Germany, which circumstance allowed West's ancestors to regard themselves as Germans rather than as ethnic Jews, and permitted Jews in general a degree of relative prosperity. "[I]n the spring of 1881," however, Martin notes, "after the coronation of Alexander III, . . . violent pogroms [broke] out, followed later by the so-called 'May Laws' " (13):

> Alexander III revoked German Home Rule in Lithuania and issued imperial edicts which forced Russification into the western departments of the empire. German officials were replaced at once and Russian was declared the official language in 1888; the right of free movement for Jewish artisans . . . was revoked, and educational quotas were established even within the Pale. These changes abruptly taught the unhappy Livonian Jews that the laws of the Russian Pale applied to them. (16)

Ironically, as Martin points out, "[t]he Wallensteins and Weinsteins . . . were in fact living at this time outside the Pale" (16), ensconced in their position of wealth and social power. Nevertheless, "all their influence, their apparently secure position, and their wealth could not protect West's family from history" (17–18). Faced with Russian anti-Semitism, Jews in Lithuania were confronted from the other side by the rising nationalism of native Lithuanians, who attacked not only Russian imperialism but also the influence of Germany as manifested in the presence of German-identified Jews and non-Jews alike. As Martin puts it, "Caught in these currents, the Jews of Lithuania, West's parents among them, turned their eyes and hopes elsewhere—to Germany, England, South Africa, Argentina, and, of course, to what they hopefully called the 'New World' " (18).

This narrative complicates the idea of marginality as we have posited it thus far. Jews who inhabited Russia during the reign of Catherine II found themselves marginalized, indeed, not only with respect to Russian culture and society but even geographically, restricted as they were to the far western edge of the empire, away from its political center. At the same time, by 1881 West's family was physically situated beyond this marginalized region, identifying primarily as Germans, not Jews, and yet subject to the laws of the Pale equally with others who were identified by the Russian state as Jewish. The impossibility of neatly mapping social marginality in terms of geography corresponds to the extensive implication of marginality itself in the larger social structure. Jewishness, in this historical context, was not a cultural identity to which individuals could lay claim or not, as they chose; rather, it was an attribute defined and manipulated by the Russian imperial forces in their attempt to forge various social elements into a structure for a stable empire. Despite appearances to the contrary, marginality is not the space beyond the limits of a given social system; it is, rather, necessarily caught up in the very structure to which it seems exterior. To the extent that its "exteriority" to the central system of power bolsters the efficacy of the system itself, marginality is never really exterior at all, but bound in a network of elements that, together, constitute the entire social structure.

This perspective throws a wrench into the idea that characters like West's Betty and Faye, who avoid the anguish of the search for meaningful signification, are, in their "self-sufficiency," exterior to the system in which such a search is founded. It embodies a tendency to totalization that allows for no "outsiders," for those whom we would class as such are actually inscribed within the structure they seem to escape precisely by virtue of their antagonistic relation to it. Betty and Faye, in this case, might be said merely to represent the blatantly insignificant against which attempts to signify the Real can be measured; they do not represent a space outside the problematic of meaningful signification, according to this rather structuralist outlook. And yet, poststructuralism teaches us that the relations that constitute a given structure are not static, and that there inheres in their instability the constant disruption of the structure, which, consequently, can no longer be "total" in the way we generally conceive of the term. These disruptions can, in fact, mark the emergence of one or more of the elements of a given structure into an altogether different system, contiguous with the first, but ordered by different laws. West's novels make explicit such a point of contiguity between the systems of language and move-

Resistance in the Novels of Nathanael West

ment, and it is this contiguity that remains to be exploited in this chapter.

The System of Movement and Its Discontents

Now, in order to get from one place to another, something must move.
Laurie Anderson, "Say Hello"

Linguistic signification can in no way be divorced from human physiology—from the operation of eyes and hands in reading and writing, of mouth and ears in speaking and listening, and, behind all these, the brain itself—for physiological operations are necessary to complete the transmission of a linguistically coded message from one person to another. Yet, the workings of the human body (and I am thinking here specifically of the visible movement of parts or all of the body) need not represent any conscious attempt at linguistic signification, nor signify anything at all exterior to the physical or psychic condition of the actor.[10] The order of physical gesture that most dramatically exemplifies a lack of external significance is the tic, that uncontrollable movement that so often frustrates and puzzles both its performer and its observers. A classic depiction of the phenomenon is provided by West in *The Day of the Locust*:

> [Homer's] big hands left his lap, where they had been playing "here's the church and here the steeple," and hid in his armpits. They remained there for a moment, then slid under his thighs. A moment later they were back in his lap. The right hand cracked the joints of the left, one by one, then the left did the same service for the right. They seemed easier for a moment, but not for long. They started "here's the church" again, going through the entire performance and ending with the joint manipulation as before. He started a third time, but catching Tod's eyes, he stopped and trapped his hands between his knees.
>
> It was the most complicated tic Tod had ever seen. What made it particularly horrible was its precision. It wasn't pantomime, as he had first thought, but manual ballet.
>
> When Tod saw the hands start to crawl out again, he exploded.
>
> "For Christ's sake!"
>
> The hands struggled to get free, but Homer clamped his knees shut and held them.
>
> "I'm sorry," he said.

Framing the Margins

"Oh, all right."

"But I can't help it, Tod. I have to do it three times." (389–90)

What is notable about Homer's gestures, above all, is that they emerge where language fails. The narrative indicates that "[s]everal times [before performing his tic] Homer started to tell Tod something, but he didn't seem able to get the words out" (389). It is in this context that Homer launches into his "manual ballet," and it is as if the physical gesture bursts forth out of the stifled attempt at verbal communication, identifying the failure of linguistic signification as the window from the realm of language (and its attendant physiological processes) into that of "pure" motion, like Faye Greener's gestures. There is an important difference, however, between these latter gestures and Homer's. Faye's movements, divorced as they are from "meaning," represent the violation of applicable laws in a system of signification. Homer's tic, on the other hand, originates with the thwarted attempt at signification and becomes "pure" by default, really; in its intricacy and precision, it represents the perversion of the laws of motion insofar as the latter are prescribed by a system, not of signification, but of power.[11]

Foucault affords us with the classic exposition of the physical "disciplines" as the manifestation, on the micro-level, of a power that seeks to impose social order through the regulation of physical movement. Using the military as his example, Foucault cites the development, in the eighteenth century, of the soldier as an entity efficiently constructed from any given subject rather than as a vocation for someone manifesting a particularly suitable physique. By the end of the 1700s, according to Foucault, the soldier

> has become something that can be made; out of a formless clay, an inapt body, the machine required can be constructed; . . . a calculated constraint runs slowly through each part of the body, mastering it, making it pliable, ready at all times, turning silently into the automatism of habit[.] [12]

This transformation is founded in several new developments in the technique of the imposition of power on the body, which Foucault details in his study:

> To begin with, there was the scale of the control: it was a question not of treating the body, en masse, "wholesale," as if it were an indissociable unity, but of working it "retail," individually; of exercising upon it a subtle coercion, of obtaining holds upon it at the level of the mechanism itself—movements, gestures, attitudes, rapid-

Resistance in the Novels of Nathanael West

ity: an infinitesimal power over the active body. Then there was the object of the control: it was not or was no longer the signifying elements of behavior or the language of the body, but the economy, the efficiency of movements, their internal organization; constraint bears upon the forces rather than upon the signs; the only truly important ceremony is that of exercise. Lastly, there is the modality: it implies an uninterrupted, constant coercion, supervising the processes of the activity rather than its results and it is exercised according to a codification that partitions as closely as possible time, space, movement. (*Discipline and Punish,* 136–37)

The disciplines, then, concern themselves with the mechanics of the body as a system of potential gestures divorced from the individual actor's attempts at signification. They aim to rationalize the activity of the body, to control its "retail" aspects in order to impress it fully with the power of the system it inhabits, and, moreover, to inscribe the wholesale body (and the collectivity of bodies) in the service of the larger goals of that system. As Foucault puts it in citing the eighteenth-century soldier's status as "a fragment of mobile space," this technique represents "a functional reduction of the body. But it is also an insertion of this body-segment in a whole ensemble over which it is articulated. . . . The body is constituted as a part of a multi-segmentary machine" (*Discipline and Punish,* 164). The regulation of this larger machine is dependent upon the discipline that operates at the level of detail within each individual body–machine that goes into constituting it. Hence the 1766 regulations for the exercise of the French infantry, which, Foucault tells us, dictate that, for marching troops, "[t]he length of the short step will be a foot, that of the ordinary step . . . two feet," and so on, and that each step will last for a specified duration (*Discipline and Punish,* 151). The discipline of the individual bodies constitutes, at the micro-level, the laws of movement for the whole assembly; for an individual to violate the rules of discipline would be for the whole regiment to commit a moving violation. The entire social order is implicated in the regulation of movement that originates in the discipline of detail.

This conception of regulated movement as fundamental to the maintenance of social order surfaces in other recent works in social theory. One sociologist, Ephraim H. Mizruchi, puts it this way in his study of the management of marginal populations: "Societies for the most part tend toward *an orderly flow* of people both from one place to the next and from one social organization to another."[13] When that flow becomes disorderly or is impeded—notably, when there is a surplus population that cannot be absorbed by the social structures operative at a given moment in a particular society—supplementary organizations must be created that can contain, for shorter or longer periods of time, the marginal population, keep it in "abeyance," as Mizruchi calls the process, and thus defuse its potential for social disruption. The Russian Pale discussed above represents a highly literalized version of such containment mechanisms. The "basic idea," according to Mizruchi, is that "organizations may be created to absorb and control the potentially dissident in our society" (ix).

There are two components in this "basic idea" that warrant further articulation and examination, and they are found in Mizruchi's reference to "flow," on the one hand, and "absorption," on the other. His discussion of "abeyance" suggests that it is through the latter phenomenon—the removal of potentially dissident elements from circulation, a type of stasis—that social control is achieved, at least when (and herein lies the second component) the system of regular "flow" or movement that normally constitutes order is overwhelmed by the number of elements that have to be kept in circulation. There is a dichotomy here between stasis and movement that needs to be explained if we are to understand fully the social regulation of potential dissidence.

That dichotomy seems to recur in the conception offered by Paul Virilio. From his vantage in the French capital, the contemporary social theorist notes that

> [f]or the mass of unemployed, demobilized workers without an occupation, Paris is a tapestry of trajectories, a series of streets and avenues in which they roam, for the most part, with neither goal nor destination, subject to a police repression intended to control their wanderings.[14]

The masses are "demobilized"—withdrawn from circulation in the sphere of production—and yet they "roam"; and, ironically, they no doubt roam precisely *because* of the efforts by the police agency to "control their wanderings," most likely formulated as an injunction against loitering, as the stereotypical order to "move along." At the same time, Virilio notes, "[t]he bourgeoisie will get its initial power and class characteristics . . . less from commerce and industry than from the *strategic implantation that establishes the 'fixed domicile' as a social and monetary value*" (9; emphasis in the original). Here, again, order is apparently based simultaneously upon enforced and regulated movement, on the one hand, and upon the stasis of the "fixed domicile," on the other. But Virilio resolves this dichotomy by insisting upon its foundation in a class differential. The stability of the "fixed domicile" is a bourgeois construct that works to dissemble the essential dynamism of social regulatory strategies. True "stability" would be completely antithetical to the mandate of a regulated society; thus, Virilio quotes a nineteenth-century military man, the colonel Delair, as articulating "the general law of this world: *stasis is death*" (13; emphasis in the original), and he himself claims that there is no stability, "there is only *habitable circulation*" (6; emphasis in the original).

In this case, a full understanding of the nature of repressive systems must entail the recognition of "the general law of this world" and thus of the implication of circulation, forced movement, in any social stability. *Resistance* to such systems will be manifested as the attempt to render such regulated circulation *un*inhabitable, using the logic of power against itself. As Virilio puts it,

> The masses are not a population, a society, but the multitude of passersby. The revolutionary contingent attains its ideal form not in the place of production, but in the street, where for a moment it stops being a cog in the technical machine and itself becomes a motor (machine of attack), in other words a *producer of speed*.
>   . . . To lead the . . . workers' army . . . means giving rhythm to the mobile mass's trajectory through vulgar stimulation, a polemical symphony, transmitted far and wide, from one to the other, polyphonic and multicolored like the road signals and traffic directions meant to accelerate the telescoping, the shock of the accident. This is the ultimate goal of street demonstrations, of urban disorder. (3, 4–5; emphasis in the original)

Thus, an attack on power would consist in the imposition of an opposing, disruptive "rhythm" onto the ordered system of movement, in an effort to subvert the rules of circulation by flouting traffic laws, disobeying directional signs, disregarding roads.

According to the Virilian conception, then, many of Nathanael West's characters must represent the potential for profound social disruption, since they approximate very closely to the condition of the picaresque hero, whose itinerary and adventures are "apparently random," [15] and evidently not governed by any regulatory system. Should these characters' waywardness be replicated on a mass scale, there would ensue exactly the sort of circulatory subversion that Virilio sees as characterizing social disorder. Elements of the picaresque are evident in West's work from the first page of *The Dream Life of Balso Snell*, which features an epigraph from Proust's Bergotte: "After all, my dear fellow, life, Anaxagoras has said, is a journey" (*Balso Snell*, 2); more than one commentator has remarked that, standing as it does at the beginning of West's first novel, this line might be taken as a gloss on the whole of his work.[16] *Balso Snell* chronicles the travels of its title character through the entrails of the legendary Trojan horse, which he happens upon inexplicably at the beginning of the novel. *The Day of the Locust* further parodies the picaresque journey, as Tod Hackett makes his way among a multitude of movie sets and the hapless performers who populate them in the Hollywood venue where he lives and works. Miss Lonelyhearts's journey is a moral one, mapped out among the letters he receives from his wretched readers, and taking its erratic nature from the necessarily oblique position of his medium—language—with respect to the "reality" he seeks. It is *A Cool Million* (1934), however, that most clearly and yet most paradoxically depicts the subversive potential of waywardness even when it is manifested by only a single individual rather than a dissident collectivity.[17]

An anti–Horatio Alger story that follows the young Lemuel Pitkin as he "seeks his fortune" in the depression-era United States, *A Cool Million* furnishes its protagonist with some comforting insight from the lips of another character, the nation's former president Nathan "Shagpoke" Whipple: "America is the land of opportunity," Whipple tells Lem. "She takes care of the honest and industrious and never fails them as long as they are both" (150). Such platitudes are offered to Lem throughout the novel, and spur him on his quest. His search is doomed to failure, of course; it cannot be otherwise in West's lampoon of the classic "rags-to-riches" story. In the nature of Lem's failure, however, we can actually locate his triumph, or at least that of West in exploding certain mythologies that subtend the social structure in which his work originates. The nature of this triumph-in-failure is suggested in Shagpoke Whipple's clarification of his position on "America" as "land of opportunity": "This is not a matter of opinion," he insists, "it is one of faith. On the day that Americans stop believing it, on that day will America be lost" (150). The country's profferment of opportunity is not an essential quality, then, but an attribute constituted by the consensus of the people. The downfall of this most necessary national feature will occur at the moment that that consensus disintegrates. This warning both foreshadows and, on a deeper level, comments upon Lemuel Pitkin's own "breakdown."

Lem's journey from his Vermont home to New York City and then to the western sierra—with innumerable side trips to prisons, brothels, and other nonmainstream establishments that Mizruchi might consider sites of abeyance—is frequently punctuated not just by setbacks in his

Resistance in the Novels of Nathanael West

financial status, which is what he seeks to amend, but also by attendant assaults on his person. These assaults—either violent or technical, illicit or sanctioned—often result in Lem's loss of sensory faculty, limb or other body part. For instance, after his honesty and naïveté lead him to become the unwitting fence for a jewel thief, Lem is kicked to unconsciousness by the police officers who arrest him. He is eventually sentenced to fifteen years in the state penitentiary (where, notably, he receives a lecture from the warden on the evils of *transgression,* of swerving from the right path in violation of the rules of the system), and there has all of his teeth extracted (163–66). In time, Lem loses not only his teeth but also his eye (184), his thumb (221), his scalp, and his leg (234). And he loses these parts not once, merely: The dentures that replace his own teeth are repeatedly taken from him and continually fall from his mouth; his glass eye drops out both accidentally and as part of an illegal ruse he unknowingly perpetrates at one point in the story; and his dismemberment is repeatedly replayed as entertainment when, near the end of the novel, he works as the straight man for a pair of slapstick comics whose "object [is] to knock off his toupee or to knock out his teeth and eye" by beating him with rolled-up newspapers (249). By the time of his death at the end of the novel, Lem's body is thoroughly fragmented.

What is notable about Lem's demise, however, is the way West designates it, for he does not refer to it as a "dismemberment," as I do above, but as a "dismantling": Shagpoke Whipple, in his eulogy, asserts that Lem was "dismantled by the enemy" (255); the subtitle of the novel is "The Dismantling of Lemuel Pitkin." In the difference between dismemberment and dismantling we can find a clue to the identity of the actual "victim" in *A Cool Million,* a victim only represented by Lemuel Pitkin himself. If "dismemberment" connotes the destruction, through fragmentation, of an organically integrated physical whole, "dismantling" suggests the division of an *assembled* entity into its constituent parts. The very form of "dismantling" suggests its origin as a designation for the removal of a person's outer garment, or mantle. Insofar as a garment and its wearer's body are not organically united, "dismantling" suggests the demonstration of essential discontinuities rather than the disintegration of essentially integrated wholes. If we look beyond Lemuel Pitkin's actual body—the organic whole—to the discontinuous assemblage affiliated with it—let us call it his "personality"—then we see that what is actually *dismantled,* or *deconstructed,* in West's novel is the notion of the human subject as an integrated, stable entity rather than the manifestation of an endless play of differences and incongruities. *Humanism*—its origin traced by Balso Snell to the Renaissance, which he "blamed . . . for throwing the artist back on his own personality" (*Balso Snell*, 31)—is what finally disintegrates in the satire of *A Cool Million*. Lemuel Pitkin himself exists still—as Shagpoke Whipple puts it, more profoundly than we would expect, "although dead, yet he speaks" (255), and in speaking shows up his actual existence in fragmentation itself. To the extent that humanism is a tool of a system in which only a select elite can actually constitute themselves as effective subjects, then Lemuel Pitkin's unregulated movement, his wandering, his *transgression* is a means to liberation at least of the theory of the subject, perhaps potentially of the subjects themselves.

The Significance of the Motion Picture

> **I went to the movies,**
> **and I saw a dog thirty feet high.**
> **And this dog was made entirely of light.**
> Laurie Anderson, "Walk the Dog," *United States*, part 1

If the violation of the rules of movement is so subversive of power, then it is logical that power would attempt to manage waywardness, not merely through antivagrancy laws, the prohibition of loitering, traffic regulations, etc.—all tactics by the legal arm of the system to keep movement in check—but also, and more insidiously, through capitalist enterprise, by the recontainment of movement within the scheme of signification. This takes place not at the level of communication between individuals but at that of the dissemination of ideology throughout the population. Power seeks to check the subversion of its laws of movement by remanaging—resubverting, as it were—the mechanism of attack against it.

Cinematic film constitutes one attempt at such recontainment in our own era and in that of West, who both worked in the motion-picture industry as a well-paid screenwriter and wrote trenchantly about it in his last novel, *The Day of the Locust*. This novel conceives of the movie business as one of a number of phenomena that draw a spiritually impoverished population to the mecca of southern California during the first half of the century. The nature of the cinema's relation to these other instances of promised enlightenment is actually suggested, however, in *Miss Lonelyhearts*, in which West takes a swipe at religious cults. The narrative presents a newspaper clipping that outlines religious leader Frank Rice's

> "plan for a 'goat and adding machine' ritual for William Moya, condemned slayer. . . . Rice declared the goat would be used as part of a 'sack cloth and ashes' service shortly before and after Moya's execution. . . . Prayers for the condemned man's soul will be offered on an adding machine. Numbers, he explained, constitute the only universal language." (*Miss Lonelyhearts*, 73)

If numbers can represent universally, can stand in for any- and everything, then they are the key to "the universal equality of things," the increased sense of which Walter Benjamin cites as a mark of twentieth-century sensibility.[18] The twentieth-century mode of perception, according to Benjamin, manifests a tendency "[t]o pry an object from its shell, to destroy its aura" (223), which is nowhere greater than in cinema. And Benjamin carefully outlines the political implications of both this tendency and the technology on which it is predicated.

Less carefully, but with vehement disgust, Max Horkheimer and Theodor Adorno, too, identify film as the central constituent of a mass culture that "impresses the same stamp on everything"; "all mass culture," they say, "is identical."[19] West, Benjamin, and Horkheimer and Adorno all comment upon a universalizing, equalizing, identifying tendency in twentieth-century mass culture, and all name film as a symbol of and commentary upon that culture. By depicting in his novels a form of resistance against the reductive effects of the culture industry, however, we might say that West follows Benjamin's suggestion to "politicize art" and turn it against the system that dissembles its own repressiveness by "aestheticizing politics" (Benjamin, 242). In order to see how this is so, we need first to determine what film signifies for West.

Film *does* signify, and not just in the obvious way of combining word, sound, and gesture in a multiplex sign that refers to something exterior to it. It goes further than this, actually subsuming some of the function of language itself, as Benjamin points out. He comments on the linguistic "signposts" that accompany photographs in magazines, and notes that

> captions have become obligatory. And it is clear that they have an altogether different character than the title of a painting. The directives which the captions give to those looking at pictures . . . become even more explicit and more imperative in the film where the

meaning of each single picture appears to be prescribed by the sequence of all preceding ones. (226)

In addition to thus referring to itself, film points as well away from the concrete world to represent an abstraction—potentiality—or, put in terms of human emotion, hope. Benjamin quotes the French novelist Georges Duhamel, who characterizes the cinema as

"a pastime for helots, a diversion for uneducated, wretched, worn-out creatures who are consumed by their worries . . . , a spectacle which requires no concentration and presupposes no intelligence . . . , which kindles no light in the heart and awakens no hope other than the ridiculous one of someday becoming a 'star' in Los Angeles." (239)[20]

The "ridiculousness" of this hope is founded, according to Horkheimer and Adorno, in the fact that "[w]henever the culture industry . . . issues an invitation naïvely to identify [with the screen star], it is immediately withdrawn." As they put it,

the starlet is meant to symbolize the typist in such a way that the splendid evening dress seems meant for the actress as distinct from the real girl. The girls in the audience not only feel that they could be on the screen, but realize the great gulf separating them from it. Only one girl can draw the lucky ticket, only one man can win the prize, and if, mathematically, all have the same chance, yet this is so infinitesimal for each one that he or she will do best to write it off and rejoice in the other's success, which might just as well have been his or hers, and somehow never is. (145)

Nor is this success that of the actor, but of the actor's image, as Benjamin points out. For what film presents to its audience is not the live performer, as in the stage play, but the performer's "estranged" image, an insubstantial apparition "made entirely of light," as Laurie Anderson would have it, mere photoplay. The public is therefore unable to manifest a genuine response to what Benjamin calls the "aura" of the live actor as element in the dramatic art, and, as a sop for this alienation, is offered instead the glamour of the actor removed from film itself. "The film responds to the shriveling of the aura with an artificial build-up of the 'personality' outside the studio," with "the cult of the movie star" in which the public's role as adulator is always clearly defined (see Benjamin, 231).

West, however, sees a limit on the movie industry's ability to manage the resistance of the masses through the fantasy it engenders. That resistance is suppressed, in *The Day of the Locust,* only so long as the public do not recognize themselves as a mass. As individuals, they can be contained in a star/fan dyad manifested in the form of autograph soliciting, for instance, or, even safer, letter writing to a cinema idol. When the fans constitute a crowd, however (at least outside of the theater, within which they form a controllable audience), this sublimation of their essentially violent nature is ineffectual, and destruction, if not of the entertainment industry itself then of those who represent it, becomes their objective. This is clear in West's famous scene of the movie premiere near the end of *The Day of the Locust*. The crowd gathered outside Kahn's Persian Palace Theatre ostensibly merely awaits the arrival of the film's stars. West's description, though, belies the benign aspect of the mass. "Individually," he says, "the purpose of its members might simply be to get a souvenir, but collectively it would grab and rend" (409). And he expands this characterization in a long passage that I quote here in full:

> It was a mistake to think them harmless curiosity seekers. They were savage and bitter, especially the middle-aged and the old, and had been made so by boredom and disappointment.
>
> All their lives they had slaved at some kind of dull, heavy labor, behind desks and counters, in the fields and at tedious machines of all sorts, saving their pennies and dreaming of the leisure that would be theirs when they had enough. Finally that day came. They could draw a weekly income of ten or fifteen dollars. Where else should they go but California, the land of sunshine and oranges?
>
> Once there, they discover that sunshine isn't enough. They get tired of oranges, even of avocado pears and passion fruit. Nothing happens. They don't know what to do with their time. They haven't the mental equipment for leisure, the money nor the physical equipment for pleasure. Did they slave so long just to go to an occasional Iowa picnic? What else is there? They watch the waves come in at Venice. There wasn't any ocean where most of them came from, but after you've seen one wave, you've seen them all. The same is true of the airplanes at Glendale. If only a plane would crash once in awhile so that they could watch the passengers being consumed in a "holocaust of flame," as the newspapers put it. But the planes never crash.
>
> Their boredom becomes more and more terrible. They realize that they've been tricked and burn with resentment. Every day of their lives they read the newspapers and went to the movies. Both fed them on lynchings, murder, sex crimes, explosions, wrecks, love nests, fires, miracles, revolutions, war. This daily diet made sophisticates of them. The sun is a joke. Oranges can't titillate their jaded palates.

> Nothing can ever be violent enough to make taut their slack minds
> and bodies. They have been cheated and betrayed. They have slaved
> and saved for nothing. (411–12)

Indeed, this sense of futility reaches its limit as the crowd West depicts gathered outside the theater erupts into a riot in the face of the movie industry's failure to make good on its promise to the masses.

Resistance thus has a most ironic beginning in *The Day of the Locust*. The interest of power lies in ensuring that the commodification of motion, action, adventure in the form of entertainment indeed defuses the tendency to unregulated, socially disruptive movement by the masses. In West's novel, however, it is precisely in succumbing to the simultaneously offered and withdrawn promise of the culture industry that the masses establish their resistance. It is as slaves of the culture industry that they take to the streets in a mob, disrupting orderly circulation as they subvert the rules of the system that mandates it. And, given what we have witnessed in the case of *A Cool Million*'s Lemuel Pitkin, we should not be surprised that the primary casualty of these marginalized subjects' resistance to containment is himself an estranged entity within the culture, one of the people on whose behalf the struggle is waged, and whose own marginality is a function of his inaptitude at signification, which system is also controlled by the power elite. Homer Simpson, the hapless midwesterner adrift in Los Angeles, becomes the convenient object of the rage that is generated in the crowd by the failure of the movie industry to live up to its promise; the film celebrities never arrive at the premiere, and the mob exacts its revenge upon Homer, whose crazed attack on a vicious child some crowd members have witnessed.

It seems inevitable, in West's novels, that the sacrifice of an individual human subject must occur at the moment of crisis for the system that has heretofore kept the resistance of said subjects in check. Rather than signifying the failure of a particular moment of resistance, however, these sacrifices might be seen as instances of heroism that identify the various local points at which totalized systems of power are vulnerable to attack.[21] In the mid-nineteenth century, Frederick Douglass asserted that "[p]ower concedes nothing without a demand";[22] it is incumbent upon those who wage the struggle to determine the proper form of that demand within their own historical context. As Foucault says, "[I]f the fight is directed against power, then all those on whom power is exercised to their detriment, all who find it intolerable, can begin the struggle on their own terrain and on the basis of their proper activity. . . ."[23] The "proper activity" for those West represents entails the subversion of the system of movement. If mere life, for West's characters, consists in traveling the thoroughfares, as is suggested by the *Balso Snell* epigraph, liberty, he tells us, consists in confronting their order. Such activity is not without its dangers, as Homer Simpson or Lemuel Pitkin might testify—or West himself, could he speak beyond the fact of his own demise. Paul Virilio alludes to the danger when he quotes Weber on the disappearance of Rosa Luxemburg and Karl Liebknecht: "[T]hey called to the streets, and the streets killed them" (Virilio, 3). The same might be said of West and the heroes of his novels.

The activity of these personages, however, represents the sort of noncentralized, dispersed attack upon a structurally totalizing system of power that poststructuralism prescribes as a mode of resistance to the repressive forces of our era. In its depiction of such local resistance, Nathanael West's work of the 1930s anticipates the modality of much late-twentieth-century social critique, and provides us with a literary vision of the form of contemporary political struggle. It also suggests that the fragmented nature of the postmodern subject has an analog in the psychic experiences of the marginalized populations that wage such resistance. The remainder of this study explores several different instances of social marginality for the specific ways that they approximate the postmodern condition, and in order to consider their relation to it.

ANAÏS NIN, DJUNA BARNES, AND THE CRITICAL FEMINIST UNCONSCIOUS

Female Self-Fashioning in Nin's "Continuous Novel"

We have seen that the social marginality of Betty, in Nathanael West's *Miss Lonelyhearts,* and Faye, in *The Day of the Locust,* is rooted in these characters' alienation from the process of linguistic signification. It is equally clear that their position in the world of the novels is a typical reflection of women's historical alienation from the centers of social and political power. The conjunction of the factors of gender and linguistic significance makes for the works' peculiar conception of the nature of the female subject, exemplified in Tod Hackett's apprehension of Faye Greener's "egglike self-sufficiency" (West, 320). Tod's perception of Faye as "egglike" underscores not only the "self-sufficiency" he himself notes in Faye's alienation from signification but also her femaleness, suggesting an essential correspondence between femininity and self-sufficiency, completeness, wholeness. This female wholeness is then held up to counter men's status as beings irremediably fragmented in their accession to language, and yet doomed futilely to attempt to mend their fragmentation through linguistic signification itself. Thus West's works, while explicating the reality of the split subject as it is known in the twentieth century, yet specify that subject as male, positing women's condition as a foil against which the "general" existential dilemma of all "mankind" can be emphasized.

It is possible, however, to see women's social marginality as bound up not necessarily with a wholeness existent outside the order of language, but rather with a radical incompleteness predicated upon the very gender politics that universalizes male experience. This female incompleteness, dialectically played against the aforementioned conception of woman's wholeness, constitutes the field of inquiry of the writers discussed in this chapter.

In the preface to her massive work of fiction, the five-volume continuous novel *Cities of the Interior,* Anaïs Nin says that her only "preconception" of the work "was that it was to be a study of women. The first book" of the series, she says, "turned out to be *Ladders to Fire.* All the women I was to write about appeared in it, including Stella, whom I later dropped because she seemed so complete in herself rather than related to the other women."[1] Stella's "completeness" (what we might call her "self-sufficiency") renders her marginal to Nin's concerns in *Cities* in much the same way that the completeness and self-sufficiency of Faye and Betty render them marginal to the significant order of West's novels. And yet there is a difference, for West attends to the condition of men alienated from themselves through language and whose condition represents that of the human race in general; Nin, on the other hand, draws characters whose incompleteness is part and parcel of their existence as women, specifically, and who are yet *interrelated* in their incompleteness in a way that suggests a structural unity among the larger community of women.

I return to the possibility of such an autonomous, self-sufficient women's community later in the chapter; first, it is necessary to trace the search for complete *individual* subjectivity that Nin's characters undertake, for Nin manifests a humanism that privileges individual subjectivity above all else, and motivates her female characters in a quest that leads them, ironically, to men as saviors from a debilitating personal fragmentation. Nin puts it this way:

> This seeking of man the guide in a dark city, this aimless wandering through the streets touching men and seeking the guide—this was a fear all women had known . . . seeking the guide in men, not in the past, or in mythology, but a guide with a living breath who might create one, help one to be born as a woman, a guide they wished to possess for themselves alone, in their own isolated woman's soul. The guide for woman was still inextricably woven with man and with man's creation. (*Ladders to Fire,* 110–11)

For woman *is* man's creation, in the view of Nin's characters, incomplete until he fashions her into a unity. The character Lillian suggests this near the very end of the work when she discusses with her male lover her relationship with another woman, Sabina. Jay has suggested that his contribution to Lillian's life has been "coarse and plain" compared to Sabina's. "No, Jay," Lillian responds, "you made me a woman. Sabina would have thrust me back into being half a woman, as I was before I met you" (*Seduction of the Minotaur,* 582).

Thus men are responsible for repairing the fragmentation of Nin's women, for forging their integrity. Sabina feels it too, though somewhat differently. Throughout *A Spy in the House of Love,* in which she is the title character, Sabina seeks her wholeness in a succession of male lovers, propelled by a fear of her own disintegration:

> [S]he was afraid because there was no Sabina, not ONE, but a multitude of Sabinas lying down yielding and being dismembered, constellating in all directions and breaking. . . . [S]he was weeping: "Someone hold me—hold me, so I will not continue to race from one love to another, dispersing me, disrupting me . . . *Hold me to one.* . . ." (439)

Sabina envisions herself making this plea directly to her husband, Alan. Typically, she imagines herself dispersed in a multiplicity, proliferating new selves over time:

> Each year, just as a tree puts forth a new ring of growth, she should have been able to say: "Alan, here is a new version of Sabina. Add it to the rest, fuse them well, hold on to them when you embrace her, hold them all at once in your arms, or else, divided, separated, each image will live a life of [i]ts own, and it will not be one but six, or seven, or eight Sabinas who will walk sometimes in unison, by a great effort of synthesis, sometimes separately, one of them following a deep drumming into forests of black hair and luxurious mouths, another visiting Vienna-as-it-was-before-the-war, and still another lying beside an insane young man, and still another opening maternal arms to a trembling frightened Donald.["] Was this the crime to have sought to marry each Sabina to another mate, to match each one in turn by a different life? (*A Spy in the House of Love,* 453)

The third of Nin's three women similarly faces the horror of fragmentation, experienced as a splitting: "[Djuna's] life was . . . divided into two parts"; she felt "as one who had been split into two pieces by some great invisible saber cut" (*Children of the Albatross,* 131). She tries at one point to explain this sensation to a "simple man," his "simpleness" suggesting the unitary nature of his being as Djuna perceives it in contrast to her own fragmentedness: "*There is something broken inside of me*" (135). But the ballet master whom she addresses represents the key to her mending, for Djuna is a dancer, and, "at the moment of dancing a fusion took place, a welding, a wholeness. The cut in the middle of her body healed, and she was all one woman moving" (132). The effectiveness of dance is predicated on its fluidity, its defiance of stasis and fixed boundaries, so that while dancing, Djuna feels spatially transported "across continents and oceans" (132). Later, an older Djuna achieves this same sense of fluidity in the company of two young men she has befriended: "Nowhere else as here with Lawrence and with Paul was there such an iridescence in the air; nowhere else so far from the threat of hardening and crystallizing. Everything flowing . . . " (168).

There is, then, a detectable pattern. By her own admission, Nin's women are incomplete subjects, and, in their incompleteness, somehow "related to" each other. Yet, rather than achieving a structural wholeness in their interrelation, Nin's characters are primarily motivated to seek completion through men, and each of them has her own savior from the threat of incompleteness. Lillian, who had been "half a woman," feels whole in her union with Jay; Sabina, fragmented in her dispersity, seeks a unifying force in Alan; Djuna, divided into two parts, finds healing first in the art of the ballet master and then in the company of the young Lawrence and Paul. The narrative is insistent in its depiction of the rescue of woman from her essential incompleteness by man, who is the creator of her integrated self. This simple explication does not address the full complexity of the interrelation of men and women in Nin's work, however, and a more extensive analysis of gender relations in the novel(s) will provide us not only with an understanding of why Nin's women fail to achieve the individual wholeness that they seek but also with a sense of why Nin finds so problematic the creation of a *collective* female subjectivity that she herself suggests as a possibility.

In order to appreciate fully the complex relation between men and women in Nin's work, let us return to the passage on the power of "man's creation," quoted above. This passage is ambiguous in that, on the one hand, it seems to affirm the integral role man plays in the creation of woman's self, underscoring the importance of this "guide with a living breath"; on the other hand, the passage asserts the "fear all women had known" in the seeking of that male guide. That this fear coexists with women's apparent desire to achieve selfhood through man indicates a deep recognition that the power men exert over women's self-fashioning is far from uniformly benevolent. Indeed, it is possible to see the disruptive function men play with respect to the female self even in the relationships between Nin's women and the very men through whom they seek psychic wholeness.

We can note, for instance, that, in addition to Alan, Sabina seeks a sort of completeness through her various male lovers. Each of her multiple selves seeks "marriage" with a different man, a conjugal union traditionally conceived as completing woman's personality. This impulse toward an assortment of marriages thus runs counter to the ameliorative effect Alan would have on Sabina's fragmented being, for while each of her different selves might find wholeness with its particular mate, the various unions serve only to crystallize the dispersity of Sabina's different selves, preventing their fusion into one whole person by Alan or anyone else, which is supposedly Sabina's objective. In the case of the lovers, then, men's status as cure for psychic dispersal predicates their status as both symptom and cause of that very fragmentation.

Thus Jay—whom Lillian credits with having "made [her] a woman" who had been only "half a woman" previously—is simultaneously the agent of women's figural fragmentation, the full force of which strikes Sabina at an exhibit of his paintings. Jay produces chaotic canvases that depict

> figures exploded and constellated into fragments, like spilled puzzles, each piece having flown far enough away to seem irretrievable and yet not far enough to be dissociated. One could, with an effort of the imagination, reconstruct a human figure completely from these fragments[,]

and the gender of this figure is pointedly specified: "By one effort of contraction at the core [these fragments] might still amalgamate to form the body of a woman" (*Spy*, 441). Jay's painting is thus no abstraction, and Sabina's further musings reveal it to be an instance of that emphatically representational genre—portraiture—for she "could see at this moment on the wall *an exact portrait of herself as she felt inside*" (441; emphasis in original).

At the same time, the accuracy with which Jay, in Sabina's view, has represented her "inner" self gives a clue to how Nin's women can view men as a unifying force for the female psyche despite these men's actual contribution to women's fragmentation, "real" or figurative. For the *accuracy* of Jay's mimetic representation—its *exact correspondence* with psychic reality—actually signals the *integrity* of Jay's art and the integrating force of Jay the artist, despite the fragmented "reality" he depicts. The good intentions of the artist thus established, the function of the narrative shifts from the explication of women's psychic status to advocacy on behalf of the artist. Thus, although the figure represented on Jay's canvas is that of a woman, specifically, Nin's narrator credits the artist with revealing "what took place inside the body and emotions of *man*" (441; my emphasis), thereby "universalizing" the import of the painting. This accomplished, the now-integrative, unifying agency of the painter is demonstrated to be subordinate to a larger, negative social force that imposes fragmentation upon the creative artist, whose plight the narrator laments:

> . . . [W]hen the painter exposed what took place inside the body and emotions of man, they starved him, or gave him Fifth Avenue shop windows to do, where Paris La Nuit in the background allowed fashions to display hats and shoes and handbags and waists floating in mid-air, and waiting to be assembled on one complete woman. (441)

Thus, what originally appeared as a man's contribution to women's figural fragmentation is recast as his essentially integrative function, subverted by the force of consumer capital into the production of a dispersed, fragmented display of women's *effects,* while the "real" woman, accurately portrayed by the painter as fragmented, walks the streets, falsely "complete." Through a process of generalization, then, this passage represents Nin's abiding (and ironic) reluctance to set forth a feminist analysis of women's psychic disorder, as the specifically feminine experience of psychic fragmentation is recast as the plight of a universalized "mankind," represented by the (male) artist whose attempts to forge subjective integrity are subverted by the dictates of the marketplace in such a way that the specific *gender* politics that contribute to women's fragmented state are completely elided.

I would not, however, attribute Nin's insistence on the economic origins of psychic disorder to a belief on her part in historical materialism. Rather, her romanticized view of the role of the artist, which implies a loathing for the commercialization of art (an attitude that I discuss more fully as characteristic of modernist ideology, in chapter 5), affords her with a fortuitous contingency whereby she can "explain" the "general" phenomenon of psychic fragmentation without recourse to feminist politics, which she is neither inclined nor equipped to undertake, as we shall soon see. Nonetheless, it is possible to identify in Nin's work points where the existence of a sort of "feminist unconscious" might be discerned—passages where there is suggested a more complex relationship between gender politics and consumer capital than is presented in the passage on the commercialization of art.

In an earlier scene, capitalism, rather than *imposing* a fragmenting function upon men, merely *enables* them in that function, providing them with particular means by and forms through which to enact the fragmentation of female subjectivity, even while they seem to promise wholeness for women. The same topos of the shop-window display that the narrator invokes in *A Spy in the House of Love* is a locus of narrative action in *Children of the Albatross*. It is in this novel that Djuna experiences the fluidity, the freedom "from the threat of hardening and crystallizing," that characterizes the company of the two young men, Lawrence and Paul. As Djuna herself puts it, these two men "hate the father" (168), by which she means, in psychoanalytic terms, that they occupy the position of the male child in the Oedipal triangle, and thus repudiate the patriarchal law (embodied in language) that mandates the child's separation from the mother and generally articulates division and fragmentation. At the same time, however, as male subjects who will necessarily eventually accede to just that position of patriarchal power that they now resist, these young men, no less than Jay or Sabina's lovers, harbor the potential for fragmenting women's figural representations, at least, if not their actual beings. The narrative provides us with a description of Lawrence's unusual avocation:

> Lawrence was now working in a place which made decorations for shop windows. He liked to work at night, to go on strange expeditions in the company of mannequins. . . . To flirt with naked mannequins whose arms came off as easily as other women's gloves, who deposited their heads on the floor and took off their wigs when they took off their hats. He became an expert at dismantling women! (169)

The image is an arresting one, and the passage recalls the discussion of the import of "dismantling" in West's fiction. After neatly distinguishing "dismantling" from "dismembering" in the previous chapter, we now come upon Nin's passage, which concisely re-conflates the two operations so that undressing and amputating become two facets of the same act, performed upon women (or their representational standins) by men. And, despite Nin's ambivalence about the gendered power differential manifest in this operation—evidenced in the lighthearted affect of the passage's final exclamation point—the subjective exercise of masculine interest is clear in this scene. For while elsewhere the capitalist marketplace seems to *dictate* man's dismemberment of the female subject, in this particular instance it merely *enables* the man in question to perform the dual function of dismantling/dismemberment. I would argue that the enabling role of capitalism here consists in its

The Critical Feminist Unconscious

assimilating to a public function the conventionally private operation of men's undressing of women, the result being the identification of disrobing with dismembering that Nin thematizes.

It is not unheard of in our culture for men to undress women quite completely, in full public view, and yet in a nonpublicized, nonphysical manner: We often say that a man undresses a woman "with his eyes," the reference being to the aggressive gaze turned upon a woman by a man who imagines her nude, available for his sexual pleasure. The function of this gaze in Nin's work is most forcefully exemplified in the character of Jay, who manifests toward woman "a violent desire to rip all her pretenses, her veils, and to discover the core of her self which . . . escaped all detection" (*A Spy in the House of Love*, 450). This desire for "discovery" of woman is the motivating force behind men's disrobing of the female figure in Nin's work, and the "socially acceptable" method of achieving this disrobing—"with the eyes"—represents the uncanny assumption of an essentially tactile operation—undressing—by the instruments of vision that seek to "know" the woman by perceiving her in her stripped state. Thus, the man's gaze, in its metaphorical overstepping of its physical limitations, represents a most powerful function in Western sexual politics.

At the same time, men's desire "to know" women represents a very specific wish in Nin's novels. Men's "discovery" of a woman does not denote the apprehension of new information regarding a particular, unique female being and its subsequent incorporation into a previously constituted core of knowledge about other individual human subjects. Rather, Nin's men seek to "discover" each woman's essential *conformity* to their own conception of woman; they seek commonality among the multiplicity of female subjects, a commonality represented, for Jay, in women's anatomy: "He had long ago found a way to neutralize the potencies of woman by a simplification all his own, which was to consider all women as sharing but one kind of hunger, a hunger situated between the two pale columns of the legs" (214). The narrative traces this technique of Jay's to his childhood experience with a European housekeeper in his family's home:

> Jay was playing on the floor with matches, unnoticed, and he found himself covered as by a huge and colorful tent by the perfoliate skirt of the German woman, his glance lost where two pale columns converged in a revelation which had given him forever this perspective of woman's being, this vantage point of insight, this observatory and infallible focus, which prevented him from losing his orientation in the vastest maze of costumes, classes, races, nationalities—no exter-

nal variations able to deprive him of this intimate knowledge of woman's most secret architecture. . . . (214)

Thus, by means of the male gaze, all women are reduced to "woman," represented solely by the female sexual organs, a "simplification" that renders women manageable for Jay, apparently by nullifying the "potency" of their difference. (We might note, as well, the simplification performed here with respect to women's "racial" identity, for, if women's essence lies at the juncture of the "pale columns of the legs," then where does even this trivialized, "stripped-down" femininity exist for women of a darker hue?)

This simplification is enacted explicitly in Nin's novel upon Sabina, whose experience of it most fully demonstrates the threat of the gaze to women's stable individual identity. At her first encounter with Philip, one of her lovers, Sabina notes that Philip

> turned his eyes . . . upon her. They were impersonal and seemed to gaze beyond her at all women who were dissolved into one, but who might at any moment again become dissolved into all. This was the gaze Sabina had always encountered in Don Juan, everywhere; it was the gaze she mistrusted. It was the alchemy of desire fixing itself upon the incarnation of all women into Sabina for a moment but as easily by a second process able to alchemize Sabina into many others.
>
> Her identity as the "unique" Sabina loved by Alan was threatened. Her mistrust of his glance made the blood flow cold within her. (380)

The power of the man's gaze is clear: Like Lawrence among the mannequins, it not only disrobes the woman but also dismantles her, undermines the coherence of her very self. If the man generalizes and sees in the single woman *all* women, this multiplication of the woman's image is the destruction of her self, for her unique person disintegrates at the moment her difference from others is denied.

Sabina's response to this situation is, appropriately, divided. On the one hand, she continues to seek a remedy for her dissociation in men, specifically in her husband Alan, caretaker of the "unique" Sabina. On the other hand, she would like to enjoy the power over her own persona that the male apparently wields. Seeing in Philip a "full assurance that he ultimately always obtained his desire," she admits to herself that "she hated this assurance, she envied it" (381). Elsewhere, Sabina contemplates "what she imagined was a quality possessed exclusively by man: some dash, some audacity, some swagger of freedom denied to woman" (366). Sabina tries to convey this quality as operative in

The Critical Feminist Unconscious

her own life, and when she is successful at it, as she sometimes is, a reversal of gender roles results, so that, for instance,

> Jay hated her, hated her as Don Juan hates Dona Juana, as the free man hates the free woman, as man hates in woman this freedom in passion which he grants solely to himself. Hated her because he knew instinctively that she regarded him as he regarded woman: as a possible or impossible lover.
>
> He was not for her a man endowed with particular gifts, standing apart from other men, irreplaceable as Lillian saw him, unique as his friends saw him. Sabina's glance measured him as he measured women: endowed or not endowed as lovers. (92)

Thus Jay, the man, is relegated to a state of nonidentity, his individuality dismantled like that of Sabina or Nin's other women in their encounters with men. And yet Sabina's achievement of this "masculine" freedom—while seeming to promise her self-coherence—entails the loss of her physical coherence. Sabina identifies as the sign of her liberation the attainment of orgasmic release in the company of a man for whom she feels no emotion, no "warmth of the heart" (394). This sensual release is described in terms of the same dissolution that characterizes women's psyches in their objectification and deindividualization by men. Having reached no climax during her first sexual encounter with Philip, she feels "Anger, Anger—*at this core which will not melt,* while Sabina wills to be like man, free to possess and desire in adventure, to enjoy a stranger" (386; my emphasis). Her desire here is for the sensation of *decenteredness*—the melting of her core—that will attend orgasm, and it is purely physical: After her first frustration,

> Sabina hoped [Philip] might tell her something that would melt the unmeltable sensual core, . . . break through her resistance.
>
> Then the absurdity of her expectation amazed her: seeking another kind of fusion because she had failed to achieve the sensual one, when what she wanted was only the sensual one. . . . (387)

The reference to "fusion" here is ironic, for it diverts attention to the "union" of man and woman in sensual pleasure, distracting from the "melting of her core" that Sabina actually seeks—her own *diffusion* or dissolution. When she does finally achieve this, it is with a sense of her newly attained effectivity as a free subject: "She opened her eyes to contemplate the piercing joy of her liberation: she was free, free as man was, to enjoy without love. . . . as a man could, she had enjoyed a stranger" (394). Thus, the physical sensation of dispersal, described by Nin as the familiar "exploding of fireworks" (394), seems to signal a subjective synthesis, insofar as Sabina now sees herself as the effective agent of her own pleasure. The site of her attainment of that pleasure, however, suggests her actual self-dispersal even in this moment of "freedom," for her liberation necessarily entails union with a "stranger"—one of her series of fleeting lovers—and we know that it is precisely when she is with these lovers that she feels most dispersed, psychically. The text makes this clear in describing the calm that succeeds her release. Noting Sabina's existence as a spy in the "war of love," Nin identifies as "her neutral zone, the moment when she belonged to none, when she gathered her dispersed self together again" (396). The conflation of psychic identity and physical being in the "self" referred to here suggests the actual loss of coherent subjectivity that plagues Sabina—like all of Nin's women—even when she seems to have achieved psychic coherence. Women seem to be denied any means of forging a stable, centered self-identity, and even when they appear to have discovered a successful method (the assumption of men's "mantle," for instance) their attempts lead circularly back to denial of individual selfhood despite all their efforts to be One. Despite her own reluctance to frame the situation in useful gender-political terms, Nin's fiction suggests that there is something inherent in the structure of gender relations that keeps women circling the territory of self-effectivity, always denied the apparently male prerogative of self-definition.

Lillian, like Sabina, has also attempted a reversal of prescribed gender roles, making aggressive overtures to her would-be lover, Gerard. She reflects upon the failure of these overtures: "I lost Gerard because I leaped" (15); and the narrative elaborates upon her statement: "Nothing could prevent her from feeling that she was not Juliet waiting on the balcony, but Romeo who had to leap across space to join her. She had leaped, she had acted Romeo, and when woman leaped she leaped into a void" (39–40). The dominant gender politics provide women with *no support* for acting as effective subjectivities, no *ground* upon which to leap. But while from her own perspective as frustrated subject, woman seems to leap "into a void"—her assertive act apparently signifying nothing—in the context of the dominant sexuopolitical order there is no void, no action that is not absorbed into the economy of signification. It remains to determine exactly what women's essays at subjective agency do signify in the governing social order, and while the ramifications of that significance are wide-reaching, they originate very specifically in the operation of the male gaze.

Theorizing Women's Divided Experience

One of the most influential theorists of the function of the male gaze in contemporary culture is the film critic Laura Mulvey. Her classic article on "Visual Pleasure and Narrative Cinema" forcefully makes the point that informs the foregoing observations on Nin's fiction: "In a world ordered by sexual imbalance, pleasure in looking has been split between active/male and passive/female. The determining male gaze projects its phantasy on to the female figure which is styled accordingly."[2] This split is manifested in narrative film as a dichotomy between "narrative" and "spectacle" that "supports the man's role as the active one of forwarding the story, making things happen." Thus, as Mulvey puts it, a feeling of "omnipotence" is engendered in the idealized male spectator of any given film, as he "identifies with the main male protagonist, . . . projects his look on to that of his . . . screen surrogate, so that the power of the male protagonist as he controls events [in the film] coincides with the active power of the erotic look," which takes as its object the female screen presence (12). The primary cinematic problem posed by the active male/passive female dichotomy is the disruption in narrative flow caused by prolonged exposure of the (diegetically superfluous) female icon to the controlling gaze. This problem is relatively minor, however, and can be resolved through any number of filmic techniques, such as incorporating the issue of man's possession of woman's image into the story line.

More problematic, claims Mulvey, is the psychoanalytic significance of the female figure, for, in addition to pleasure, "[s]he also connotes something that the [man's] look continually circles around but disavows: her lack of a penis, implying a threat of castration and hence unpleasure" (13). Following Freud, Mulvey asserts that

> [t]he male unconscious has two avenues of escape from this castration anxiety: preoccupation with the re-enactment of the original trauma (investigating the woman, demystifying her mystery [cf. Jay's impulse to "simplify" women in Nin's novels]), counterbalanced by the devaluation, punishment or saving of the guilty [female] object . . . ; or else complete disavowal of castration by the substitution of a fetish object or turning the represented [female] figure itself into a fetish so that it becomes reassuring rather than dangerous. . . . (13–14)

Mulvey then posits Alfred Hitchcock's *Vertigo* (Paramount, 1958) as an example of the complex cinematic employment of both these techniques for escape from castration anxiety. The male protagonist of the film, Scottie (James Stewart), in his capacity as private investigator, "watches and falls in love with a perfect image of female beauty and mystery" (Mulvey, 16). That image, however, is a "false" one, an imposture perpetrated by a woman whose "real" life is radically divergent from the one she represents to Scottie's scrutiny. Eventually, he unwittingly meets this impostor, and succeeds in recreating her in the very likeness she had earlier worked to produce, which he now fetishizes. The woman herself (played by Kim Novak) takes an appropriately passive role in this re-creation, but, in the end, her acquiescence to the makeover results in proof of her own "real" duplicity—her "truth" is discovered and she must pay the consequences. Fetishization and demystification work together in *Vertigo* to defuse the threat of castration represented in the female figure.

The overview of *Vertigo* provided by Mulvey gives us an idea of the general operation of the heterosexual male gaze in narrative cinema, but in addition to the effects that Mulvey cites, the film offers in one particular a graphic illustration of the interrelation between the function of the male gaze and the "void" encountered by Nin's women when they attempt to invert the sexuopolitical hierarchy in which the gaze derives its power. A more extensive review of the film's story line will help us to understand both the "void" and the apparently inescapable fragmentation that Nin's female characters face in their search for individual subjectivity.

Hitchcock's Judy Barton is a salesclerk in a clothing store, transplanted to San Francisco from Kansas, and taken up by an unscrupulous industrialist, Gavin Elster, first as mistress, then as accomplice in the murder of his wife. His plan is to make his wife's death look like a suicide, and to ensure that there will be a witness to testify to that effect. Consequently, he calls on his old college friend, John Ferguson ("Scottie"), newly retired from active duty as a police officer due to his fear of heights and associated vertigo, and requests him to follow and watch his wife, Madeleine. Madeleine, says Elster, is not herself lately; she is surely possessed by the spirit of her great-grandmother, the Spanish dancer Carlotta Valdes, and he fears that she will commit suicide as Carlotta did when she was Madeleine's age. Scottie does trail "Madeleine"—actually Judy disguised to look like Madeleine looking like an old portrait of Carlotta that hangs in a local museum; the real Madeleine lives away in the country. He becomes entranced by her beauty and mystery, and determines to break the spell that he, too, now believes afflicts her. He is unsuccessful in this; "Madeleine" seems driven to death, once attempting suicide by throwing herself into the San

Francisco Bay, and finally succeeding in it at the old mission where Carlotta was born. Visiting the site with Scottie, she tells him there is something she must do in the church. She breaks from him and runs up the stairs of the church tower. He tries to follow her, but his acrophobia prevents him. All he can do is listen to the shriek she emits upon reaching the top of the tower, and watch her body fall past the tower window from the landing where he sits, paralyzed with vertigo.

But it is all a charade. Gavin Elster is positioned at the top of the tower when the disguised Judy arrives. In his arms he holds the body of his wife, already dead with a broken neck, and when Judy reaches the landing he hurls the body from the tower, as Judy screams. The point, of course, is that when "Madeleine" leaps into the void, as it were, it is for Scottie's visual benefit. He must see her take her plunge in order to act as a witness in Elster's interest. Similarly, the leap "Madeleine" makes into the bay earlier in the film is calculated precisely for Scottie's visual consumption, apprising him of "Madeleine's" apparent suicidal tendencies. The phenomenon of an "illusory" Madeleine created solely as an object for Scottie's gaze, however, simultaneously implies a "real" woman—Elster's actual wife, certainly, but, more important here, Judy—behind this facade. Thus the figure of the woman in the film is from the very first constituted as a duality: the "public" woman, meant for visual consumption by the male, and the "private" woman, whose mystery the man seeks to uncover.

Scottie succeeds in discovering the "real" woman. He accidentally comes upon Judy in her "normal" aspect some months after Madeleine's death. Though he has been released from the mental hospital where he was incarcerated after the incident, he is still obsessed by his love for Madeleine. He is struck by Judy's resemblance to her, approaches her, and convinces her to commence dating him (for she, the "real" Judy, has always secretly loved him); but she must allow him to make her over into "Madeleine's" image, which he fetishizes. She reluctantly concedes, and is transformed to appear as "Madeleine" did, to Scottie's pleasure, until one evening when she puts on a piece of jewelry that "Madeleine" had worn. Scottie becomes suspicious and coaxes Judy to the scene of the crime. Once at the mission, he induces her to confess her guilt in Madeleine's death as he forces her to climb the tower stairs, himself determined to make it to the top this time despite his fear. At the top of the tower, Judy begs forgiveness, pleading her love for Scottie, and while they are thus engaged one of the mission nuns appears in the belfry, curious about the noise. Apparently convinced that the shaded figure is Madeleine's ghost, Judy leaps from the tower to her death, the status of her "real" self now coinciding with that of the illusion she had perpetrated. Of course, it was not really she who perpetrated the ruse or the murder, it was the man, Gavin Elster, but by now the film's complicity with male self-interest is completely established. Thus, the camera, homologous (according to Mulvey) with the eyes of both the film's (male) spectator and the male protagonist, does not witness Judy's plunge as it did that of "Madeleine." The "private" nature of this latter leap seals the essential duality of woman according to the reality/appearance dichotomy noted earlier, with the precipitating factor in the dichotomy the male gaze itself.

Vertigo's treatment of male/female relations illuminates the sexuopolitical problematic depicted in Nin's fiction, for it is now clear that the "void" into which Lillian (or any of Nin's women) leaps when she takes the initiative with a man is a figure for her ineffectivity as an active subject within the general sphere of heterosexual relations, in which she serves merely to consolidate men in a patriarchal social structure that furthers their interests. This is not to say that women do not ever succeed as active subjects in concrete instances, but rather that their actual success or failure is potentially irrelevant, since any assertive action they take might always be assimilated, by the consuming male gaze, to the category of woman's "public" persona, and thus implicated in the buttressing of patriarchy. At the same time, no matter what the nature of her activity, this "public" woman also always constitutes a foil against which an "essential," "private" woman—Jay's reductive vision of genitalia, for instance—is formulated as an object for men's "discovery." The patriarchal context in which women's action originates continually threatens to determine the ultimate significance and function of that action, no matter what the intention of the woman performing it.

This is not a new observation; numerous commentators have noted that a primary function of woman in patriarchal society consists in the establishment of the very ties between men that constitute that patriarchy. Eve Sedgwick has extensively demonstrated how, on the one hand, the woman is ostensibly the object of the man's erotic desire; on the other hand, and less obviously, she functions to further homosocial bonding *between men,* to men's sociopolitical advantage.[3] Before Sedgwick, Gayle Rubin cited Claude Lévi-Strauss's claim that "the total relationship of exchange which constitutes marriage is not established between a man and a woman, but between two groups of men, and the woman figures only as one of the objects in the exchange, not as one of the partners. . . ." [4] Rubin has offered her own comments:

> This analysis of society as based on bonds between men by means of women makes the separatist responses of the women's movement thoroughly intelligible. Separatism can be seen as a mutation in social structure, as an attempt to form social groups based on unmediated bonds between women. It can also be seen as a radical denial of men's "rights" in women, and as a claim by women of rights in themselves. (175n)

This passage is a product of its time, which saw the rise of a feminist separatism strongly identified in the United States with a "political lesbianism" that perceived women's continued social and sexual servicing of men as a barrier to the realization of their own personal and political autonomy. This politics was articulated in radical feminist documents published during the early 1970s, in particular, "The Woman-Identified Woman" and "Realesbians and Politicalesbians." [5] Whatever the status of separatist politics presently (and separatism is still a political strategy undertaken by many women in the name of radical feminism), [6] Rubin's commentary cogently suggests both the importance to feminist politics of the extensive analysis of sociopolitical bonds between men and the potentially powerful effects to be generated in the uniting of women in a politicized collective subjectivity. Both of these phenomena—the bonding of men in patriarchy and woman-identified feminist resistance to that patriarchy—though intent on different political ends, are predicated on the function of homo*sociality* as a dynamic distinct from homo*sexuality*. It is Anaïs Nin's failure to conceive of such a dynamic (in the case of men *or* women) that prevents her from understanding either women's individual psychic fragmentation as a political phenomenon deriving from patriarchy or women's collective subjectivity as a potential remedy for that fragmentation.

It is easy enough to find, in Nin's fiction, an instance of woman serving as a bond between men; indeed, *Children of the Albatross* presents a literal realization of that classic triadic structure. In that novel, Djuna wonders about her relation to her erstwhile lover, Michael, and his new liaison, Donald, as they drink at a Paris cafe:

> Why should she be sitting between Michael and Donald?
>   . . . [Michael] had this need to invent a trinity: to establish a con-

necting link between Djuna and all the changing, fluctuating Donalds.

As if some element were lacking in his relation to Donald.

. . . Love flowing now between the three, shared, transmitted, contagious, . . . *the missing dimension of their love accomplished in space like an algebra of imperfection, an abstract drama of incompleteness at last resolved for one moment by this trinity of woman sitting between two incomplete men.* (156, 159)

The passage that I emphasize is both the answer to Djuna's question and the obfuscation of the pertinent issue. For Nin's female character does indeed represent a bond *between men,* to the diminishment of her own subjectivity, and yet Nin seems to locate the source of that diminishment specifically in the *erotic* nature of Michael's and Donald's relation, rather than in the essential structure of male homosocial union.

Nin's Djuna evinces an exasperation with her implication in male homosocial bonding ("When," she asks herself, "will I stop loving these airy young men" [160]) that is founded more on her sense of the "incompleteness" or "insufficiency" of male homoeroticism than on the detrimental effect upon women of male homosocial union *per se.* When Donald confides to her, "I am not sure I love Michael," it is "exactly what she expected to hear. Always this admission of incompleteness" (157). Djuna's interpretation of this confession implies her conviction of the inadequacy of male–male erotic union and indicates a heterosexism and a homophobia that obscure the pertinent sexuopolitical issues Nin's work raises. An extensive excerpt from her voluminous *Diary* serves to illustrate Nin's views on male homosexuality. In the homosexual, she says,

> I never see perversion, but rather a childlike quality . . . [as] when one hesitates to enter the adult world. The relationship based on identification . . . or "the double," on narcissism, is a choice more facile and less exigent than that between men and women . . . whenever I came close to a homosexual, . . . I found . . . a fixation on preadolescence, . . . and always some traumatic event which caused fear of woman, hence the hatred of her . . .
>
> This hatred of woman I had never experienced until I came to America. The Spanish homosexual or the French homosexual loved men but did not hate women. Paradoxically, they romanticized her. . . .
>
> In the American homosexual it was the hatred of woman which was a perversity, for it distorted reality. . . . The constant presence of an enemy makes for the opposite of innocence. . . . It may have

The Critical Feminist Unconscious

been for this reason that there were no romantic love stories. Homosexual novels were stories of promiscuity, not love.

. . . It is totality the homosexual fears. He separates love and sexuality.[7]

This passage is highly problematic, for a number of reasons. First, Nin identifies in male homosexuality (at least in the "American" variety) a fundamental misogyny. She is not altogether wrong in doing this *insofar as* male homosexuality can represent an example of male homosocial bonding that serves to consolidate masculinist subjectivity against the interests of women. The fact is, however, that in U.S. culture, male homosexuality has very rarely, if ever, constituted a plank in the implicit masculinist platform on which the dominant social structure has been built, regardless of the gender politics of any given homosexual or group of homosexual men. It is not male homoeroticism *per se* in which misogynist attitudes are manifested but rather in the homosocial structures of patriarchy. Homoerotic relations might derive some benefit from these structures, but they do so *in spite of* their erotic nature, which is conventionally seen as completely at odds with masculinist interests.[8] So it is that homosocially constituted patriarchy often effects its most potent misogyny in the context of heterosexual relationships. Nin's failure to see this precludes her as well from gaining insight into the interrelation between the male homosexual condition and female existence in U.S. society.

Further, in the above passage Nin evinces but a shallow understanding of the various means by which misogyny is manifested in Western culture. If it is true, for instance, that "the Spanish homosexual or the French homosexual . . . romanticized" woman (and it is by no means clear that this is the case), it still is not necessarily true that they "did not hate [her]," if by "hatred" we designate the conviction that women are essentially "inferior to" men and thus not worthy of the same personal and political privileges that men enjoy. Such an attitude is in no way incongruent with the "romanticization" of a feminine ideal.

Finally, Nin reveals the homosexual's fear of "totality," a discovery that informs her depiction of the relationship between Michael and Donald as essentially "incomplete." And yet, it is her own tendency to totalization that has led her to homologize male homoeroticism and misogynistic male homosocial bonding in the inappropriate way outlined above, and thus to blur the relevant sexuopolitical issues that her work raises. And it is the condescending pop-psychology-based homophobia—evidenced in her reference to the homosexual's "childishness"—that is the engine of this obscurantism, not only affecting Nin's understanding of male–male relations but also preventing her from considering the possibility of a politicized female collective subjectivity. For Nin's negative attitudes about homosexuality do not exhaust themselves with the consideration of the male example. Her *Diary* cites her remark to her psychoanalyst, Otto Rank: "I have always felt that there *is something beyond* Lesbianism, narcissism, masochism . . . ," and Rank seems in accord with her assessment of the *selfishness* of lesbianism when he replies, "Yes, there is creation" (vol. 1, 271; italics in original). So Nin's homophobia cuts both ways. At the same time that her attitudes about male homoeroticism prevent her from accurately assessing the effect of male homo*social* relations on women's condition, her negative view of lesbianism, coupled with her tendency to conflate homo*sexuality* and homo*sociality*, blinds her to the possibility of women's redressing their diminishment in patriarchy through collective political action. The result is the paradoxical gender politics of Nin's novel, in which men are both the creators of women's complete selves and the agents of their psychic fragmentation, and in which Nin seems to attempt to present "an exact portrait of [woman] as she [feels] inside," without being able to imagine how to alter that condition.[9]

It is crucial to recognize that, while homosociality and homosexuality might coincide in any given social formation, we must nevertheless insist on the distinction between them. I have been at pains to show, after all, that women's psychic fragmentation is founded in a sociopolitical order that denies them full subjectivity. The means for rectifying that debilitation is to be found, then, not in the erotic component of same-sex relations—though that component may certainly be deployed as a powerful political tool—but in the political alliance that those relations can represent. In other words, if we are to move "beyond lesbianism," as Nin puts it, this will signal not our renunciation of it but rather our recognition of the profoundly political problematic that attends it, a problematic that must be engaged if the psychic debilitation of gender and sexual minorities is to be redressed.

The Feminine Condition and Existential Angst in Djuna Barnes's *Nightwood*

Nin's interest in the exact representation of women's emotional experience is evidenced not only in her novels but also in her comments on another writer whom she claims as a primary influence on her work.

In addition to appropriating her name for one of her own fictional characters, Nin invokes the genius of Djuna Barnes throughout her famous *Diary*. A letter she wrote to Barnes in the 1930s notes Barnes's achievement in consciously writing "as a woman" (vol. 1, 225–26; vol. 2, 239–40). Moreover, Nin continually emphasizes the stylistic influence that Barnes's most famous novel had on her:

> *Nightwood* did have enormous influence on me, the level on which she writes, between conscious and unconscious, poetry and prose. . . .
>
> I have always mentioned *Nightwood* in lectures, written about Djuna Barnes, praised her work whenever the occasion arose. I still think it is a perfect example of the poetic novel, a classic.
>
> In the forties . . . I repeated that I owed my formative roots to Djuna Barnes. . . . It did not seem to me that America had given her the recognition she deserved. . . .
>
> I am glad to pay tribute to the depth, the power and vision of *Nightwood*. (vol. 6, 224, 366)

And this tribute continues into the 1970s, during which Nin reaffirms that "I learned a great deal about the poetic novel from Djuna Barnes's *Nightwood*" (vol. 7, 250).

It seems that one of the things Nin must have learned from Barnes was that an "exact portrait" of woman would require her depiction as a profoundly fragmented psychic entity, for Barnes's women, like Nin's, are portrayed as just such incomplete beings. And while Barnes does not shy from the depiction of lesbian attachments—indeed, the plot development of her novel actually depends upon them—Barnes's characters are no more capable than Nin's of forging an effective collective feminine subjectivity through their relations with one another. On the contrary, it is in the lesbian relationships in the novel that women's incompletion seems most glaring. An examination of Barnes's classic work will allow us to trace this phenomenon to the failure to distinguish a political homosocial component attendant to the homoerotic, and to illustrate more vividly the necessity of such a distinction to any progressive gender and sexual politics. We will also see that, in her inability to conceive a political alliance among her women that incorporates and rearticulates their lesbianism, Barnes, like Nin, takes recourse in a strategy of generalization in order to "explain" the psychic ineffectivity of her characters.

One way in which Barnes's work differs from Nin's is that although Nin discerns in *Nightwood* (1937) Barnes's impulse to frame an accurate representation of feminine experience, nowhere does Barnes herself specify or explicate such an intention.[10] While it is crucial to avoid assimilating the array of issues Barnes treats to the single problem of feminine subjectivity, I do think that we can interpret Barnes's reticence on gender relations as a mark of the overgeneralization that her novel, like Nin's, manifests. Nonetheless, it is clear that the action of *Nightwood* centers on the personality of one particular female character. The cover notes to the New Directions Paperbook edition of *Nightwood* call it "the story of Robin Vote and those she destroys—her husband the 'Baron,' their child Guido, and the two women, Nora and Jenny, who love her."[11] This description is misleading because it imputes to Robin Vote a degree of subjective agency in the "destruction" of others that she really does not enjoy, and because, consequently, it suggests that Robin somehow "survives" the fate visited upon the other characters, when in fact it is she who finally "gives up" at the end of the novel (170), exhausted in her attempt at self-integration. The crucial point here is that Barnes's novel, an exemplar of modernist alienation, manifests characteristics of fatalism and predestination conventionally associated with literary naturalism, but which are often comprised in the modernist project.[12] As we shall see, it is these attributes of Barnes's work that enable her to bury the specific sexuopolitical import of her text beneath the representation of a generalized existential malaise, and thus to dissemble the political bases and ramifications of subjective fragmentation.

If Robin Vote is the central character in *Nightwood,* then Nora Flood is the central consciousness. By this I mean that it is Nora whose reflective and contemplative nature leads to a development in her understanding of herself in relation to Robin. Nora is the first lover Robin takes after abandoning her husband, the "Baron" Felix Volkbein. The Baron himself is a highly thoughtful character, but his concentration is spent on trying to discern the true nature of Robin and, later, of their son, Guido, rather than the significance of his relation to either of them. Similarly, the Doctor, Matthew O'Connor—a sort of one-man Greek chorus to whom both Felix and Nora turn for psychic illumination—projects his incisive analytic skills for the most part outwardly onto the surrounding characters; when they are turned upon his own existence, it is to consider himself as an anomaly among other human beings, not in relation to them. Jenny Petherbridge, Robin's other lover, has no powers of reflection, and the shallowness of her character is revealed in the paucity of her activity in the narrative. If we are to seek the

The Critical Feminist Unconscious

significance of Barnes's story, then, we will have to do so through the character of Nora and, especially, through the relationship between Nora and Robin Vote.

There are eight chapters in *Nightwood*. Three of them are devoted to the quest of Nora Flood to understand and maintain her relationship with Robin. That quest takes place alternately in an anguished solitude (chapter 3) during which Nora waits for Robin to return from the mysterious sojourns she makes nightly, or in equally anguished consultation with the Doctor (chapters 5 and 7), from whom she seeks philosophical enlightenment about her existence with Robin. The difficulty of that existence derives from its status as a paradigm of incompletion. Barnes describes the intensity of Nora's and Robin's relationship in chapter 3 of the novel, "Night Watch": The two women, "going about the house, in passing each other, . . . would fall into an agonized embrace, looking into each other's face, their two heads in their four hands, so strained together that the space that divided them seemed to be thrusting them apart" (57–58). This paradigm is repeated in Robin's later relationship with Jenny; in chapter 4, " 'The Squatter,' " Barnes describes Jenny and Robin together at dinner,

> Jenny leaning far over the table, Robin far back, her legs thrust under her, to balance the whole backward incline of the body, and Jenny so far forward that she had to catch her small legs in the back rung of the chair, ankle out and toe in, not to pitch forward on the table—thus they presented the two halves of a movement that had, as in sculpture, the beauty and the absurdity of a desire that is in flower but that can have no burgeoning, unable to execute its destiny; a movement that can divulge neither caution nor daring, for the fundamental condition for completion was in neither of them; they were like Greek runners, with lifted feet but without the relief of the final command that would bring the foot down—eternally angry, eternally separated, in a cataleptic frozen gesture of abandon. (69)

The curse of eternal separation, represented in both scenes by the physical space between Robin and the women who love her, is most fully illustrated in Robin's relationship with Nora, who in chapter 3 suffers Robin's absence as "a physical removal, insupportable and irreparable" (59), so that the psychic fragmentation she feels at the loss of Robin becomes rendered as an actual physical lack, which Nora struggles to repair. Dr. O'Connor identifies this psychic and physical disintegration when, spying Nora out on the street in search of Robin, he ruminates to himself: "There goes the *dismantled*—Love has fallen off her wall. . . . She sees her everywhere. . . . Out looking for what she's afraid to find—Robin. There goes mother of mischief, running about, trying to get the world home" (60–61; my emphasis). These passages make clear the profound sense of incompletion that characterizes Nora's relationship with Robin, but they do not in themselves suggest the full import of that incompletion. For Nora's sense of fragmentation—her lack of communion with Robin—is not a function merely of Robin's physical removal from Nora; it is rather—and as is suggested in the scene in which the two women hold each other's faces in close proximity—an aspect of their very togetherness, of their relationship as two women.

The clue to this fact is located late in the novel, in Nora's assertion to Matthew O'Connor that "when a woman gives [a doll] to a woman, it is the life they cannot have, it is their child, sacred and profane" (142). And she goes further: "A man is another person—a woman is yourself. . . . If she is taken you cry that you have been robbed of yourself" (143). These are Nora's only two references to the specifically homosexual nature of her relationship with Robin, and yet their uniqueness is as important as their content. We can see through these statements that the incompleteness that characterizes the relationship is not a consequence of mere fate; rather, it is a function of the dominant conception of lesbianism itself. In the one instance, the hypothetical doll exchanged between the two women is the symbol of the "barrenness" of their relationship in a social context that can only construe vitality in terms of reproductive heterosexuality. Thus what Nora refers to as this "effigy" (142), while representing the union of the two women, also represents the fundamental lack that that union constitutes. In the other instance, for a woman to become another woman's "self" in a lesbian attachment is for their relation always to underscore their radical incompleteness as women; for, as is demonstrated in the image of the women's faces strained together, mere physical proximity does not constitute the integration of one subject with the "self" that is represented in another. To identify one's self in another, fundamentally inassimilable entity is thus to establish oneself as an irremediably incomplete subject.

This analysis is, of course, based on the conception of lesbian relationships (and of femininity) that Barnes herself posits. At this juncture, we would certainly want to reject such a view entirely, and argue that it originates in a social context that is itself predicated on a conception of both the feminine subject and homosexual relations as fundamentally ineffective. We are able to make such an assertion, however, precisely because our thinking about sexual politics has benefited from the profound social changes that have occurred in Western culture since *Nightwood* was written. The context in which Barnes wrote, on the other hand, was characterized by just such attitudes about women and lesbian relations as we see reflected in the novel, despite Barnes's own lesbianism and that of the women in the Paris literary community she occupied in the 1920s and early 1930s. According to Shari Benstock, "[A]mong homosexual women of the Left Bank community, most . . . demonstrated that they had internalized both homophobia and misogyny" (115).[13] This may account for the statement that biographer Andrew Field claims Barnes made during the 1970s, while recalling her relationship with the sculptor Thelma Wood: "I'm not a lesbian. I just loved Thelma."[14] In any event, this resistance to being identified in terms of her homosexual relationship indicates Barnes's related inability to conceive of lesbianism as potentially implicated in a feminist politics constituted through homosocial identification. This limit to Barnes's conception of the gender politics that predicates her characters' status as fragmented subjects is represented in her text by the assimilation of women's specific concerns (manifested in the relationship between Robin and Nora) to a more general problematic of existential disorientation. If the limit to Barnes's feminist analysis is a product of the social context in which she lived, however, so too is the necessity for her to generalize women's particular dilemma dictated by the context in which she worked, as we will soon see.

In examining the scene in which Nora suffers Robin's absence as a physical removal, we have traced that phenomenon to a gender politics that conceives of women as radically incomplete subjects. That conclusion, however, is the result of what might well be called a "forced" reading. For Barnes herself, rather than explicating her conception as grounded in a gender-political reality, actually construes it as part of a grave existential dilemma—more "general" than gender—in which all of her characters are implicated. The interpretation that I propose, on the other hand, necessitates that we pry from the textual elaboration of this dilemma the small kernel of gender-political analysis represented in Nora's ruminations on her relationship to Robin and from it derive our understanding of Barnes's text. Far from being undesirable, however, such a forced reading is essential to a consciously politically motivated criticism that recognizes that crucial social commentary is regularly suppressed beneath the surface features and ostensible subject matter of literary texts. The novel's reflection on Nora's and Robin's relationship represents an irruption of that commentary into the narrative discourse itself—one that provides us with the means both to understand how the political import of Barnes's work is managed in the text and to discover into what larger existential problematic it is generalized.[15]

We already know that, for Nora, "Robin's absence . . . be[comes] a physical removal, insupportable and irreparable." This is so because, as even Robin herself acknowledges, she "belong[s] to Nora, and . . . if Nora did not make it permanent by her own strength, she would forget" (55). Thus, the violation of that belonging through Robin's absence is a specific and uniquely painful experience: "As an amputated hand cannot be disowned because it is experiencing a futurity, of which the victim is its forebear, so Robin was an amputation that Nora could not renounce" (59). The complexity of this formulation is startling. First of all, it is clear that Robin is integral to Nora's being—she "belongs to" Nora in the way that one of Nora's limbs "belongs to" her and contributes to her physical integrity, her wholeness in space. But when that limb (to continue with Barnes's metaphor) is cut off from the rest of the body, the resulting spatial fragmentedness suggests as well the entity's existence in time, as the amputated limb "experienc[es] a futurity" in which the amputee is implicated, as "forebear" of the removed limb. This futurity consists ultimately in the severed limb's death, resulting from its separation from the life force of the body; it is this death that the body itself will eventually come to experience, hence its stake in this "future." And yet here the irony is particularly deep, in that if the body is the "forebear" of this death experience on the part of the severed limb—the limb seen as offspring of the body—it experiences the peculiar agony of having its progeny precede it in death, inverting the conventional, or "natural," order of relations between parent and offspring. In order to stave off the intrusion of the disruptive temporal element into the spatial unity represented by their domestic life together, Nora seeks to be reunited in space with Robin, and, as Barnes tellingly puts it, she "would go out into the night that she might be 'beside herself' " (59), "herself" consisting in Robin, now so painfully severed from Nora's being.[16]

What this passage represents, then, is the explication of Nora's fragmentation not in terms of gender politics—her particular construction as a feminine subject—but rather as a problematic of physical dimensions (time and space) that affect not just Nora or Robin, or even Barnes's female characters, but the population generally. This engagement with the interrelated effects of time and space on human subjectivity characterizes Barnes's treatment of all her characters, and very early on sets the stage for the vicissitudes they will experience. Let us

The Critical Feminist Unconscious

consider, for instance, Dr. O'Connor's observations about the Baron Felix even before he has met Robin Vote:

> "There's something missing and whole about the Baron Felix—damned from the waist up, which reminds me of Mademoiselle Basquette, who was damned from the waist down, a girl without legs, built like a medieval abuse. She used to wheel herself through the Pyrenees on a board. What there was of her was beautiful in a cheap traditional sort of way, the face that one sees on people who come to a racial, not a personal, amazement. I wanted to give her a present for what of her was missing, and she said, 'Pearls—they go so well with everything!' Imagine, and the other half of her still in God's bag of tricks! Don't tell me that what was missing had not taught her the value of what was present." (26)

In this ostensible rumination on the condition of the Baron, O'Connor actually articulates the paradox upon which Barnes's treatment of fragmentation is founded, and to which we can trace her engagement with the exigencies of time, on the one hand, and space, on the other: In the first place, the fragmentedness of the human entity results in the impulse to mend it, hence the doctor's desire to give the legless woman "a present for what of her was missing," a replacement for her loss. But in the second place, and contrarily, absence of the missing fragment results in the overvaluing of the present entity so that it attains a completeness in itself that both compensates for and yet emphasizes the lack—what is missing teaches us the value of what is present. In this case, the doctor's giving the woman "a present for what of her was missing" reads not as a compensation for the missing limbs but rather as an adornment of that lack. "For" can signify not only "in the place of" but also "in service to," and, in the latter case, the gift operates analogously with the present upper body, which itself serves to make amends for what is missing through its increased value, rather than by creating a whole unity in conjunction with an additional element. Consequently, Barnes's novel thematizes two modes of self-integration: an organic mode, in which the fragmented subject figuratively regenerates its missing parts, and a structural mode in which the fragment interrelates with other, similarly incomplete entities to form a new unity. These two modes, in turn, seem to correspond to two different ways of ordering experience, especially as Barnes develops them: The organic mode operates through a temporal order, and the structural mode operates spatially.[17] The consequence of conceiving the problem of personal fragmentation and its rectification in this way is that the fragmentation attending a specifically female experience is not interrogated for the gender-political import that it embodies, but rather it functions as a window onto a general consideration of the existential dilemma of the twentieth-century subject, for the impulse to self-completion is the motivating force not just for Barnes's female characters but for all of the personages who inhabit her novel.[18] The characters' different modes of attempting self-integration—the organic and the structural—provide for the overarching dualistic conception that governs Barnes's fiction, and which itself, rather than gender politics, becomes the primary ordering principle in her novel.

I want to examine in some detail the full rendering of time and space as existential dilemmas in Barnes's novel. First, however, it is necessary to recognize that a large part of what makes these dimensional considerations problematic in Barnes's ontology is that she construes time and space not as the interrelated functions that our experience tells us they must be but rather as radically separate phenomena, mutually opposed and essentially antagonistic. Such a conception seems to indicate Barnes's impulse to structure human experience along polarities and dualities—sharply divided extremes—in order to render it intelligible.[19] Indeed, Barnes seems convinced both of the necessity of division in human experience—its fundamental implication in linguistic practice, for instance—and of the impossibility of maintaining a distinction between the terms of any given polarity, the blurring of distinctions that she sees as humankind's inescapable horror. Matthew O'Connor is the spokesman for this view in *Nightwood,* expounding on the import of distinctions in human existence. Declaiming to Nora in one of his many rambling diatribes in the book, Dr. O'Connor recalls his role in a dispute in a tavern regarding prime Paris "pissing ports" and other venues for the illicit nighttime liaisons he seeks:

> "I said that the best port was at the *Place de la Bastille.* Whereupon I was torn into parts by a hundred voices, each of them pitched in a different *arrondissement* . . . ; I banged the table with a *formidable* and yelled out loud: 'Do any of you know anything about atmosphere and sea level? Well,' I says, 'sea level and atmospheric pressure and topography make all the difference in the world!' My voice cracked on the word 'difference,' soaring up divinely . . ." (92)

The cracking of the voice is not merely the manifestation of the very "difference" the word is meant to denote, but also the exaltation of difference by means of the "divine" nature of the cracking itself. And the narrative consistently plays upon the importance of distinctions— dualities—in its treatment of time versus space, past versus present, presence versus absence, and, the persistent leitmotif, innocence versus guilt. As the Doctor, again, puts it, "Man was born damned and innocent from the start, and wretchedly—as he must—on those two themes—whistles his tune" (121). Accordingly, Barnes herself aligns the major dichotomy in *Nightwood*—that of time and space—along the governing distinction between commission and recuperation, for, according to the Doctor, "[i]n time everything is possible and in space everything forgivable . . . There is eternity to blush in" (126–27); Yet this final clause gives the key to the realization of these extremes of time and space, for eternity—and infinity, too—is an experience reserved for the dead; the living have no access to the certainty afforded by the extremes of time and space. On the contrary, life is "the middle condition," as the Doctor puts it (118), it "is but the intermediate vice" (127), and their condemnation to this intermediacy—where all distinctions ultimately blur—represents the horror of existence for Barnes's characters.

The embodiment of this condition is the character Jenny, whom Robin takes as a lover after leaving Nora. Barnes describes Jenny Petherbridge as "a 'squatter' by instinct" (68), by which she means that Jenny's primary mode of experience is the appropriation of others' effects, emotional or otherwise. None of the significant experience of her life originates with Jenny herself; rather, "[s]he had a continual rapacity for other people's facts" (67). And,

> [s]ince her emotional reactions were without distinction, she had to fall back on the emotions of the past, great loves already lived and related, and over those she seemed to suffer and grow glad.
>
> When she fell in love . . . she became instantly a dealer in secondhand and therefore incalculable emotions. As . . . she had stolen or appropriated the dignity of speech, so she appropriated the most passionate love that she knew, Nora's for Robin. (68)

Matthew O'Connor tells Nora that Jenny "has a longing for other people's property, but the moment she possesses it the property loses some of its value, for the owner's estimate is its worth"; consequently, he continues, "all her life she has been subject to the feeling of 'removal' " (98). What this last term suggests is Jenny's inability to experience "presence" fully, for those entities with which she most strongly identifies are always elsewhere, the identification lost the moment she claims them for herself. These alienated effects represent, as Dr. O'Connor puts it, a "present that she can't copy" (124), and underscore her inability for lived experience. At the same time, Jenny (like the other characters, as we will soon see) longs for reengagement with the past, embodied in Robin, whom neither Jenny nor anyone else can satisfactorily approach. Robin thus represents for Jenny (as for all of Robin's suitors) "the past that she can't share" (124). Unable to identify with either term in the past/present dichotomy, Jenny more than any of the others represents the anguish of modern life, and occupies the limbo of indistinction that all of Barnes's characters struggle to escape.

Thus distinction—difference—is of critical import in Barnes's world. Ironically, however, in the novel's elaborate construction of a general phenomenon in which time and space are the governing principles of universal existential angst, distinctions and differences that are operative in the lived reality of the social world are elided as meaningful phenomena. Specifically, differences of gender and sexual orientation are diffused—we might almost say sublimated—in a metaphysical consideration on the problematic distinction between time and space.

Some analysis of the function of Barnes's different characters will be helpful to understanding how the distinction between time and space becomes thematized in the novel. In particular, it will be helpful to see how Barnes constructs a dichotomy between Robin Vote, on the one hand, and those who love her, on the other. Robin, along with these other characters, is seeking a way to correct her psychic fragmentation, and she does this, like Nin's Sabina, through her successive relationships with different people in the story. The key to her motivation, however, is not in the various liaisons into which she drifts, but rather in the point from which she has come. Long after his marriage to Robin has dissolved, the Baron Felix muses with Dr. O'Connor on Robin's origins. She had, he says, "an undefinable disorder, a sort of 'odour of memory,' like a person who has come from some place that we have forgotten and would give our life to recall" (118). In responding to this formulation, Dr. O'Connor clarifies that it is not primarily a "place" that is Robin's formative point of origin, but a time—a time in the past: "So the reason for our cleanliness becomes apparent," says the Doctor, referring to most people's *lack* of this "odour of memory." "[C]leanliness is a form of apprehension; our faulty racial memory is fathered by fear. Destiny and history are untidy; we fear memory of that disorder. Robin did not" (118). The "disorder," then, is the "primitive" past in which humans lived their prehistoric state—a state of untamed nature, which, according to the Doctor, we both fear and long to recall:

"The almost fossilized state of our recollection is attested to by our murderers and those who read every detail of crime with a passionate and hot interest . . . It is only by such extreme measures that the average man can remember something long ago; truly, not that he remembers, but that crime itself is the door to an accumulation, a way to lay hands on the shudder of a past that is still vibrating." (118–19)

It is this "shuddering," primitive past that the narrative insists Robin represents, above all in her animality, suggested with her introduction into the story:

Sometimes one meets a woman who is beast turning human. . . .

Such a woman is the infected carrier of the past: before her the structure of our head and jaws ache—we feel that we could eat her . . . for only then do we put our face close to the blood on the lips of our forefathers. (37)

The assertion of Robin's primal nature is constantly repeated: "[S]he . . . carried the quality of the 'way back' as animals do" (40); she possesses the sensory abilities of animals—when she lives with Nora, the latter worries that Robin "might lose the scent of home" (56); the Doctor says, "Robin was outside the 'human type'—a wild thing . . ." (146); Jenny, the lover who succeeds Nora, notes that Robin "neglects [her pets], the way that animals neglect themselves" (115).

This insistence on Robin's primal quality makes clear her identification with the past, but it is the exact *nature* of that identification that constitutes her uniqueness. For she does not simply *represent* the past—though she certainly does this in the view of those who know her—but is completely *of* the past; she not only represents a "racial" memory, the record of the time in which she originates, she *is* that time. Robin's relation to the past might be called "monumental" in that, as the Baron says, she has the "quality of one sole condition," a "condition that *cannot vary*" (112; my emphasis). If this is the case—if Robin is unshakably identified in the past, unable to develop beyond it, not subject to the effects of time—then she is fundamentally *ahistorical,* necessarily alien in the present, and her psychic integrity must be predicated upon her reimmersion in the moment in which she originates. Yet, our experience of time is such that we can only traverse it in one "direction," into the future, so Robin can only avail herself of the altogether-inadequate means the human condition offers for her reintegration; hence her attempts to reassociate with the past through, for example, her choice of clothes, which "were of a period that [Felix]

Framing the Margins

could not quite place" (42), and her itinerancy ("strangely aware of some lost land in herself, she took to going out" [45]), strikingly manifested in her movement from one lover to another.[20] It is as she comes into contact with these various people that what has been described as the "destruction" evident in the novel manifests itself, and that destruction is the result of the ironic incompatibility of Robin's "pastness" and the other characters' longing for historical rootedness—a duality that cannot be bridged.

We can read the impulse behind her acquaintances' fascination with Robin in the very passage, cited earlier, that identifies the source of her own alienation. It is precisely *because* Robin is "the infected carrier of the past" that "we feel that we could eat her . . . for only then do we put our face close to the blood on the lips of our forefathers." What informs "our" desire to assimilate a woman like Robin to our own substance is the implicit *need* we have to commune with the essence of our forebears. There seems to be some lack of historical grounding on the part of Barnes's contemporary characters that results in the need to forge a direct relation between themselves and the past, which they see represented in Robin Vote. What becomes problematic in these characters' relations with Robin, however, is that their attempts to commune with the past through her necessarily entail their physical proximity to her, a closeness in space that they hope to maintain as static, providing a comforting—though always partial and unsatisfactory—rootedness in their "racial" history. At the same time, however, Robin's own desire to resituate herself in time must entail movement through space, insofar as our experience of time is contingent upon motion in space, so that in order to continue her quest for reintegration with her origins, Robin is continuously propelled away from those who are most drawn to her, and a fundamental opposition between her interests and theirs becomes manifest.

From her marriage to Felix Volkbein, through her subsequent affairs with Nora Flood and Jenny Petherbridge, the conflict between Robin's objective and those of her liaisons is clear. The struggle is emblematized in the passages quoted above, which describe Robin's relations with Nora and with Jenny. For if, when Nora and Robin hold each other's faces in their hands, "the space that divided them seemed to be thrusting them apart," this is due to the incompatibility of Nora's desire for union in space and Robin's need for relocation in time, which propels her away from that spatial union. Similarly, in the dinner scene with Robin and Jenny, Jenny's impulse to fuse with Robin—represented in her "leaning far over the table" toward Robin—is comparable to

Nora's desire for a spatial proximity. And yet, the impossibility of such union is represented in Robin herself, whose interest in what might be called "historical integrity" rather than in spatial unity is suggested by the far backward incline of her body *away* from Jenny, her gesture of retreat indicating her proper location in the "way back" of the "racial" past. It is the conjunction of the impulse to spatial unity (present in Jenny and Nora) and the desire for temporal integrity (represented in Robin) that results in the mutual repulsion of Robin and her lovers, even as they seem to desire fusion.

The same condition seems to obtain in the union between Robin and the Baron Felix, whose obsession with what he calls the "great past" (38) is based upon his conception of it as populated by a venerable nobility, graced with a class of people and manners most worthy of honor. A deep moral classicism is manifest in the Baron's unyielding reverence for this bygone era, and he hopes that, even if that great past itself is not extended into contemporary life, a full appreciation of it will be. Explaining his devotion to the doctor, he says, "To pay homage to our past is the only gesture that also includes the future" (39).

This concern with infusing the present and the future with the vitality of the past explains the Baron's fascination with Robin, for she seems to embody such an admixture of the vibrant past in the contemporary condition. "Yes," Felix admits to Dr. O'Connor, as they discuss the Baron's failed marriage to Robin,

> "[S]omething of this . . . was in the Baronin . . . in her walk, in the way she wore her clothes, in her silence, as if speech were heavy and unclarified. There was in her every movement a slight drag, as if the past were a web about her, as there is a web of time about a very old building. There is a sensible weight in the air around a thirteenth-century edifice . . . that is unlike the light air about a new structure; the new building seems to repulse it, the old to gather it. So about the Baronin there was a density, not of age, but of youth. It perhaps accounts for my attraction to her." (119)

And perhaps it does, for it is not a personal sense of age Robin exudes—not "the density of age"—but rather a sense of the age of the human race, manifested as traces of its "primitive" stage, as the "youth" that is so dense about her.

It is this density of youth about Robin, however, that marks the difference between her relation to the past and that of the Baron. It is not an *appreciation* of the past that Robin embodies, but rather the past itself. The Baron misinterprets that embodiment as a feeling about the great past that Robin, like him, wants to pass on to posterity; for the Baron "wished a son who would feel as he felt about the 'great past' " (38). Yet, when the Doctor asks him of which nationality he would want the mother of his son to be, Felix betrays his own situation in the present—the only point of view from which one can formulate an "attitude" about the past—by affirming that he would choose "the American": "With an American anything can be done" (39). With this seemingly trivial assertion of the import of national identification, the Baron unmistakably evinces a consciousness grounded in the contemporary political era (and in the geographic, the *spatial* demands of that era) regardless of his great *interest* in the past, and thus underscores his difference from Robin, an ahistorical being whose nationality is immaterial in the context of her predicament.

Robin is not interested in inheritance or legacy or in informing the future by means of the past. Her problem is how, as a being in the present, to live in the past whence she springs. Hence her impulse, after their son, Guido, is born, to "hold . . . the child high in her hand as if she were about to dash it down" (48), or her furious exclamation to Felix regarding Guido: "I didn't want him!" (49). The incompleteness that characterizes Robin's existence—rooted in temporal displacement—is of a different order than that which characterizes Felix, which we might call historical misidentification, and neither can be remedied through union between the two characters. Their son might be seen to represent the reconciliation of the functions of time and space, as a physically separate entity that issues from his parents' union and embodies their "futurity"; and yet Guido is no means of access to the past but, rather, through his Catholic mysticism, the renunciation of all temporal concerns. Felix meditates at one point upon the "profound elasticity" of the Catholic church (108), manifested in its embracement of both the Roman and the French—two extremely dissimilar—religious examples. His son, on the other hand, in his embracement of the Church, which is the denial of history—and in his "mental deficiency," which renders him incapable of comprehending either of his parent's relation to it (107)—represents the limits of another elasticity, the failure to bridge his mother's implication in the past and his father's devotion to it. As the "snapped elastic" that fails to encompass his parents' various existences, Guido stands not for the realization of their wholeness through sexual union but as the underscoring of their incompleteness, and their inability to meet the dual demands of time and space.

Here, then, we can see Barnes's construction of a parallel function, in her consideration of the tension between temporal and spatial concerns, to that described in her suppressed consideration of the politics of gender and sexual difference. For what does Guido recall in his representation of the incompleteness of Robin's and Felix's union but the doll exchanged between Robin and Nora, which similarly underscores the lack and ineffectivity that characterize that relationship? As the product of the more conventional heterosexual union, however, Guido serves as the means by which the text's consideration of lack is rendered not in gender- or sexuopolitical terms, but as a function of the more "general" existential dilemma that Barnes depicts.

In a passage that recalls his earlier discernment of something both "missing and whole" about the Baron, Dr. O'Connor informs Felix that "[a] man is whole only when he takes into account his shadow as well as himself." He is referring to Guido, who, he tells the Baron, "is the shadow of your anxiety" (119–120). Guido's insubstantiality—his representation of a lack, of Felix's inability to gain the great past he so reveres—is underscored in his rendering here as a mere "shadow." And yet, the Doctor suggests, by assimilating to oneself that part which is insubstantial, one comes to realize a condition of wholeness that was hitherto unattainable. Nightwood shows psychic "wholeness," then, to inhere in the comprehension of both one's presence and one's lack, in the very incompleteness that "wholeness" supposedly would alleviate. This is a radical observation, anticipating the lessons of poststructuralism and their possible application to theories of the subject—especially the socially marginalized subject, whose effectivity this new conception of psychic integrity might greatly enhance. And yet, the efficacy of the observation in the novel is undercut, as it is invoked not in order to theorize the specific political status of the fragmented feminine subject but rather to illuminate the general existential dilemma of all "mankind," beneath which Barnes's treatment of the feminine condition is strategically and inevitably buried. Strategically, because the modernist ethic that dominated the context of Nightwood's publication would squelch the novelistic thematization of an overly specific and personalized women's experience; [21] inevitably, because, whatever attachments Barnes (or Nin, too, for that matter) might have had to other women, neither of them was personally and/or historically enabled to identify explicitly a political component either in women's psychic debilitation or in lesbian affiliation—the specific and potentially political homosocial dynamic attendant to homosexual relations.

And yet the point is most emphatically not that Barnes's work, or Nin's, is not "feminist enough," for it is precisely such historical contextual factors that will largely determine the degree to which an author can develop a feminist critique. The point is that, for all its insistence on the non-gender-political nature of the psychic disorder that it represents, Barnes's work, along with Nin's, is informed by a feminist political unconscious that actually provides the narrative tension necessary to bind the work in a coherent whole. The suppression of that feminist content beneath the depiction of a generalized existential malaise reproduces the very disenfranchisement of women that the text simultaneously represents, in the form of psychic fragmentation. A politically conscious criticism will entail the excavation of that feminist content through a reading designed to illuminate the various specific conditions that will become inscribed in the postmodern moment of the late twentieth century. Our insistence on such specificity will not diminish the theory of the postmodern; on the contrary, it will make clear the wide array of conditions that must obtain in order for the postmodern to emerge as the cultural dominant of our era. The result will be a deeper understanding of the postmodern moment, and a concomitant necessary revision of our conception of it.

GWENDOLYN BROOKS AND THE VICISSITUDES OF BLACK FEMALE SUBJECTIVITY

Beyond the Sex/Gender System: The Complex Construction of Feminine Identity

Our examination of works by Anaïs Nin and Djuna Barnes has made it clear that any discussion of the female subject as merely an opposition to the masculine is bound to be fraught with difficulties. A study of the specific *gender* politics of those authors' works—questions of feminine identity, for instance—inevitably implicates us in an equally crucial exploration of issues related to *sexuality* and *sexual orientation*—the erotic relationships among different subjects, lesbian identification—issues that, while closely related to gender in our social context, are not homologous with it. And yet, just as gender is a constitutive factor in our understanding of sexuality and sexual orientation, these latter phenomena are similarly important factors in the constitution of gender, and then only two among many. For the system in which the various gender and sexual identities that characterize our society are constituted—what Gayle Rubin has called the "sex/gender system"— is not closed.[1] The constitution of any given gender identity, for instance, depends upon factors from social categories conventionally conceived of as distinct from sex and gender—race, for example, or class, or physical ability or bodily configuration. And the converse is also true: Any individual's experience of racial identity, for example, will be contingent upon that person's gender. This dynamic might be multiplied infinitely, depending on the way that various social categories are inscribed in any given individual subject: Any one of the different social identities with which a given subject might be affiliated is inevitably intersected by a number of other social factors, with the multitude of possible such intersections constituting the various complex, conflicted, and contradictory "subject positions" that a particular individual might occupy at any moment.[2] What this means is that any analysis that focuses solely on one particular social category without recognizing its imbrication with other pertinent categories—an imbrication that determines its meaning in a given context—will inevitably tend toward a universalizing of one particular social experience that is both false and obfuscating, no matter how insightful certain elements of the analysis might be. I mention this not just as a general observation that ought to inform any work of social or cultural criticism (though I do conceive of it in that way); more crucially, I mention it because I take it to represent a vital lesson for anyone who wishes to understand the import of the postmodern condition for the multiplicity of human subjects that constitute the U.S. body politic. I do not pretend to engage the myriad facets of that multiplicity in this study. Their sheer number, let alone the necessarily contingent nature of their intersection, would render such an undertaking impossible. I do, however, hope to engage in this work a model for conscientious cultural analysis as I explore the relations among some of the categories that have been most effectively deployed in the construction of socially marginalized group identities in the U.S. context.

Having discussed the shortcomings of social analysis that fails to take into consideration the multiplicity of subject categories that any given individual must necessarily occupy, we will nonetheless find it useful to refer to just such a study, which falsely "isolates" gender from the various other social factors with which it is intertwined and considers one way in which women's position in Western culture has contributed to the specific psychic fragmentation that they must experience. Jean Baker Miller's influential work in feminist psychology is enlightening for us to study, not just because of the faulty universalizing that it manifests but because it nevertheless has great explanatory power for the literary works that I want to examine in this chapter, as we see later on.

Writing on women's experience of anger, Jean Baker Miller has suggested that "women's traditional roles and internalized cultural concepts of 'femininity' . . . entwine to characterize their expressions of anger as pathological." [3] Consequently, according to Miller, "women generally have been led to believe that their identity, as women, is that of persons who should be almost totally without anger and without the *need* for anger. Therefore, anger feels like a threat to women's central sense of identity . . ." (3). Nonetheless, Miller asserts, even in the context of the systematic invalidation of women's anger,

> [a] major exception may be noted. There is one place in which anger and aggressive action have been permitted to women—usually spo-

ken of in terms of an animal metaphor—that is, in defense of her young, as a lioness defends her cubs. In such an instance, as in almost everything, the woman is allowed anger *in the interest of someone else*. (3; emphasis in original)

We can see, early in this excerpt, the problem of universalizing that I have mentioned above. Rather than acknowledging the cultural specificity of her claims, Miller instead implicitly posits "women" as merely oppositional entities with respect to masculine norms of behavior. Thus, while undertaking the feminist project of *de*universalizing masculine experience by specifying the dynamics of anger along gender lines, Miller simultaneously reinscribes as a feminine universal the experiences of a particular group of women about and for whom she is writing—a group we can roughly identify as occidental, probably living in the United States, middle to upper middle class, heterosexually identified, and conversant in cultural codes that derive from a Eurocentric tradition, that is to say, "educated"—for in her easy and unqualified references to "women's" experiences as opposed to "men's," she generalizes this group's experiences of anger as applicable to all women, whoever they may be and in whatever sociocultural context they may live. The explicit embodiment of this universalizing tendency in Miller's essay is to be found not so much in these uninterrogated nominative references to "women," however, but rather in her invocation of a particular condition considered to bind women across whatever social, political, and cultural differences distinguish their experiences. I am referring to the condition of motherhood, identified by Miller as a particular context in which women's anger, normally suppressed, might be given full sway. I return to the ramifications of this claim later on in the chapter, for I think that they are very useful for understanding the constitution of some women's subjectivities (and, paradoxically, those of African-American women, in particular) as radically fragmented entities both before and during the postmodern era. Right now, however, I would examine in depth some representations of the condition of motherhood itself, to see if it really does function, as Miller suggests, uniformly to consolidate women's experiences, even in the limited context of the mid-twentieth-century United States.

Given what I have said above about the necessary imbrications of the sex/gender system with various other systems of social categorization, it would seem clear that a full interrogation of the role of motherhood must entail a consideration of the import of other social phenomena—phenomena operative outside the sex/gender system proper—in the construction of that role. The verse of Gwendolyn Brooks will, I think, offer us the opportunity for such a consideration, and make completely clear the problematic nature of any claims for the unitary significance of motherhood in the era and locale under consideration.

Two Brooks "Mothers" and the Politics of Identification

Critics normally conceive of Gwendolyn Brooks's poetic achievement as comprising two distinct phases. From the early 1940s through the mid-1960s, as Maria K. Mootry notes in her "introduction" to the poet, Brooks's work derived from two intersecting traditions: that of modernist aesthetics, epitomized by T. S. Eliot, Ezra Pound, and Wallace Stevens; and that of midwestern populism, represented by such poets as Carl Sandburg, Vachel Lindsay, and Edgar Lee Masters.[4] Most crucial about these influences, as is evident to commentators whose approach to African-American literature has been founded in the post-1960s critical context, is that they both represent the suppression of specifically African-American experience—the one through an emphasis on formal precision and semantic obscurity, and the other through a conception of the U.S. melting pot in which, even while romanticized working-class allegiances might be celebrated, ethnic and racial specificity would be effaced. Such poetic effacement of racial politics has had an effect, argues Houston Baker, on the critical reception of Gwendolyn Brooks:

> The world of white arts and letters has pointed to her with pride; it has bestowed kudos and a Pulitzer Prize. The world of black arts and letters has looked on with mixed emotion, and pride has been only one part of the mixture. There have also been troubling questions about the poet's essential "blackness," her dedication to the melioration of the black American's social conditions.[5]

While the question of "essential 'blackness'" is one that demands rigorous and intense examination, I do not wish to focus directly on it here except insofar as it underlies the apparently bifurcated nature of Gwendolyn Brooks's poetic career.[6] For in 1967 Brooks achieved a new understanding of the aesthetic demands of an "essentialized" blackness that led her consciously to reorient her poetic practice in the late 1960s and since. By the time she developed this new black consciousness, Brooks had already received most of the honors to which Baker refers—among them, five Midwestern Writers' Conference Awards, two Guggenheim Fellowships, fellowship in the American Academy of Arts and Letters, the Pulitzer Prize, and an invitation from President

Kennedy to read at the Library of Congress.[7] This last honor, representing as it did the imprimatur of state authority, perhaps most vividly suggests the degree to which Brooks was appreciated not only by white publishers and reviewers, as Baker notes, but by the representatives of institutions designed to consolidate white power in the United States. It is precisely this aspect of the recognition accorded Brooks that accounts for the "mixed emotion" with which many African-American commentators have received her work.

In 1967, however, Brooks attended the Second Black Writers' Conference at Fisk University, where she first heard the articulation of the "black aesthetic" by writers such as Imamu Amiri Baraka, John Oliver Killens, and David Llorens (Mootry and Smith, 284). Transformed by this experience, Brooks became committed to the ideals of the Black Arts Movement and developed a new set of artistic objectives, which she outlined in her 1972 autobiography, *Report from Part One*:

> My aim, in my next future, is to write poems that will somehow successfully "call" (see Imamu Baraka's "SOS") all black people: black people in taverns, black people in alleys, black people in gutters, schools, offices, factories, prisons, the consulate; I wish to reach black people in pulpits, black people in mines, on farms, on thrones[.] (cited in Baker, *Journey Back*, 109)[8]

Brooks began putting these new ideals into poetic practice with *In the Mecca*—her epic work of 1968, which focuses explicitly on the violent realities of black life in a Chicago tenement slum—and, especially, *Riot* (1969), a meditation on urban civil disturbances, which she published through the black-owned and -operated Broadside Press.

Given the highly self-conscious shift in Brooks's concerns after 1967, it has been easy for critics to categorize her work into either an "early" period, in which considerations of racial politics are muted through a stylized poetic formalism, or a "late" period informed by the Black Arts Movement, in which issues of black cultural nationalism seem of paramount concern. It should be made clear, though, that such a sharp dichotomy must be highly problematic, for, while it is true that much of Brooks's earlier work manifests a concern with formal detail that is conventionally identified with the Eurocentric aesthetic of high modernism, it is equally true that many of the poems from the period through 1960 engage issues of profound import with respect to both racial and gender politics in the United States.

This is particularly true of what we might call Brooks's "meta-ballad," "A Bronzeville Mother Loiters in Mississippi. Meanwhile, a Mississippi

Mother Burns Bacon," published in *The Bean Eaters* (1960). Houston Baker summarizes the theme of the poem by saying that, in it, "[t]he ignominies of lynching are exposed" ("Achievement of Brooks," 27–28). While this is true, Baker's abbreviated formulation does not suggest the full complexity either of the ignominies that he mentions or of the sociopolitical commentary embodied in the poem. A close examination of the piece will help us to understand the interrelatedness of gender and racial concerns in Brooks's work and thereby help to clarify how those problems become managed in the postmodern U.S. context.

I should state explicitly that my interest in this poem is due, in large part, to its apparent positing of motherhood as a condition that binds women universally, across an array of social differences that would otherwise separate them. I do intend, after all, to return to the problems posed by such universalizing as is manifested in Jean Baker Miller's article, examined above; and the very title of Brooks's poem—presenting as it does the activities of two different mothers in an ostensibly parallel construction that renders them "equal"—bespeaks a tendency to universalization that I would want to interrogate. Before I can do that, however, it is necessary to examine in some detail Brooks's poem as a whole, to determine the historical facts and social logic upon which it is founded.

The narrative of "A Bronzeville Mother . . ." is based on the 1955 murder of Emmett Till, and as such it evidently must treat issues of racial violence in the southern United States.[9] Additionally, however, the poem thematizes the relative ineffectuality of the (white) female subject in the historical context it depicts. The focus of the poem is the woman on whose behalf the fourteen-year-old black boy has been killed. The setting, as the poem opens, is a domestic one, with the woman in her kitchen preparing a meal for her husband and children. Ruminating on the recent dramatic events that have befallen her, she tries to fit them into a manageable narrative structure, reflecting that "From the first it had been like a / Ballad . . . / . . . Like the four-line stanzas of the ballads she had never quite / Understood—the ballads they had set her to, in school."[10] Despite her attempts to render events into a coherent form, however, the woman's never having understood any of the ballads to which she now recurs indicates her abiding inability to impose meaningful order upon the circumstances of her life; and, as Maria K. Mootry suggests, it becomes quite clear that the ballad structure itself is inadequate to accommodate the complexity of the social forces that bear upon her existence, as Brooks's poem is spun out in unwieldy free-verse lines that undo the regular meter and stanza pattern of the traditional form.[11]

Mootry further suggests that Brooks's undermining of poetic order mirrors the decline of the traditional social order of the South that the poem depicts, as the narrative ends with the blossoming, in the woman's consciousness, of an intense hatred for her husband, who had been her savior—a hatred "[b]igger than all magnolias," which symbolize Southern tradition. The metaphorical eclipsing of that tradition by the conscious antagonism of its white female victim thus represents, according to Mootry, the fundamental unsettling of the oppressive social order and the potential for widespread social and political liberation—the fact that "the myth of the benign, patriarchal magnolia'd South must end, for the sake of women, of blacks, and of society itself" (" 'Tell It Slant,' " 185). Even if we read the climax of the poem in this way, however—which seems perfectly plausible given what elements of it we have considered so far—we must recognize that this potentially revolutionary undermining of the social context does not originate external to the traditional order. Rather, that society's fundamentally contradictory nature is made manifest in the very existence and experience of the white woman herself, whose subjectivity is profoundly fragmented *as a matter of course* within the system she inhabits, and whose psychic life is thus necessarily disordered. That personal disorder is suggested in stanza six of the poem, in which the woman, reflecting on her husband's murder of the black boy and associated events, acknowledges to herself her status as a fundamentally dis-integrated psychic entity:

> The one thing in the world that she did know and knew
> With terrifying clarity was that her composition
> Had disintegrated. That, although the pattern prevailed,
> The breaks were everywhere. That she could think
> Of no thread capable of the necessary
> Sew-work. (lines 46–51)

In the next stanza she seeks to conceal any outward sign of this disintegration by carefully attending to her physical appearance with comb and lipstick, for

> Whatever she might feel or half-feel, . . . He must never conclude
> That she had not been worth it. (62–63)

The introduction of the husband in this stanza suggests the source of— or at least the referent against which we might measure—the woman's lack of integrated subjectivity, since throughout the poem, it is the masculine figure of the husband who actually manifests subjective agency. And the exact nature of the acts he commits is crucial, for it is not just that he avenges his woman's honor—though he does do this,

> . . . rushing
> With his heavy companion to hack down (unhorsed)
> That little foe (41–43);

more important, however, is the act of violence that he commits within the private, domestic sphere itself, in the context of his own family. For once the woman has prepared the meal, composed herself in the mirror, "made the babies sit in their places at the table," and called "Him" to eat (52–53), there is played out a small domestic drama that interrupts the husband's ruminations on the "larger" political issue at hand. Having been acquitted of the black youth's murder, the husband is now certain that

> Nothing and nothing could stop Mississippi.
> They could send in their petitions, and scar
> Their newspapers with bleeding headlines. Their governors
> Could appeal to Washington. . . . (82–85)

But the more immediate appeal, following directly upon this last elliptical line, is from one of the children, and it redirects the violence associated with racial confrontation back within the confines of the white household:

> "What I want," the older baby said, "is 'lasses on my jam."
> Whereupon the younger baby
> Picked up the molasses pitcher and threw
> The molasses in his brother's face. Instantly
> The Fine Prince leaned across the table and slapped
> The small and smiling criminal. (86–91)

The woman's response to this action is first to envision her child's cheek as having been overtaken by a violent, blood-red wound; then to leave the table and look silently out the window, where her husband follows her and begins to kiss and caress her while she thinks about the children, who are "whimpering" in the background:

> Such bits of tots. And she, their mother,
> Could not protect them. . . . (111–12)

It is in this last line that we begin to discern the ramifications of the politics of motherhood as they have been outlined by Jean Baker Miller in the essay cited above. For according to Miller, it is precisely in defense of her children that a woman is allowed to act in anger. Indeed, to the extent that maternal nurture is considered to be women's primary social function (as it traditionally is), then to act in defense of her child is not only allowed of a woman but, second only to childbearing itself, actually impressed upon her as a necessary duty if she is to manifest evidence of her conformity to the essential characteristics of Woman—her fundamental femininity. Brooks's Mississippi mother, then, finds herself in an untenable position, because her ability to achieve even the extremely limited feminine identity that has been prescribed for her has been thwarted by the masculine personage for whose benefit such highly circumscribed gender roles have been established in the first place, and against whom she cannot rebel. Prevented from fulfilling the gender function that is dictated for her, this woman consequently recognizes in herself a profound lack of subjective agency. And yet, this awareness, because it is accompanied by her sense of entrapment in a patriarchal order that she cannot escape, provides Brooks's character with no recourse but to nurture a hatred for her husband that, while enormous, is nonetheless silent and impotent ("She did not scream. / She stood there." [131–32]), and thus detrimental not so much to the social order that constrains her but to her own sense of psychic subjectivity.

Thus, the profound passivity that evidently characterizes Brooks's Mississippi mother as she assimilates "[t]he last bleak news of the ballad" and comes to a full awareness of her social status seems to preclude the liberatory reading of the poem posited by Maria Mootry. But Mootry's sense that the poem holds out hope for progressive social transformation is based not only on the Mississippi mother's new knowledge about the Southern social order but also on the idea that this new awareness allows the white character to "enter . . . into sisterhood with the grieving black mother" of the murdered boy (" 'Tell It Slant,' " 185). Were this "sisterhood" to exist, it would represent a radical force for change in the historical context of Brooks's poem—an interracial emotional and political alliance aimed at eliminating the racist and sexist social formation dominant in the southern (and northern) United States. In order to see whether the potential for such an alliance is articulated in the poem, however, we need first to consider what form it would have to take in order to be effective.

If Mootry is right in suggesting that the conclusion of Brooks's poem represents the possibility of a progressive alliance between her Mississippi and Bronzeville mothers, then we might well be able to identify in the narrative elements of a "hegemonic articulation" in which the interests of the two women intersect in a mutually supportive way that would enable their furtherance in the political arena. Ernesto Laclau and, especially, Chantal Mouffe, building their analysis primarily on the Marxist thought of Antonio Gramsci, have been instrumental in theorizing a "post-Marxist" hegemonic practice that would eschew the primacy of class (or any other social factor) as the articulating principle of political struggle. Rather, Mouffe suggests, effective progressive action depends upon the establishment of "a true hegemonic counter-offensive" to oppressive forces—a "political construction articulating all the struggles against different forms of inequality."[12] She derives this model from Gramsci's concept of an "expansive hegemony"—"a chain of equivalences between all the democratic demands to produce the collective will of all those people struggling against subordination . . . an 'organic ideology' that articulates all those movements together" (99). In positing this model, Mouffe categorically rejects any interpretation of hegemony "as the imposition of a class ideology on undergroups" (102), and she distinguishes expansive hegemony from "hegemony by neutralization," in which a central organizing constituency "take[s] account of the demand of some group, not to transform society so as to resolve the antagonism it expresses, but only so as to impede the extension of that demand" (103).[13]

To return to Brooks's poem, then, the two demands represented by the Bronzeville and Mississippi mothers would have to do with the abolition of racial injustice on the one hand and of sexist oppression on the other, and their articulation in a progressive structure of "expansive hegemony" would require that neither interest be neutralized by the expression of the other. At the same time, their ability to be "articulated together" depends upon the recognition of what Laclau and Mouffe call a "nodal point" that would partially and temporarily fix their political meaning in the field of discursivity that constitutes the social realm (*Hegemony and Socialist Strategy*, 112). That nodal point, in Brooks's poem, is represented by her two characters' common motherhood, and while that shared condition might constitute the basis for their political alliance, it is questionable whether its particular articulation in the poem allows for an "expansive hegemony" in which the specificity of both women's demands is recognized and maintained. An examination of the semantic and syntactic structures of Brooks's work will allow us to see whether the conditions for "expansive he-

Gwendolyn Brooks and Black Female Subjectivity

gemony" are represented in the poem, and to determine the true nature of the "sisterhood" whose possibility Mootry sees reflected in Brooks's conclusion.

Let us remember Brooks's title: "A Bronzeville Mother Loiters in Mississippi. Meanwhile, a Mississippi Mother Burns Bacon." It is conventionally shortened to "A Bronzeville Mother . . . ," yet this abbreviation belies the title's actual semantic significance and that of the poem as a whole. It is crucial to note the function of the adverb "meanwhile" in the second sentence of the poem title. This adverb indicates that the action denoted in the succeeding clause is related in a particular way to another action, which is described, in this case, in the preceding sentence. That relation is one of simultaneity—the Mississippi mother burns bacon *at the same time as* the Bronzeville mother loiters. And yet we must not equate simultaneity with parallelism, for the adverb "meanwhile," while not itself a subordinating conjunction—that is, it does not serve to introduce a dependent clause—nonetheless has the effect of rendering the action whose description *precedes* it subordinate to the action in the clause it introduces; the former becomes mere background against which the latter takes place.

One reason for this lies in what Saussure has identified as the linear nature of linguistic signification. Since, in the process of reading or otherwise assimilating linguistic information, we can only attend to one semantic unit at a time, what is under our consideration at any given moment must necessarily predominate over what we have just previously encountered, and must also necessarily become subordinate to what will gain our attention in the next instant, barring any grammatical configuration or semantic factor that signals to us an overriding hierarchy of value in which to order the elements we discern.[14] Brooks's title offers no such marker to suggest the primacy of the Bronzeville mother's action over that of the white woman. Indeed, when considered more closely and, especially, in conjunction with the structure of Brooks's poetic narrative, the form of the title seems only to underscore the linearly organized hierarchy of value to which I have referred.

The appearance of parallelism between the actions of Brooks's two mothers that I note above does not derive solely from their evident "real" simultaneity, *per se*; it is bolstered by Brooks's particular deployment of tense in her title. Each of the sentences that constitute the title is constructed in the simple present tense. Yet, the actions that the sentences represent actually take place in two different types of "present time," both of which can be rendered in English through the simple-present-tense construction. The first sentence, "A Bronzeville mother loiters in Mississippi," denotes an action in progress, without specifying the length of its duration or its beginning and end. The second sentence, on the other hand, refers to a finite action in its entire carrying out: "A Mississippi mother burns bacon [at this very moment, which ends with the sentence]." The distinction between these two types of present tense—progressive and finite—is not necessarily clear in the grammar of the example at hand. It might be made more so by some changes in the title's syntax. For instance, the title might be rendered as one complete sentence—"While a Bronzeville mother loiters in Mississippi, a Mississippi mother burns bacon"—in which the subordinating conjunction, "while," would make clear the relatively "inferior" status of the Bronzeville mother's action. Or, were we to retain the two-sentence construction, the first sentence might be rendered in the present-progressive form, through the use of the present participle: "A Bronzeville mother is loitering in Mississippi." To make these syntactic changes, however—thus making clear the relative importance of the two mothers' actions—would be to beg the question of that importance somewhat, since, leaving aside the effect of the linearity of the signifier, the converse revisions might just as easily be made: "A Bronzeville mother loiters in Mississippi while a Mississippi mother burns bacon," or "A Bronzeville mother loiters in Mississippi. A Mississippi mother is burning bacon." Thus, the justification for positing the relative value of the mothers' actions in the way that I suggest must be derived from the language and logic of the poem itself, which can be discerned if we examine first the nature of the title verbs specifically and, second, the events described in the poetic narrative as a whole.

It is clear enough, I think, that the action of loitering is constituted by its extended duration. The lingering quality that characterizes loitering works counter to its possible occurrence in a finite instant that would be conveyed by the simple present tense. Conversely, the burning of the bacon that is noted in Brooks's poem takes place in just such a limited span of time. This is evident not so much through the nature of burning generally but certainly in the particular *type* of burning to which Brooks refers: the burning of a foodstuff, which tends not to go on and on, as a forest fire might, and which, at any rate, would be relatively more finite than the loitering denoted in the poem. The limited duration of this burning is made perfectly clear in the text of the poem, in which it is one of a number of occurrences whose discrete finiteness is indicated by their being rendered in a rapid sequence of simple-past-tense constructions:

> Her bacon burned. She
> Hastened to hide it in the step-on can, and
> Drew more strips from the meat case. . . . (13–15)

In contrast, the loitering of the black mother—already necessarily of extended duration, as I have indicated—is denoted in the text merely through the white characters' recurrence to her existence as a catalyst for their own (specific and finite) actions. There are only two references to the Bronzeville mother in the poem. The first occurs through the reverie of the white woman's husband, who muses that, despite the annoyance of the events attending the murder,

> . . . it had been fun to show those intruders
> A thing or two. To show that snappy-eyed mother,
> That sassy, Northern, brown-black— (75–77)

in short, to humble the Bronzeville mother, who has been a continuous presence throughout the proceedings—a presence against which the white man's actions take place.

The black woman serves a similar function for the Mississippi mother, who, as she becomes conscious of her entrapment in the dominant social system, recalls the presence of the Bronzeville mother in the courtroom. That presence continues to affect her as she stands at the window near the end of the poem, feeling revulsion at the kisses that her husband presses upon her:

> . . . She wanted to bear it.
> But his mouth would not go away and neither would the
> Decapitated exclamation points in that Other Woman's eyes.
> (128–30)[15]

It is at this point that the white woman's hatred for her husband "burst[s] into glorious flower" (133)—the discrete, highly significant climactic action of the poem, against which the existence of the black woman is mere backdrop, a loitering presence.

The import of all of this, of course, is not merely grammatical. My point is to demonstrate how, in a work whose title suggests an alignment of the interests of black and white female subjects—particularly in its invocation of the "universal" function of motherhood—the active subjectivity of the black woman is actually suppressed beneath that of the white actors in the poem, including the white woman. Indeed, the black woman never does take center stage in "A Bronzeville Mother . . . "; she becomes an active subject only in the much shorter poem, "The Last Quatrain of the Ballad of Emmett Till," a sort of envoy to the longer piece that is regularly printed immediately after it in volumes of Brooks's poetry. This poem—ironically constructed in spare two-line stanzas characterized by regular, though slant, end rhyme—presents a world unpeopled by whites in which Emmett's mother "sits in a red room, / drinking black coffee," "kisses her killed boy," and "is sorry." [16] The profound disjuncture between the experiences of the Mississippi mother, depicted in the long poem, and the activity of the Bronzeville mother, which takes place in "The Last Quatrain . . . ," indicates not the binding effects of motherhood on the two women but rather the specificity of their experiences as mothers, a specificity predicated on their racial difference. The suppression of the Bronzeville mother's subjective agency in "A Bronzeville Mother . . ." is thus highly significant: It indicates the inability of the Mississippi mother—the articulating subject in "A Bronzeville Mother . . ."—to take account of the specificity of the Bronzeville mother's experience in her new conception of her own relation to the dominant social order. Consequently, it also indicates the degree to which political demands deriving from the specific experiences of African-American subjects are "neutralized" in the hegemonic articulation represented in "A Bronzeville Mother. . . ." However logical and possible it may be, then, there is no progressive, "expansive" hegemonic alliance between Brooks's black and white female subjects.[17] Rather, the "sisterhood" that Maria Mootry discerns as nascent in "A Bronzeville Mother . . ." is actually a counterproductive one, as it depends upon the negation of an element of the Bronzeville mother's identity that is actually constitutive of her experience as a mother, which the "sisterhood" is supposed to affirm.

The failure of effective political coalition in Brooks's poem does not, however, denote the poem's failure to register trenchant social critique. On the contrary, "A Bronzeville Mother . . ." does a great service in that, by demonstrating as false the ostensible "universality" of the condition of motherhood, the poem suggests the great variety and specificity of experiences that constitute the array of subjectivities in the social body of the United States. To make explicit that variety and specificity is to enable us to consider with increased rigor the sociopolitical ramifications of any given cultural development, which is precisely our task here with respect to postmodernism.

Now it is crucial to recognize that to say that the concept of *universality* is invalid is not to suggest that the myriad different subjectivities that constitute a society are not all impinged upon by certain social forces that tend toward *totalization*. In the contemporary era, the various forces that conspire to produce the "postmodern condition" affect all of the different individual subjects existent within the social context; these forces will not affect all of those subjectivities in the same way or to the same degree—this is not what I mean when I suggest that the forces tend toward totalization. Rather, an identifiable logic that governs a given social force will produce various effects for different individual subjects, according to a number of factors such as I have outlined above. Nonetheless, an awareness of how those factors are organized in various individual identities can be very helpful to us as we consider the relation of one specific subjectivity to a particular social system. Our knowledge of the social construction of the subject can enable us to extrapolate from a particular example to speculate on some general strategies by which systems work to inscribe individual subjects within them.

In order to do this, let us turn from Gwendolyn Brooks's poetic work to her novel *Maud Martha* (1953), so that we can identify the particular ways in which a particular black female subjectivity is inscribed within a totalizing social and economic system in the mid-twentieth century. If "A Bronzeville Mother . . . " represents, through its focus on a white woman's psychic and political development, the suppression of black women's subjectivity and its circumscription by racist and sexist social codes, *Maud Martha* focuses specifically on the experiences of a black woman to represent her conscious resistance against such suppression and her consequent achievement of active subjectivity. It also, however, demonstrates how that subjectivity, once achieved, is inscribed within a system of consumer capitalism such that the status of subjectivity itself becomes highly problematized in ways we have come to associate with the postmodern condition.

Maud Martha and the Issue of Black Women's Anger

In her groundbreaking essay on *Maud Martha*, Mary Helen Washington asserts the need for critics to establish a "relationship between the protagonist's personal experiences and the historical experiences of her people." [18] Within the novel itself, according to Washington, that relationship is thematized in Maud Martha's frustrated attempts at self-expression—in "the truncated stutterings of a woman whose rage makes her literally unable to speak" (249). To follow Washington's suggestion and historicize Maud Martha's stifled anger requires us to identify specific historical factors in that silent rage and specific historical instances of its function in the experiences of African-American women. That is what I attempt to do in the remainder of this chapter, in order to arrive at broader claims about the implication of Brooks's work in the early representation of postmodern subjectivity.

Maud Martha is Gwendolyn Brooks's autobiographical account of the life of a young black woman living on the South Side of Chicago during the 1930s and 1940s. The narrative traces Maud Martha Brown's development from a child of seven to a deeply self-aware young woman with a family at the close of World War II. The chapters of the novel are centered on the various relationships, events, and observations that characterize Maud Martha's existence: her interactions with her parents, brother, and sister; the death of her grandmother; her relations with the few whites with whom she comes into contact; her first love affairs; her marriage to Paul Phillips; her domestic life and her forays into black and white society; the birth of her daughter, Paulette; her encounters with her South Side neighbors; and the tentative, and not altogether satisfying, resolution to Maud's dilemma of how to function in mid-twentieth-century U.S. society as a conscious and intelligent black woman.

The anger that Mary Helen Washington identifies as characteristic of Maud Martha's existence is precipitated, to a large degree, by the instances of humiliation that she faces even within her own familial and community context: for instance, the marked preference that her family (and most other people, too) show for her sister, Helen, who is lighter skinned and "prettier" than Maud, though not nearly so smart, thoughtful, or considerate; or when, at a social function sponsored by the private black men's club known as the Foxy Cats, Maud's husband Paul forsakes her to take to the dance floor with the glamorous Maella, who is "red-haired and curved, and white as white." [19] There is the time, as well, when she is compelled to "celebrat[e] Christmas night by passing pretzels and beer" for Paul's friends, rather than establishing her own set of holiday customs for her family, as she had envisioned (102). These episodes induce a great degree of rage within Maud Martha that, nonetheless, is suppressed beneath her silent and self-effacing demeanor. The narrative's short, relatively unmodified declarative sentences and the extreme brevity of its chapters underscore Maud's laconic nature and, as Washington further notes, emphasize the fact that, despite the intensity of her emotions, "Maud Martha rarely speaks aloud to anyone else" in the novel (249).

This is true not just of Maud's experience within the black community but also in the case of her interactions with whites, who represent

Gwendolyn Brooks and Black Female Subjectivity

the impingement upon that community of the ideology of the dominant culture. Three chapters in particular indicate Maud Martha's bafflement in the face of white effrontery and emphasize the position of Brooks's character within the specific historical context of the 1940s United States. Chapter 25, "the self-solace," depicts Maud Martha at a beauty salon awaiting her turn in the chair. During this interval, the black owner of the shop, Sonia Johnson, is approached by a white saleswoman who is urging her to carry a new line of cosmetics. After Mrs. Johnson agrees to take a few lipsticks on trial, the saleswoman, Miss Ingram, makes small talk with her:

> "I'm mighty glad . . . that the cold weather is in. I love the cold. It was awful, walking the streets in that nasty old August weather. And even September was rather close this year, didn't you think?"
> Sonia agreed. "Sure was."
> "People," confided Miss Ingram, "think this is a snap job. It ain't. I work like a nigger to make a few pennies. A few lousy pennies." (138–39)

Maud Martha, waiting for Sonia Johnson in her chair, overhears this comment, and her response is characteristic:

> Maud Martha's head shot up. She did not look at Miss Ingram. She stared intently at Sonia Johnson. Sonia Johnson's sympathetic smile remained. Her eyes turned, as if magnetized, toward Maud Martha; but she forced her smile to stay on. Maud Martha went back to *Vogue*. "For," she thought, "I must have been mistaken. I was afraid I heard that woman say 'nigger.' Apparently not. Because of course Mrs. Johnson wouldn't let her get away with it. In her own shop." Maud Martha closed *Vogue*. She began to consider what she herself might have said, had she been Sonia Johnson, and had the woman really said "nigger." "I wouldn't curse. I wouldn't holler. I'll bet Mrs. Johnson would do both those things. And I could understand her wanting to, all right. I would be gentle in a cold way. I would give her, not a return insult—directly, at any rate!—but information. I would get it across to her that—" Maud Martha stretched. "But I wouldn't insult her." Maud Martha began to take the hairpins out of her hair. "I'm glad, though, that she didn't say it. She's pretty and pleasant. If she had said it, I would feel all strained and tied up inside, and I would feel that it was my duty to help Mrs. Johnson get it settled, to help clear it up in some way. I'm too relaxed to fight today. Sometimes fighting is interesting. Today, it would have been just plain old ugly duty." (139–40)

The key point here is not that Miss Ingram really does say "nigger," and that Mrs. Johnson later tries to explain to Maud Martha why she has let it go by. What is most significant is that, through the entire interaction, Maud Martha says nothing, either to the white woman, Miss Ingram, or to Mrs. Johnson, to whose explanation Maud Martha responds by staring "steadily into [her] irises. She said nothing. She kept on staring into Sonia Johnson's irises" (142). This gaze by which Maud Martha meets Mrs. Johnson's point that "that word 'nigger' can mean one of them just as fast as one of us, and in fact it don't mean us, and in fact we're just too sensitive and all . . . " (142)—this gaze represents the displacement of Maud Martha's anger onto Mrs. Johnson for having failed in her duty, and the simultaneous distraction of the reader's attention from the fact of Maud Martha's own silence, which implicates her as well in the offensive interaction. This focusing of anger at Sonia Johnson rather than at the white woman suggests the detrimental consequences of her suppressed rage for the black female subject herself, and the psychic fragmentation that is the primary result.

Given this, then the efficacy of Maud Martha's silent rebellion even when she is removed from the triadic structure exemplified in the beauty parlor scene is inevitably called into question. In chapter 29, "millinery," Maud Martha disdains to pay $7.99 for a particular hat, offering "[n]ot a cent over five" to the white saleswoman with the haughty demeanor ("[w]hen she looked at Maud Martha, it was as if God looked" [155]). When she discovers that Maud Martha is adamant in her decision, the clerk offers to speak to "the owner" of the shop, who might reduce the price, since, as she says to Maud Martha, "you're an old customer. I remember you. You've been in here several times, haven't you?" The woman is oblivious when Maud Martha replies, "I've never been in the store before," and rushes off to confer with the store "owner"—indicated by the narrative to be the saleswoman herself (156). She soon returns with "permission" to sell the hat for five dollars. In apparent retaliation for the clerk's reduction of her to a generalizable entity, however, Maud Martha tells the woman, "I've decided against the hat," and quietly exits the establishment (156). The white woman's bewilderment at Maud Martha's action is evidenced in her stuttering response to it—she sputters incoherently, "Black—oh, black—" (157); but in addition to suggesting her own incomprehension, the saleswoman's broken utterance indicates as well the unarticulated quality of Maud Martha's rebellion, which, precisely *because* it is unarticulated, is not fully effective.

Maud Martha's own attitude about the significance of these quiet rebellions is demonstrated in chapter 30, "at the Burns-Coopers'," in which she decides to take a job as a domestic in order to sustain her family while Paul is laid off from work. While peeling potatoes in the white family's kitchen and listening to the mistress of the house go on about her expensive indulgences, Maud Martha is accosted by Mrs. Burns-Cooper, Sr., her employer's mother-in-law:

> There was no introduction, but the elder Burns-Cooper boomed, "Those potato parings are entirely too thick!"
>
> The two of them, richly dressed, and each with that health in the face that bespeaks, or seems to bespeak, much milk drinking from earliest childhood, looked at Maud Martha. There was no re-monstrance; no firing! They just looked. But for the first time, she understood what Paul endured daily. For so—she could gather from a Paul-word here, a Paul-curse there—his Boss! when, squared, up-right, terribly upright, superior to the President, commander of the world, he wished to underline Paul's lacks, to indicate soft shock, controlled incredulity. As his boss looked at Paul, so these people looked at her. As though she were a child, a ridiculous one, and one that ought to be given a little shaking, except that shaking was—not quite the thing, would not quite do. One held up one's finger (if one did anything), cocked one's head, was arch. As in the old song, one hinted, "Tut tut! now now! come come!" Metal rose, all built, in one's eye.
>
> I'll never come back, Maud Martha assured herself, when she hung up her apron at eight in the evening. She knew Mrs. Burns-Cooper would be puzzled. The wages were very good. Indeed, what could be said in explanation? Perhaps that the hours were long. I couldn't explain *my* explanation, she thought.
>
> One walked out from that almost perfect wall, spitting at the firing squad. What difference did it make whether the firing squad under-stood or did not understand the manner of one's retaliation or why one had to retaliate? (162–63)

This final passage sums up Maud Martha's philosophy of resistance to the oppressive circumstances in which she finds herself, a philosophy that underlies her actions not only at the Burns-Coopers' but also in the two other situations that we have examined, in which Maud Mar-tha's proud refusal to acknowledge her humiliation outwardly actually prevents her effective rebellion within those situations.

The mode of resistance that Maud Martha uses at the Burns-Coopers', however unarticulated and thus unsatisfactory it may be, is, neverthe-less, recognizable within the context of black women's historical situ-ation in northern U.S. cities during the 1940s. Documentation of the domestic "slave markets" operative in New York City through the beginning of the decade offers a context within which we can situate Maud Martha's mode of rebellion. A 1940 *Daily Worker* article by Louise Mitchell detailed the trials of black women who gathered daily in middle-class urban neighborhoods, waiting to be hired by white families looking for cheap domestic labor. In addition to providing statistics regarding the number of black female domestic workers in the United States as of her writing and the state of wage and hour legislation across the country, Mitchell describes the routine of the women who sell their labor on these street-corner markets:

> They come as early as 7 in the morning, wait as late as four in the afternoon with the hope that they will make enough to buy supper when they go home. Some have spent their last nickel to get to the corner and are in desperate need. When the hour grows late, they sit on boxes if any are around. In the afternoon their labor is worth only half as much as in the morning. If they are lucky, they get about 30 cents an hour scrubbing, cleaning, laundering, washing windows, waxing floors and woodwork all day long; in the afternoon, when most have already been employed, they are only worth the degrading sum of 20 cents an hour.
>
> Once hired on the "slave market," the women often find after a day[']s backbreaking toil, that they worked longer than was arranged, got less than was promised, were forced to accept clothing instead of cash and were exploited beyond human endurance. Only the urgent need for money makes them submit to this routine daily.[20]

Mitchell ends with a call for legislative and executive action on behalf of domestic workers.

Similarly, in an earlier article on "The Bronx Slave Market," published in the November 1935 edition of the Negro magazine *The Crisis,* Ella Baker and Marvel Cooke identify general antilabor sentiment, the "artificial" class divisions between white-collar professionals and laborers, and racism within the labor movement as the primary obstacles to the fair treatment of black domestics in U.S. cities. Moreover, the anecdotes they relate indicate the overdetermined nature of the social divisions they critique. An interviewee from among the women gathered at one of the "slave marts" gives this perspective on employer/worker relations:

> "Say, did you ever wash dishes for an Orthodox Jewish family? . . . Well, you've never really washed dishes, then. You know, they use a different dishcloth for everything they cook. For instance, they have

one for 'milk' pots in which dairy dishes are cooked, another for glasses, another for vegetable pots, another for meat pots, and so on. My memory wasn't very good and I was always getting the darn things mixed up. I used to make Mrs. Eisenstein just as mad. But I was the one who suffered. She would get other cloths and make me do the dishes all over again."[21]

Eventually, this woman leaves the situation in which cultural difference functions merely as a means to make her "suffer," and she does this under circumstances similar to those facing Maud Martha at the Burns-Coopers':

> . . . [A]fter I had been working about five weeks, I asked for a Sunday off. My boy friend from Washington was coming up on an excursion to spend the day with me. She told me if I didn't come in on Sunday, I needn't come back at all. Well, I didn't go back. . . . (270)

This act of resistance, like Maud Martha's, constitutes an expression of self-respect on the part of the woman performing it, but it also necessarily represents a sense of her autonomy from the exploitative system of domestic labor—a sense proven to be false by her eventual installment in the Bronx "slave market," with the thoroughly degraded condition that it implies.

A similar sense of autonomy from the system of exploitation is evidenced in another of Baker's and Cooke's subjects:

> We sidled up to a friendly soul seated comfortably on an upturned soapbox. Soon an old couple approached her and offered a day's work with their daughter way up on Jerome avenue. They were not in agreement as to how much the daughter would pay—the old man said twenty-five cents an hour—the old lady scowled and said twenty. The car fare, they agreed, would be paid after she reached her destination. The friendly soul refused the job. She could afford independence, for she had already successfully bargained for a job for the following day. She said to us, after the couple started negotiations with another woman, that she wouldn't go way up on Jerome avenue on a wild goose chase for Mrs. Roosevelt, herself. (268)

This invocation of First Lady Eleanor Roosevelt is significant for the way it evidences a refusal to be implicated in the white woman's scheme; but the autonomy upon which this resistance is predicated is crucially belied—not just by Baker's and Cooke's reminder that it is a luxury contingent upon the financial circumstances in which the worker finds herself at any given moment, but also by black women's appeals, dur-

Framing the Margins

ing FDR's presidency, to the very representatives of state power whose authority they would deny. Historian Gerda Lerner has compiled a number of black women's letters to FDR and Mrs. Roosevelt that exhibit simultaneously a sense of righteous independence from these influential figures and a tone of pleading for recognition by the white power structure that they represent. One letter to FDR from a young Chicago woman manifests anger and a vaguely threatening tone:

> Why must our men fight and die for their country when it won't even give them a job that they are fitted for? They would much rather fight and die for their families or race. Before it is over many of them might. . . . We are real citizens of this land and must and *will* be recognized as such! (Lerner, 301)

Elsewhere, though, the same letter is more plaintive:

> Won't you help us? I'm sure you can. I admire you and have very much confidence in you. I believe you are a real Christian and non-prejudice. I have never doubted that you would be elected again. I believe you can and must do something about the labor conditions of the Negro. (301)

A young woman of twenty five writes a similarly pleading letter to Mrs. Roosevelt:

> I'm in need of food and closes. I don't have any relative at all so help me. . . .
> Could you do something for me help me to fine something. Tell me what to do if you could give me some to do in the hospitial or in a hotel or any where I will do it. I will take a day job are a night job anything. Please help me. You can see I'm in need of help Mrs. Roosevelt. (403)

A Michigan woman puts her appeal to the President in terms of a powerfully suggestive metaphor:

> You are the Father of this country and a Father are suppose to look out for all of his children so we are depending on you. (405)

The rendering of FDR as a "father" in this letter suggests simultaneously the writer's assertive sense of the president's responsibility to the people and a degree of passive obedience to the patriarch's will. Or as Gerda Lerner herself puts it, these letter writers' "faith in the all-powerful benevolence of the President is as pathetic as is their need. Yet these letters also reveal a strong self-assertion, an insistence on being given their rights, an attitude of exasperation with unfulfilled promises" (399). It is the simultaneous faith and self-assertion evident in these letters that complicates our understanding of Maud Martha's mode of resistance in Gwendolyn Brooks's novel. For Maud Martha herself does make at least one direct, assertive demand to a benevolent and omnipotent white figure; the structure of that demand, however, indicates not only Maud Martha's self-assertion but also the fact of her entrapment by a system in which the meaning of her self-assertiveness is predetermined.

The site of Maud Martha's verbal self-assertion is, as Mary Helen Washington points out,

> [a] large downtown department store in the 1940s—a place where black women were generally allowed to work only as "stock girls" or kitchen helps[. It] is fundamentally alien territory for Maud, and yet it is on this hostile ground that Maud finally asserts herself. (256)

This is all true enough, but the point of the scene, as I hope to show, has less to do with black women's assigned place within the sphere of *labor*—where they are allowed to *work*—than with their function as potential *consumers,* for it is through this latter category that they will become integrated into the larger U.S. culture in the late 1940s and beyond.

In the chapter entitled "tree leaves leaving trees," set during the Christmas season, Maud Martha takes her young daughter Paulette to visit with Santa Claus and give him her list of holiday wishes. The introductory passages of the chapter describe Santa's interactions with the children who come to see him:

> . . . Santa pushed out plump ho-ho-ho's! He patted the children's cheeks, and if a curl was golden and sleek enough he gave it a bit of a tug, and sometimes he gave its owner a bit of a hug. And the children's Christmas wants were almost torn out of them.
> It was very merry and much as the children had dreamed. (172)

Then, the intrusion into this happy scene of Maud Martha and her daughter:

> Now came little Paulette. When the others had been taken care of. Her insides scampering like mice. And, leaving her eyeballs, diamonds and stars.
> Santa Claus.
> Suddenly she was shy. (172)

And, to alleviate this shyness, Maud Martha gives her daughter bits of encouragement:

> Maud Martha smiled, gave her a tiny shove, spoke as much to Santa
> Claus as to her daughter.
>
> "Go on. There he is. You've wanted to talk to him all this time.
> Go on. Tell Santa what you want for Christmas."
>
> "No."
>
> Another smile, another shove, with some impatience, with some
> severity in it. And Paulette was off. (172–73)

Insofar as Maud Martha's words of encouragement are directed "as much to Santa Claus as to her daughter," this scene might be understood as depicting Maud Martha's own overture to the Santa figure, with Paulette merely functioning as the intermediary in the interaction. Thus, it is a harbinger of the more direct encounter that ensues, and whose confrontational nature is suggested in the "impatience" and "severity" with which Maud Martha compels Paulette to approach Santa. Paulette does move toward Santa and makes her overture:

> "Hello!"
>
> Santa Claus rubbed his palms together and looked vaguely out across
> the Toy Department.
>
> He was unable to see either mother or child.
>
> "I want," said Paulette, "a wagon, a doll, a big ball, a bear and a
> tricycle with a horn." (173)

And, in response to Santa Claus's evident lack of interest in Paulette, Maud Martha intervenes:

> "Mister," said Maud Martha, "my little girl is talking to you."
>
> Santa Claus's neck turned with hard slowness, carrying his unwilling face with it.
>
> "Mister," said Maud Martha. (173)

And Santa responds by mechanical rote:

> "And what—do you want for Christmas." No question mark at the
> end.
>
> "I want a wagon, a doll, a bear, a big ball, and a tricycle with a
> horn."
>
> Silence. Then, "Oh." Then, "Um-hm."
>
> Santa Claus had taken care of Paulette.
>
> "And some candy and some nuts and a seesaw and a bow and
> arrow." (173–74)

Maud Martha intervenes again, but this time she addresses her daughter:

"Come on, baby."

"But I'm not through, Mama."

"Santa Claus is through, hon." (174)

And mother and daughter exit the department store, into a world of "wonderful snow" and "blue twinkles" that represents the fantasy of social harmony within which Maud Martha had wanted to keep Paulette, protected, for just a little longer (174).[22]

The dynamics of Maud Martha's interaction with Santa Claus strikingly exemplify Jean Baker Miller's point that women's anger is typically deployed in the interests of others, particularly in defense of their children. The result of this very specifically mandated deployment of women's anger would necessarily seem to be a degree of psychic splitting on the part of the female subject, insofar as her emotional agency is realized only when she projects it away from herself and into the context of another's experience. In Maud Martha's case, this splitting is concretized in the actual articulation of the black female's demands, not only by Maud Martha herself but by Paulette, who finally addresses Santa Claus directly to make her appeal. It is crucial for us to examine fully this appeal to understand the significance of the Santa Claus scene with respect to black female subjectivity. Before we do this, however, it is important to note that the splitting of Maud Martha's subjectivity that I have identified in this scene—her approximation to the condition of postmodernist psychic fragmentation—is a function not merely of Maud Martha's *femininity,* as Miller would suggest, but also (and significantly) of her *blackness,* indicating once again the inflection of the purportedly universal experiences of femininity and motherhood by other social factors, in this case, race.

The further import of the Santa Claus scene derives from the fact that, even in the fragmentation of her subjectivity that would seem to be debilitating for Maud Martha, she actually exercises most strongly her subjective will through her (and Paulette's) demands to Santa Claus. And yet, that apparently potent new subjectivity is mitigated by the social context in which it emerges, as we can see if we examine the dual nature of Maud Martha's address to Santa Claus. Our examination of black women's letters to FDR has taught us to discern the simultaneously assertive and suppliant character of such appeals to the white patriarch. Maud Martha's appeal is no different in that, while it strongly urges upon Santa the fact of black female subjectivity—that Paulette is, indeed, talking to him—it also represents a plea for her inclusion within the order that seems designed precisely to exclude her. That plea, though implicit in Maud Martha's words to Santa, is made explicit in Paulette's listing of the Christmas presents she hopes to receive. "I want," she begins, and this verb phrase is set off from its objects by the narrative explication "said Paulette." This abstracted, generalized wanting can be said to represent the fundamental lack that has historically characterized the social and political existence of the African-American female subject, and the desire for the dominant sociopolitical order to rectify that deficiency. It is a demand for inclusion within the "mainstream" social order that seems necessarily to exclude black subjects from it, and thus to conceive such a demand as a fundamental threat.

The remainder of the sentence, however, comprising the various specific objects that Paulette wants—"a wagon, a doll, a big ball, a bear and a tricycle with a horn"—actually suggests the mechanism by which the African-American woman's integration into the U.S. "mainstream" can be effected, without damage to the existing sociopolitical order. For once the general desire for redress within the dominant system is reduced to the particular wanting of specific *commodities,* then the black female subject who is articulating these wants no longer represents a threat to the political order so much as she represents an element that is easily assimilable within that order. Specifically, she is a consumer, a subject ready-made for incorporation into the late-capitalist economy of the post–World War II United States, and into the postmodernist "cultural logic" that attends it.[23]

To historicize *Maud Martha,* then, is to illuminate the effects of an increasingly totalized capitalist system upon the subjects whom that system touches. We achieve such illumination by theorizing the specificity of the experiences of Gwendolyn Brooks's black female subject, whose status as a fragmented entity both prefigures and coincides with her inscription in the postmodern condition. The founding of that fragmentation in the different "differences"—of race and gender—that characterize the black woman's existence in the U.S. context should remind us that effective theorization of the postmodern moment will take account not just of division in the individual human subject but of divisions and inequities in the social realm in which that subject is constituted. By charting the negotiation of that fragmentary social realm by those subjects who are marginalized within it, we can begin not only to understand the cultural logic that is postmodernism but to take the full measure of the political logic through which it is developed.

Gwendolyn Brooks and Black Female Subjectivity

"To Become One and Yet Many"

Psychic Fragmentation and Aesthetic Synthesis

in Ralph Ellison's *Invisible Man*

Reflections on the Black Subject

To a great degree, the difficulty confronted in the constitution of the African-American subject is a function of the social interrelation of blacks and whites in the United States. The nature of that interrelation casts black identity necessarily as a problem, an objective never to be realized, hardly to be imagined, so that the black subject exists not so much as the negativity conventionally believed to emblematize it but rather always as potentiality unfulfilled, simultaneous promise and disappointment.[1] Ralph Ellison's *Invisible Man* (1952) is the classic text of the problems and possibilities of black (male) identity, and in its figuration of the difficulties of the marginalized subject, it suggests the degree to which individual subjectivity generally will become problematized in the postmodern era.

The unrealized nature of black identity is manifested on many levels in Ellison's novel—in the fact, for instance, that its protagonist has no name; more complexly, the character's very assertions of self-identity indicate his incompleteness as a subject: "I am nobody but myself," he says at one point,[2] and later, "I am who I am" (263). These declarations seek to gain force through their tautologousness, but their very redundancy bespeaks a line of reasoning that, in its figurative circularity, suggests nothing so much as the zero that actually represents the protagonist's identity.[3] The Invisible Man harbors a suspicion of his own "nothingness," and it troubles him, as is attested in his frequent admissions to suffering an "obsession with [his] identity" (253 for this particular confession); and it is this obsession that motivates his search for validation of his subjective self, or, in his words, "a proper reflection of my importance" (160). The metaphor is apt, for it both refers to a recognized mechanism in the formation of individual identity and points to an episode in Ellison's novel that demonstrates the preemptive role played by U.S. race relations with respect to the constitution of the black subject.

The function of "reflection" in the establishment of individual identity has been very specifically theorized in psychoanalysis by Jacques Lacan, after the example of an infant first noticing its image in a mirror. By means of the "mirror stage," says Lacan, "the *I* is precipitated in a primordial form, before it is objectified in the dialectic of identification with the other . . . [; b]efore its social determination."[4] Lacan's wording suggests a two-part process of formation of the individual subject: The first comprises the mirror stage's "reflective" function, by which the child perceives a wholly integrated image of itself that it ever after strives to achieve in "reality," though it can only approach this ideal asymptotically; the second is the "social determination," by which the subject is distinguished from others with whom it comes into contact, thus achieving a degree of individuality. Leaving aside the many subtleties of Lacan's theory, we can designate the two parts of the "self"-formative process as "idealization" and "differentiation," and any analysis of the Invisible Man's attempt to forge individual identity will have to assess his achievement in these two areas of self-definition.

It is clear, then, that the mere achievement of one's "proper reflection" does not in itself constitute subjective identity; rather, this would represent idealization without differentiation, the figuration of a whole, integrated "ideal-ego" with no trace of an Other against which the subject can be delimited. For the irony of differentiation is that though its objective is the distinction of an individual subject against all others, it is predicated upon admission of the inevitable traces of difference that always laterally, as it were, infect any given "identity." Without this ironical process, a "whole" subject can never be constituted—the "social determination" of the subject is not to be bypassed. The problem for Ellison's protagonist, however, in the early stages of his search for selfhood, is that the social structure itself, as it manifests inequities based on racial difference, impinges deleteriously upon the supposedly nonsocial process of self-idealization. Thus, the character does not actually fail at differentiating himself from surrounding subjects; he never gets that far because a politically skewed social structure allows those surrounding subjects to prevent him from ever conceiving a reflection of himself in the first place, from idealizing a "self" for himself.

This predicament is illustrated in the early chapters of the novel, which depict the protagonist's experiences as a student at a respected Southern Negro college. During his tenure there, he is assigned to escort a wealthy white benefactor of the school, a genteel Yankee banker named Mr. Norton, who makes an official visit to the campus. One of the Invisible Man's responsibilities is to chauffeur Mr. Norton among the environs of the college, and while they are taking their tour, he looks continually into the rearview mirror of the car to see not his own reflection but that of Mr. Norton, who sits in the back seat. The protagonist makes repeated references to this phenomenon: "Through the rear-view mirror I could see him" (37); "Through the glass I saw him" (41); "I [saw] him smiling through the mirror" (43); "[O]ur eyes met for an instant in the glass" (43–44). The suggestion of transparency in the preposition "through," so oddly used in this context, hints at the relative ease with which Mr. Norton's image is observed in the reflective apparatus, whereas the protagonist is thwarted from glimpsing his own image—from experiencing a successful mirror phase—and thus from achieving a workable self-conception.

The Invisible Man's failure at self-idealization is rooted not in any fundamental psychic deficiency on his part but rather in the politics that govern his social relations with Norton and other whites. We can see this most clearly if we examine the effects of the rearview-mirror episode on the character of Norton. If the Invisible Man meets Mr. Norton's eyes when he looks in the mirror, the parallel and reverse situation must obtain from Mr. Norton's vantage; and yet, rather than disrupting the white man's sense of self, this phenomenon seems only to reaffirm his identity. At one point, as they gaze at each other's images in the mirror, Mr. Norton says to his driver, "[Y]ou are my fate, young man. Only you can tell me what it really is" (41). He has previously declared to the protagonist his conviction that "your people [are] somehow connected with my destiny" (41). Clearly, Norton means in some sense to "find himself" through the protagonist and other blacks, and we might wonder why the Invisible Man should not similarly seek his own self in the image offered by the white businessman. Norton himself gives a clue to this. By way of explaining what he means in saying that the Invisible Man is his "fate," Mr. Norton asserts that his "real life's work" has been his "first-hand organizing of human life" (42). If this is so, and if the Invisible Man himself is representative of the human life Mr. Norton has "organized," through his philanthropy, for instance, then the protagonist might be seen to stand in relation to Mr. Norton as a "congealed form" of the white man's labor, after Marx's theory of commodity fetishism and Georg Lukács's concept of reification, which derives from it.[5] Insofar as his "work" is an alienated dimension of his own essence, then Mr. Norton is able to see himself projected back to himself in the person of the Invisible Man. This cannot function reciprocally, however: The manifest power imbalance between Norton and the protagonist precludes the reversal of their "worker/product" relationship since, paradoxically, the type of "labor" Mr. Norton performs in the production of an Invisible Man requires an amount of monetary capital that is denied to the protagonist, due primarily to his status as a black youth. What this scene in the novel represents, then, is the intersection of psychology by politics, such that the achievement of self-image that helps constitute psychic "stability"—however imperfect that achievement must of necessity be—is the privilege only of the few of optimum economic, social, and political standing, whose very success at self-definition sets them up as an impediment to the self-constitutive efforts of those less fortunate.[6]

If this is manifested symbolically in the aforementioned mirror play in Ellison's novel, it soon becomes lived reality for the protagonist, whose experiences with Mr. Norton quickly lead to the destabilization of what he has heretofore conceived of as his "identity." During his jaunt with Norton, the protagonist unwillingly exposes to the white man's scrutiny elements of the local black community deemed to be unrespectable by the educated Negroes at the college: a sharecropper known to have fathered the child his daughter is carrying and a "sink-hole" of a saloon frequented by a group of "insane" black war veterans. Emotionally overwrought and physically jarred during the outing, Norton confers with the college president, Dr. Bledsoe, upon his return to campus, and the latter man expels the protagonist from school—ostensibly temporarily—as punishment for the "poor judgment" he has exercised while escorting Mr. Norton. The Invisible Man reflects upon his impending exile from the sylvan campus with a sense of grave doom: "Here within this quiet greenness I possessed the only identity I had ever known, and I was losing it" (97). This loss of "identity" appears to result from the impingement of "exterior" politics (in the form of the white businessman) upon the protagonist's life within the confines of the school, in much the same way that the failure of the Invisible Man's "mirror stage" results from the intrusion of Mr. Norton's image into his process of self-idealization. Yet, this idea of an interior/exterior dichotomy is a false one, and on close scrutiny the essential implication of "outside" political forces in the operation of the school becomes clear, even in the person of Dr. Bledsoe himself.

The protagonist faces off with the college president when Bledsoe announces that he will punish the student for his misadventures with Norton even after assuring the white man that the protagonist won't be faulted. The Invisible Man threatens to expose Bledsoe's duplicity to the community—"I'll tell everybody," he exclaims (139)—but Bledsoe is unmoved, conveying his disdain in a telling rejoinder:

> "Who, Negroes?" Negroes don't control this school . . . , nor white folk either. True they *support* it, but *I* control it. I's big and black and I say 'Yes, suh' as loudly as any burrhead when it's convenient, but I'm still the king down here. . . . When you buck against me, you're bucking against power, rich white folk's power . . . " (140)

This declaration is beautifully self-consuming, for it begins with an assertion of Dr. Bledsoe's sovereignty at the college, but then immediately suggests the compromising of his authority in his "convenient" posturing for white benefactors—for the fact that he occasionally judges such minstrel-like dissembling to be prudent indicates the subordination of his power to the implicit demands of some higher authority, and that higher authority is explicitly designated when he tells the protagonist that to buck him is to buck "white folk's power." Hence, the "big, black" college president is both a screen before and a manifestation of white political sovereignty, despite his self-aggrandizing assertions to the contrary. This is true regarding both his capacity as administrator of the college and, through that role, his personal self, as we see in his interaction with Mr. Norton.

Exasperated with the protagonist for having taken Norton to meet the disgraced sharecropper simply because the white man "asked" him to, Bledsoe has exclaimed, "We take these white folks where we want them to go, we show them what we want them to see" (100). Yet, what Bledsoe wants the white man to see appears to coincide with what he knows the white man himself wants to see, as evidenced in the peculiar type of self-fashioning he performs as he prepares to meet with the distraught Norton. Approaching a mirror on his way to confer with Mr. Norton after his harrowing experience, Bledsoe stops at the glass and "compose[s] his angry face like a sculptor, making it a bland mask" suitable for presentation to Norton (100). The mirror provides a no more accurate reflection of Bledsoe here than of the protagonist in the car earlier; rather it indicates the intervention of the white man, willy-nilly, in the process of the fashioning of the black self, which consequently can only be manifested as the "mask" of the minstrel.

The reason for such performance by Bledsoe is no mystery; as he says to the protagonist of whites such as Norton, they "support" the school. His providing these benefactors with an appropriate image of himself as leader guarantees the continued flow of funds necessary to keep the institution afloat and himself in his position of "control." Thus, the form of the black self-image is governed at all points by an extensive racial politics, regardless of how veiled its function may be, and, in any case, the impingement of that politics upon even the most "insulated" black community can be traced along the flow of capital from the centers of "white folk's power" to the farthest reaches of the black diaspora.[7]

Once we recognize the implication of the operative political economy in the psychic affect of the black subject, it is clear that the campus of the Negro college is by no means separate from the site at which industrial capitalism operates but rather continuous with it, and the Invisible Man's seeming exile to the world of business emerges as his unwitting strike toward the very root of his problem of psychic self-definition. Yet, the root of his problem does not necessarily hold the key to its solution, cannot in itself offer up a self for him to assume, as is demonstrated soon after his arrival in New York with letters of introduction from Dr. Bledsoe to a number of white industrialists. It is these men whom the protagonist hopes can be induced to give a "proper reflection of [his] importance," to affirm his identity, but he soon learns the impossibility of this when he meets the son of one of the tycoons, the young Mr. Emerson. This man is himself a nonentity—a "nonidentity"—by virtue of his apparent homosexuality, suggested by allusions to his "hip-swinging stride" (177) and patronage of the "Club Calamus" (182). As he says, his father considers him to be "one of the unspeakables" (184). If, as Gates suggests, identity and self-presence are ultimately established through speech in Ellison's novel, then the fact that the young Emerson is "unspeakable" renders his personality void, and this ironically, given that his father, who passes judgment on his son's "speakability" is himself never an actual "presence" in the novel, but exists only through verbal allusions by his own son and the protagonist.

It is because he is aware of his own position outside the realm of recognized identity that Emerson can confront the protagonist with *his* existential dilemma. He hints to the Invisible Man that all is not right with the letters Dr. Bledsoe has given him (they actually record Bledsoe's intention not to allow the protagonist to return to school). At this the protagonist plaintively insists to Emerson, "[I]f there's someone who has tampered with my letter, I'll prove my identity." But Emerson, as a self-acknowledged void in the economy of identity, does not speak this language; he exclaims, "Identity! My God! Who has any identity any more anyway?" (184). We might say that Emerson is an emblem of the twentieth-century crisis of the individual, whose integrity of identity has been threatened by the increasingly rationalized mode of production that characterizes industrial capitalism in the era.[8] In his exclamation to the protagonist, however, Emerson himself posits as inevitable the forces that confront the individual in search of identity. With their actual basis in capitalist production thus veiled, mystified, these now apparently natural forces seem to offer an intangible foe to be confronted by the Invisible Man in a metaphysical quest for individual identity.

Given this, we can see *Invisible Man*'s relation to literary modernism, a movement that, according to Lukács, "by exalting man's subjectivity" presents "man as a solitary being, incapable of meaningful human relationships," with the result that "man's subjectivity itself is impoverished."[9] Fredric Jameson has both critiqued and assimilated Lukács's claim that modernism, in Jameson's words, "is some mere ideological distraction, a way of systematically displacing the reader's attention from history and society to pure form, metaphysics, and experiences of the individual monad"; expanding and deepening Lukács's position, Jameson goes on to assert that modernism "is all those things, but they are not so easy to achieve as one might think. The modernist project is more adequately understood as the intent . . . to 'manage' historical and social, deeply political impulses, that is to say, to defuse them, to prepare substitute gratifications for them, and the like."[10] According to Jameson, one classic modernist means of "management"—or "strategy of containment," as he also calls the phenomenon—is the narrative manifestation of just such a metaphysical struggle between "man" and "nature" as Ellison's protagonist seems to face after his discussion with the young Emerson. Thus, his foray into the teeth of a naturalized industrial capitalism ironically constitutes precisely the modernist strategy of containment that supposedly works to "manage" politics in literary narrative. Yet, at the same time that politics (in its economic manifestation) is managed, it reemerges in the form of a problematic of race relations to disrupt the very site upon which such management is achieved.

Having been sent forth by the junior Emerson to make his way in the seemingly autonomous world of industry, the Invisible Man seeks work at the Liberty Paints Company. Approaching the company plant for the first time, he notes that "a huge electric sign announced its message through the drifting strands of fog: KEEP AMERICA PURE WITH LIBERTY PAINTS" (192). Apparent here is the paradox of purity inhering in a surface coating that itself could be said to render what it covers impure. The sign's message is an invitation to conflate surface and depth, "appearance" and "reality," signifier and signified in what quickly becomes manifest as a politics of color. For we soon learn that the company's "best selling paint . . . , the one that *made* [the] business," is called "Optic White" (212–13), suggesting the very duplicity inherent in the notion of a painted surface's "purity," for if the word means "with reference to the eye," then *"Optic* White" may present a pure white facade to visual scrutiny, but it simultaneously masks a "reality" that undoubtedly manifests some darker hue.

This theme is reimplicated in the Invisible Man's first job at the plant, as a "doper" who measures ten drops of a "dead black" liquid into each bucket of Optic White paint, then follows directions to "stir it 'til it disappears" (195). The "disappearance" of the dark substance (the ten drops of which might correspond to the roughly 10% of the U.S. population represented by blacks) into the "glossy white" paint is really its disguising behind a facade of purity that belies the nonwhite nature of one of its constituents. Kimbro, the protagonist's supervisor, articulates the paradoxical nature of his paint's purity when he comments not only that "[i]t's the purest white that can be found" but that it is "paint that'll cover just about anything!" (197). This encomium is repeated by Lucius Brockway, the ancient black plant engineer who oversees the Invisible Man's subsequent assignment in the factory boiler room. "Our white," says Brockway, betraying his sense of a personal familial bond with the company, "is so white you can paint a chunka coal and you'd have to crack it open with a sledge hammer to prove it wasn't white clear through!" (213). Brockway's investment in surface appearances in the inanimate world is quickly shown, however, to correspond with a similarly shallow Uncle Tomism in the realm of racial politics. He displays his contempt for the labor union that seeks to organize the plant's black workers by exclaiming to the protagonist, "For one of us [blacks] to join one of them damn unions is like we was to bite the hand of the man who taught us to bathe in a bathtub!" (223). The perversion of the familiar injunction not to bite the hand that feeds one is, of course, Ellison's jab at black accommodationism as manifested in authors from Phillis Wheatley to Booker T. Washington (whose words, especially as found in *Up from Slavery*, echo most loudly here[11]); but it also demonstrates Brockway's bias in favor of a "whitewashing" of manner and outward appearance as opposed to demands for more substantial effects that would sustain the black body itself. It is appropriate, then, that Brockway's system of valuation should be inverted by the union members he so despises,

Fragmentation and Synthesis in Ellison's *Invisible Man*

who, initially suspicious of the protagonist's affiliation with Brockway, charge that he is "[a] first-class enameled fink!" (215), thus casting the moral whitewashing of the black man as a tool of repressive forces out to crack their "brotherhood."

The mere reversal of hierarchy is not, however, an adequate means of redressing the grievances of the marginalized against the central powers, as the experience of Ellison's protagonist attests. When he needs to replace the dope Kimbro has provided him, he draws liquid from the wrong canister in the factory tank room. He recalls the result of mixing this new "dope" with the Optic White paint and applying a sample coat to some planks of wood: "The paint was not as white and glossy as before; it had a gray tinge" (198–99). Though Kimbro apparently corrects the mistake and again supplies the protagonist with the proper substance, the Invisible Man still notes the imperfection in the paint samples: "All were the same, a brilliant white diffused with gray," but this time, as he notes, "Kimbro had failed to detect it" (201).

What the protagonist alone seems to bear witness to is the true nature of the relation between white surface and black interior, between white dominance and black subordination, for, rather than their opposition resulting from their profound alienation from each other, blackness, as represented by the paint dope, for instance, is actually implicated in the very whiteness of whiteness. The few drops of black dope that seem to intensify the brilliance of "Optic White" are merely a figure for a marginalized black population in relation to which the white power structure establishes itself, not unlike the manner in which Mr. Norton recognizes his own identity through the black man. The "diffusion" of grayness throughout the glossy white surface of the painted planks shows up the fact that whiteness is no "pure" entity, but a function of the blackness against which it positions itself.

The protagonist's simultaneous recognition of the nature of whiteness and of the inability of blackness similarly to establish itself due to the interrelated factors of economics and racial politics is figured in the text as an explosion in the factory boiler room, which the Invisible Man recalls by noting, "[I]n that clear instant of consciousness I opened my eyes to a blinding flash" (225). The flash, which is both a revelation and a blinding—which both marks and terminates the "clear instant of consciousness" in which eyes are opened—represents the beginnings of the Invisible Man's true crisis of identity. The boiler-room accident sends him to the company hospital, where he wakes to a disorienting array of voices, mirrors, and elements of a "white world" (233) that, he says, "I could no more escape than I could think of my identity" (237). His inability to remember his name—which he equates with his "identity"—in the face of the white medical staff's questions, racial jokes, and mirrored equipment indicates his inability to posit his own ideal image through either conventional "reflective" techniques or the color-coded opposition by which white identity distinguishes itself. The protagonist does recognize that his "freedom" and his identity "are involved with each other," thinking to himself, "when I discover who I am, I'll be free" (237). Yet his discovery of his identity seems equally contingent upon the achievement of his freedom—freedom from the limits on black self-achievement that seem endemic in the interrelation of blacks and whites, and thus escapable through reimmersion in the black community.

The Collective Entity and Individual Identity

The Invisible Man's recurrence to the black community is notable for at least two reasons: First, it signals his repeated attempt to escape politics by avoiding manifestations of racial difference, despite what we know of the essential implication of racial politics even in the most insular black "community," such as the Negro college; second, it might be said to indicate his immersion in the realm of "signification." For it is clear that, despite all efforts at "whitewashing" nonwhite entities— coating them with Optic White paint so that their surfaces might signify a deep "purity"—the true signifier of whiteness thus far in the narrative is blacks themselves, in their confirmation of white identity. When Mr. Norton looks into the mirror, he sees a black face that he unperturbedly recognizes as a signifier for his own self, to put the matter in Saussurean terms. Thus, the protagonist's repatriation aligns him with the level of the "signifier" in Saussure's diagram of the linguistic sign.[12] The negative aspects of this alignment are clear, as blacks in this case constitute a population whose own "destiny" seems to be never to stand for itself, but always for an Other who appears to control the very means of self-definition. This sort of identification of blacks with the signifying function thus implies blacks' role in creating their own invisibility.

There is, of course, an alternative process of signification that characterizes the black community—the witty verbal play so important in black folk culture. "Signifyin'," in this sense, is a distinctly oral tradition, tending to the aggrandizement of those in the community with the most impressive verbal facility. A common mode of signifying is for the canny "tropiste" to humiliate humorously a witless foil who is said to be "signified" upon. To "signify" or "play the dozens," then, is to perpetrate a sort of joke upon another person, and *Invisible Man* gives a particularly appropriate example of the phenomenon in the protagonist's account of his experience at the Liberty Paints infirmary. He describes the actions of one of the medical staff who vainly attempts to jar his memory of his "identity": He "produce[d] a child's slate and a piece of chalk, writing upon it: WHO WAS YOUR MOTHER?" This unwitting variation of the signal utterance of signification sparks an unspoken reply by the protagonist: "I looked at him, feeling a quick dislike and thinking, half in amusement, I don't play the dozens. And how's *your* old lady today?" And later, the chalk message: "BOY, WHO WAS BRER RABBIT? He was your mother's back-door man, I thought," the irreverent invocation of the foil's mother marking the "cap" on this instance of signification, its object being wholly unaware of the process (235–36).[13]

Thus, blacks' status as "signifiers" with respect to whites has dual implications. On the one hand, blacks' destiny always to affirm white identity at the expense of their own seems inevitably to lead to their invisibility. On the other hand, when blacks act as effective "signifiers" in the folk sense of the term, then the joke is on the white power structure itself, and the possibility for such a joke derives, ironically, from a property of the Saussurean signifier. Illustrative of this is the most explicit trick pulled by the Invisible Man on the dominant system—his theft of electricity from the Monopolated Light & Power company:

> [T]hey suspect that power is being drained off, but they don't know where. All they know is that according to the master meter back there in their power station a hell of a lot of free current is disappearing somewhere into the jungle of Harlem. The joke, of course, is that I don't live in Harlem, but in a border area (5).

That is to say, the *joke* inheres in the protagonist's liminality, his un-locatability, his instability—a definitive characteristic of the Saussurean signifier, whose propensity for "slippage" has been widely noted. Through his identification with the function of the signifier, then, the Invisible Man seeks once again to establish his individual self, both by "slipping" beyond the apparent physical limits of whites' scope of power and by making expert use of the properties of the linguistic signifier through the activity of public speaking, a vocation he enters soon after his arrival in Harlem's black community. The undertaking of this latter activity seems to signal further the protagonist's desire to escape the detrimental impingement of politics upon his attempts at psychic individuation, insofar as he conceives activities of personal expression (we might call them instances of aesthetic production) to be fundamentally unrelated to political existence.

The use of public oratory is appropriate for the forging of individual identity within the black community, as it seems to address the specific difficulties the locale poses for the Invisible Man's attempt at self-definition. For, if the protagonist, as a black man, interrelates with whites only to the detriment of his ability to *idealize* his own self-image, his existence among other blacks poses problems for his attempts to *differentiate* himself from surrounding subjects. Indeed, the Invisible Man sees the problem of forging individual identity as endemic in the black community, as is attested in his ruminations upon relics from his college's early days—"photographs of men and women in wagons drawn by mule teams and oxen, dressed in black, dusty clothing, *people who seemed almost without individuality,* a black mob that seemed to be waiting, looking with blank faces." In contrast to this impression of an unindividualized black mob, however, is that made by whites, who manifest individual identities in the photograph. For though the protagonist despairs at the photo's representation of blacks, he sees "among them the inevitable collection of white men and women in smiles, clear of features, striking, elegant and confident" (39 for both excerpts; emphasis mine). The protagonist's successful establishment of his individual identity, then, would entail his extrication from the "mob" that is the black community.

The Invisible Man's impulse to effect such an extrication is evident early on in the novel, during the account of the battle royal episode. In recalling the event, the protagonist announces his disdain for the other young men who participated in the white-sponsored fray, seeing himself as set apart from the ranks of the black community due to his role as featured speaker during the smoker following the battle:

> I suspected that fighting a battle royal might detract from the dignity of my speech. In those pre-invisible days I visualized myself as a potential Booker T. Washington. But the other fellows didn't care too much for me either, and there were nine of them. I felt superior to them in my way, and I didn't like the manner in which we were all crowded together into the servants' elevator. (17–18)

Of course, the major obstacle to the Invisible Man's distinguishing himself from other blacks is the fact of his own "blackness," which at the same time he can never escape as his social identity, causing a seemingly irresolvable tension within the protagonist's psyche as the will to individual identity confronts the fact of community heritage and identification. To evade this personal dilemma, the protagonist reformulates his internal tension as a struggle between himself—the radical individualist—and other blacks who, in his view, have "[n]o respect for the individual" (313). This outward projected tension is manifested in his relationship with Mary, the maternal black woman who takes in the Invisible Man upon his retreat from the paint factory, and with whom he lives until he begins his more significant work. It is against Mary's conception of black subjectivity that the protagonist articulates his own belief in the importance of the individual. In speaking to the protagonist of his future, Mary says, "It's you young folks what's going to make the changes. . . . Y'all's the ones. You got to lead and you got to fight and move us all on up a little higher" (249). Mary, insofar as she acknowledges the importance of individual subjectivity at all, conceives of it as a means of bettering the whole community; she identifies with the collective. The Invisible Man rejects this conception as he ruminates upon his relationship with Mary:

> [T]here are many things about people like Mary that I dislike. For one thing, they seldom know where their personalities end and yours begins; they usually think in terms of "we" while I have always tended to think in terms of "me"—and that has caused some friction, even with my own family. (309)

The invocation of the "family" here is telling, for it reillustrates for us the protagonist's conception of his problem as a primarily "private" one; in spite of his efforts to project his personal psychic dilemma into the larger field, that field still consists only of the black community, and thus the problem appears to be kept "in the family," safe from the deleterious effects of politics that seem to threaten the minute blacks and whites interact. Yet the very means the protagonist uses to resolve his problem with the family that is the black community lead him inevitably into the threatening world of politics that he would avoid.

The Invisible Man has every desire to resolve the tension between himself and his community in his own favor, as a blow for the individual. It is ironic that he sees a way to do this by inadvertently taking the advice that Mary urges on him—he becomes a "race leader" (252; 308). Signs of his interest in assuming such a position are evident as early on as his comments about being a potential Booker T. Washington, and become quite salient by the time he reaches Harlem. Soon after his aforementioned conversation with Mary, the protagonist finds himself on the scene when an elderly black couple are being evicted from their Harlem apartment. Realizing the potential for violence at the site, he uses his oratorical skills to calm a riotous mob of blacks who threaten the evicting agents. "Black brothers!" he exclaims, "That's not the way. . . . We're a law-abiding people and a slow to anger people" (269). This "we" reference—which seems to indicate the Invisible Man's acceptance of his place within the black community—is really the cleverly disguised positing of an individual "I" who wishes to gain control over the collective. The pluralization represents not the protagonist's reconciliation to his membership in the group but a tactic designed to subordinate the force of "grass-roots" sentiment to an individual subjectivity whom the group would "choose" as its guide. This is evidenced when the Invisible Man suggests to the crowd, "Let's follow a leader . . ." (269), and that leader soon emerges in the person of the protagonist himself.

The Invisible Man's accession to this position of leadership does not occur spontaneously, however; rather, it is precipitated by the machinations of a force other than the protagonist's own, and whose externality even to the larger black community suggests the inevitability of the political realm's intervention into perfectly personal family matters, or, more accurately, the ways in which the personal is itself political. For the Brotherhood is a blatantly political force in the world of the novel. It is the fictional analog to the Communist party, and its influence is foreshadowed in the operations of the labor union at Liberty Paints. The man at the helm of the organization approaches the Invisible Man after witnessing his performance before the crowd at the eviction. Brother Jack cannily suggests that his group can provide the protagonist with the opportunity to become "the new Booker T. Washington" (298); yet his further comments clearly indicate that such an achievement by the Invisible Man must necessarily entail an affront to collective black identity. When Brother Jack asks him if he is related to the evicted couple, the protagonist, in a rare moment of identification with his community, says, "Sure, we're both black." Jack, enraged at the black man's refusal to view the "larger" political picture, snaps, "Why do you fellows always talk in terms of race!" (286). Clearly, if the Invisible Man is to become a race leader under the auspices of the Brotherhood—and he sees no other way to do so—all conception of the effectivity of black collective identity must go by the wayside. But even this is not so simple as it seems: The concept of leading one's people itself embodies a paradox in that leadership implies an individual subjectivity that, in its very force, stands in opposition to the community meant to be led, but of which the leader, too, is supposedly—and, in the Invisible Man's case, inescapably—a member. Thus, the very tension the protagonist had hoped to evade by casting his inner struggle as one between himself and the community confronts him again when he seems to have won his battle for individual subjectivity, and he is hard-pressed to maintain the delicate balance necessary to his continued success as a leader of his people.

This balance between representing and leading a constituency is one maintained by the Brotherhood only because it sacrifices its integrity to an "end justifies the means" credo that allows it simultaneously to direct its followers along a particular course of action and to impose upon them a sense of the rightness of that path. Brother Jack puts it bluntly late in the novel, when he insists to the protagonist that the Brotherhood's job with respect to its constituents is "not to *ask* them what they think, but to *tell* them!" (462). Of course, in public the Brotherhood vigorously denounces individualism as a barrier to the progress of the properly political entity that is the collective population: "[I]ndividuals . . . ," says Brother Jack, "don't count" (284); and he cajoles the protagonist into seeing the value of working for collective goals through the Brotherhood: "I can't believe that you're such an individualist as you pretend" (286). But it is precisely by appealing to the Invisible Man's sense of individualism that Brother Jack induces him to join the organization, and that appeal takes the form of a very subtle compliment on the black man's ability to "*tell*" people what to think. Referring to the Invisible Man's impromptu speech at the eviction, which has actually fueled rather than curtailed the crowd's anger, Brother Jack tells him, "That was a masterful bit of persuasion, brother . . . You aroused them so quickly to action" (281; 283). It is this praise for his oratorical skills, which the protagonist sees as an element of his individual identity, that moves him eventually to accept the Brotherhood's offer, thinking, "It was, after all, a job that promised to exercise my talent for public speaking" (291). At the same time, it is precisely his tendency to see public address as a "talent" to be exercised rather than a politically teleological activity that obscures the Invisible Man's sense of the full implications of his decision. He cannot understand, for instance, how his persuasive ability works; surveying the melee that follows his address at the eviction, he repeatedly wonders, "What had I said to bring on all this?" (277; 280), implying his knowledge of some causative force in his oratory but indicating, too, his ignorance of its operative mechanics. Similarly, he is puzzled by Brother Jack's reference to his ability to rouse people to action, stating simply, "I wanted to make a speech. I *like* to make speeches. What happened afterwards is a mystery to me" (286). The Invisible Man's insistence on this "art for art's sake" attitude—a mere fondness for speechmaking in and of itself—and his failure to understand the "mysterious" power of oratory to produce action by others are manifestations of his suspicion of politics as an "external" force that has heretofore served to thwart his attempts at psychic individuation. He conceives of public oratory as a realm in which he can discover his self, representing both the uniqueness of his attributes and a privileged space of verbal signification that seems impermeable to the threat of politics. Ironically, it is the nature of his affiliation with the Brotherhood that allows him to conceive of this false aesthetics/politics dichotomy, despite his mandate to channel the aroused energy of his listeners in the political paths deemed proper by the Brotherhood. For, as a lecturer for the Brotherhood, the protagonist is merely *doing his job,* and the cash payment he receives for his services, while inextricably binding him to a world charged with economic and raciopolitical factors, appears to him merely as freedom from worry about his material needs, and hence to concentrate solely on his "art." The effect is that of the minstrel show mentioned earlier, and it recalls the prize briefcase given to the protagonist by the school superintendent after his speech at the smoker. "He makes a good speech," the administrator has said of the young black student, "and some day he'll lead his people in the proper paths" (32). The briefcase is no "gift," but actually prepayment for the Invisible Man's "proper" use of his public-speaking skills—that propriety having been determined by the superintendent and other like-minded whites. Similarly, his salary from the Brotherhood ensures that the Invisible Man will give an appropriate public performance, linking him willy-nilly to the political structure he so desperately wants to avoid, and yet simultaneously shielding him from material concerns. The result is that Ellison's protagonist develops a false sense of an autonomous, apolitical aesthetic realm in which he believes he can express his individual will, fiddling—or orating—while Harlem burns.

For the Invisible Man's concern with his individual identity does not abate during his time with the Brotherhood. Rather, he is constantly reminded of the threat to individual black identity figured in the mob, as in the school photograph discussed above; he is continually confronted by his supposed constituency in the form of an indistinguishable mass. He recalls his first speech for the Brotherhood:

> I seemed to move in close . . . my eyes flying from face to face, swiftly, fleetingly, searching for someone I could recognize, for someone from the old life, and seeing the faces become vaguer and vaguer the farther they receded from the platform. . . .
>
> The light was so strong I could no longer see the audience, the bowl of human faces. (332)

But while the features that distinguish the audience members as individual human beings become blurred before the protagonist's eyes, he conceives of himself in contradistinction to the mass and claims that he has become "more human" before the crowd (337). So the terms are set: The collective, represented by the audience for the protagonist's speeches, is a consuming mass that obliterates the distinguishing features of the individuals who constitute it, but it is also the entity against which an effective leader can distinguish himself as an individual subject; the crowd both opposes the individual and demonstrates him to himself, becoming, for a moment, that mirror which serves to confirm individual identity. In this moment, it seems that the protagonist has fulfilled, for himself at least, the task articulated by his college literature professor in discussing James Joyce's hero. He remembers his instructor saying: "Stephen's problem, like ours, was not actually one of creating the uncreated conscience of his race, but of creating *the uncreated features of his face*. Our task is that of making ourselves individuals" (345–46; emphasis in the original). In opposing himself as orator to the indistinguishable mob of his audience, Ellison's protagonist seems to succeed in this to some degree.

The minute the Brotherhood alters its support for the protagonist, however, his ability to sustain individual identity in the face of the black community is undermined. This development evidences the radical connection between the protagonist's ability to produce speeches and the politics of the Brotherhood, but it further indicates his dependence upon the black community for his achievement of individual identity. It isn't as if the Invisible Man hasn't been warned against "going too fast" or "getting too big"—he has received an anonymous note (later learned to have been penned by Brother Jack himself) reminding him, "[Y]ou are one of *us* . . . you know that this is a *white man's world* . . . *They* do not want you to go too fast and will cut you down if you do" (374). Yet he is still stunned when the organization pulls him out of Harlem and reinstalls him downtown, to lecture on the "Woman Question." The move is ostensibly a response to charges of "petty individualism" brought against the Invisible Man by an associate in the organization's Harlem section; the Brotherhood will review the case while he is temporarily transferred. No matter what the intent, though, the action serves to remind the protagonist that he is unlikely ever to reach the Brotherhood's center of power, or, as he puts it, "to approach some of the aspects of the organization about which I knew nothing . . . higher committees and the leaders who never appeared . . ." (397). For the Invisible Man demonstrates a fierce ambition with respect to the Brotherhood, recalling that the Brotherhood "was the one organization in the whole country in which I could reach the very top and I meant to get there" (372); and, when faced with his reassignment, "my ambitions were too great to surrender so easily . . . my main concern was to work my way ahead in the movement" (397). Geographically, the Invisible Man's transfer downtown does seem to signal his "approach" to the center of the Brotherhood, since the lower regions of Manhattan represent the seat of the organization's leadership no less than that of the capitalism championed by Norton and the elder Emerson, while Harlem's location at the northern end of the island, far from these centers, indicates the estrangement of its people from true political power. Yet it is identification with the people of Harlem *as well as* affiliation with the Brotherhood that sustains the protagonist's newfound individual identity, as he begins to realize: "I had learned that the clue to what Harlem wanted was what *I* wanted; and my value to the Brotherhood . . . depended upon my complete frankness and honesty in stating the community's hopes and hates, fears and desires" (398).

This becomes clear later, when the Invisible Man is whisked back to service in Harlem as suddenly as he was remanded downtown. He can no longer interact with the community as he had before his reassignment, and at least one resident of Harlem views his return with skepticism, which he voices openly in a neighborhood bar. In defense of the protagonist, his bartender friend says, " 'This here man's done more for the community than you'll ever do.' *'What* community?' " asks the skeptic, " 'I hear he got the white fever and left' " (415). The distinction between the individual and his community, apparently necessary if he is to be conceived as a leader, has become overly marked, the result being not simply the establishment of individual identity but the dissolution of ties between the two entities, ties necessary to the political efficacy of either. The capricious actions of the Brotherhood authorize this fate for the Invisible Man, simultaneously demonstrating to him his political marginality.

That marginality is underscored by the protagonist's mandate to speak on the "Woman Question." The Invisible Man himself fights his initial

Fragmentation and Synthesis in Ellison's *Invisible Man*

impulse to regard his new assignment as "an outrageous joke" (397), asking himself, "[W]hy shouldn't I speak about women, or any other subject? Nothing lay outside the scheme of our ideology . . ." (397). Yet his very contention that women are a "subject" for ideological debate rather than a constituency to be represented betrays their double marginalization in their reduction to an abstract dilemma and the concomitant shuttling of that dilemma to the periphery of the Brotherhood's business.

This bracketing of women is figured in the Invisible Man's own actions as an agent for the Brotherhood, when he "dismisse[s] a woman seeking to free her husband, who had been jailed for beating her" (382). This seemingly gratuitous final clause jars precisely because it points up the circumscription of women's activity in the novel. The narrative severely limits mention of this woman's action, telling us only that she seeks to free her husband; similarly, it tells us nothing of him but that he beats her. Thus, the conceptual window it very deliberately opens for us onto this woman's life is exceedingly narrow, for if she succeeds in what appears to us as her only activity, this would merely provide the possibility for her husband to engage in his only apparent activity—beating her. This narrative cul-de-sac thus illustrates the pointless circularity of women's action and its predication on the actions of men, which appear as an unambiguously destructive force in women's lives. The protagonist's "dismissal" of this woman is the icing on the cake, transcending its local status as a mere conclusion of business and representing, more sweepingly, women's expulsion from the focus of the Brotherhood's concern.

Even the Invisible Man's selfish attempt to use women for his own political gain within the Brotherhood is undermined precisely by their marginal status. He contrives to have a sexual liaison with one Sybil, wife of a top man in the organization, in order to gain information about the Brotherhood's leadership. But she can tell him nothing, the white women who form the outer fringe of the Brotherhood being just as estranged from any real effectivity as he is himself, and representing, if anything, a boundary around and not a means to the powers that control the organization. Any contact between the black man and the (white) women in the novel represents, then, a sort of meeting of the marginals, as the protagonist himself realizes. During an encounter with another white woman whom he meets at his first lecture on the "Woman Question," he is struck by the sense that "the discordantly invisible and the conspicuously enigmatic were reaching a delicately balanced harmony" (401). Even this moment of synthetic stability shared by the two politically decentered figures is disrupted, however, at the instant their union is consummated: The couple face a looking glass in the woman's bedroom and

> in the mirrored instant I saw myself standing between her eager form and a huge white bed, myself caught in a guilty stance, my face taut, tie dangling; and behind the bed another mirror which now like a surge of the sea tossed our images back and forth, back and forth, furiously multiplying the time and the place and the circumstance. (405–406)

The mirror that, in other circumstances and for other people, had promised a fixing of individual identity here operates as a monstrously multiplying apparatus, figuring not the stabilization of identity but rather its instability—represented as multiplicity—which seems to be the fate of those traditionally denied the means of establishing themselves as subjects, such as women and black men.

The Invisible Man's reassignment, then, is a catalytic event, reminding him of his true marginality within the order he inhabits, and pointing out to him both his dependence, as a creative "author," on the power of the Brotherhood—the crucial link between art and politics—and the importance of his identification with the black community if he is to achieve individual identity. He realizes the necessity of embracing the "we" he has hitherto rejected if he is to constitute the "me"—or, more appropriately, the subjective "I"—he so desires, for he can lay claim to individual identity in no other way.

Aesthetic Synthesis and Collective Experience

We know that Ellison's protagonist has thus far conceived of the tension between the individual and the collective as cause for distress, and yet there is precedent within Afro-American aesthetic theory for seeing this tension as a productive force. Ellison himself, writing of Afro-American musical form, invokes the tension as a generative power, even while he acknowledges the danger to the individual inherent in that tension:

> There is . . . a cruel contradiction implicit in the art form itself. For true jazz is an art of individual assertion within and against the group. Each true jazz moment (as distinct from the uninspired commercial performance) springs from a contest in which each artist challenges all the rest; *each solo flight, or improvisation, represents* (like the

successive canvases of a painter) *a definition of his identity: as individual, as member of the collectivity and as a link in the chain of tradition.* Thus, because jazz finds its very life in an endless improvisation upon traditional materials, the jazzman must lose his identity even as he finds it. . . . [14]

Similarly, speaking of blues form, Houston Baker asserts that "[t]he viability and energy of the blues derive from the bluesman's improvisational skill. . . . His effective performance depends on his knowledge of the tradition of which he is a part and his deft improvisational energies." [15]

If these formulations of the operative aesthetic of jazz and blues read as analogs of T. S. Eliot's claims in "Tradition and the Individual Talent," it is because the musical forms, according to Ellison and Baker, manifest what can be called the "modern classicism" the achievement of which Eliot campaigns for in his modernist "manifesto." When Eliot says that "the historical sense involves a perception, not only of the pastness of the past, but of its presence," that it "is . . . what makes a writer most acutely conscious of his place in time, of his contemporaneity," [16] he is placing his writer at the point occupied by Ellison's and Baker's musical improvisationist, and he, before them, has articulated the inevitability of the loss of the individual to the collective that is scripted as a simultaneously past and present artistic "tradition": "What happens [to the poet] is a continual surrender of himself as he is at the moment to something which is more valuable. The progress of an artist is a continual self-sacrifice, a continual extinction of personality," or what he refers to in the same essay as a "process of depersonalization" (52–53).

This depersonalization seems not to trouble Eliot, and, though it apparently troubles Ellison, the focus of his anxiety is the loss of individual personality, not to the artistic tradition whence it springs but to a commercialism manifested in the usurpation of the artist's individuality by the context of artistic production. He laments: "[H]ow often do we see even the most famous of jazz artists being devoured alive by their imitators, and shamelessly, in the public spotlight?" ("Charlie Christian," 234). The object of Ellison's disgust—the *commercialization* of the "true jazz moment"—is telling, for it indicates why, with respect to the loss of personality to artistic tradition, both Eliot and Baker (and Ellison, too, apparently) can be quite complacent, in evident contradiction to Lukácsean characterizations of the modernist project as one that privileges the individual. The collective "tradition," the loss of personality to which evokes only the slightest hint of melancholy in Ellison and none in Eliot or Baker, represents a privileged aesthetic, a "more valuable" category to which the modernist ethic would easily sacrifice the "individual monad." On the other hand, the *commercialization* of jazz by a disrespectful collective posterity or consumer population represents the profanation of the individual by means of the mode of production. This profanation is the very subordination of the individual subject to politics that Marxism claims is opposed by modernist ideology.

Ellison's fear and loathing of commercialization can be seen as a cognate of the Invisible Man's dread of absorption by the body politic of the black community. In order for Ellison's protagonist to find value in the tension between the individual and the collective; to experience with exhilaration what Ellison, recalling his own boyhood experience of jazz, sees as "[t]he delicate balance struck between strong individual personality and the group"; [17] potentially to reconcile himself to what Eliot identifies as the "continual extinction of personality"—to achieve these things, the Invisible Man must absorb the lessons of Eliot and Baker, and Ellison in his essays, and recast the battle between the collective and the individual in aesthetic rather than political terms. We have seen him do this in his position with the Brotherhood, where he—as aesthetic producer—is effectively shielded from the political realities that ground his aesthetic production. The rescripting operative here underscores *Invisible Man*'s relation to modernism, since the shift in the terms of the problematic of subjectivity results in the privileging of an aestheticism generally associated with "high modernism." We know, however, that the aestheticization of the tension between the individual and the collective is predicated upon an aesthetics/politics dichotomy that must be false; thus, any merely aesthetic "resolution" of that tension in favor of the individual must necessarily result in a human subject that is, ironically, radically incomplete, as attested by the protagonist's inevitable remarginalization even within the apparently liberatory realm of the Brotherhood.

A successful resolution of the conflict between collective identity and individual subject can only take place in a context that supports both aesthetic production and psychopolitical subjectivity. When this is not the case, as with the Brotherhood, there occurs, for example, the apparent validation of one individual subject (the speechmaking protagonist) at the expense of the community (the faceless audience). Similarly, early in the novel, the protagonist recalls a college assembly at which a young woman has given a vocal performance of a striking nature: "[A]t times the voice seemed to become a disembodied force

Fragmentation and Synthesis in Ellison's *Invisible Man*

that sought to enter her, to violate her, shaking her, rocking her rhythmically, as though it had become the source of her being, rather than the fluid web of her own creation" (114); and, after finishing, "she sank slowly down; not a sitting but a controlled collapsing . . ." (115). What achieves subjectivity here is not the woman who sings but the song, the aesthetic product itself, which is figured as threatening the singer's material being, not unlike the way the repressive milieu of the college threatens any effective black subjectivity. When politics and artistic production do meet face to face in the novel, rather than across the screen of monetary exchange, it is as a result of a tragic contingency—witness the scene of eviction at which the protagonist makes his original speech. A similar circumstance marks the apparent resolution of politics and aesthetics in the novel, consisting in the case of Tod Clifton, the Invisible Man's colleague in the Harlem section of the Brotherhood.

The protagonist *is* reassigned to Harlem after his stint as a lecturer on the Woman Question, as noted earlier, and his new task there is to combat the forces of "Ras the Exhorter," a black nationalist organizer whose politics the Brotherhood has denounced as racist. His principal ally in this battle had been Tod Clifton, a "Brother" who continued work in Harlem during the Invisible Man's absence. The protagonist returns to the Harlem section only to find, however, that Clifton has inexplicably disappeared. Clifton's situation had been parallel to that of the protagonist: A young black rendered ineffectual as a leader within the black community due to his affiliation with the Brotherhood, he is equally unable to find validation of his identity in the white power structure. Like the protagonist, Clifton has appeared to be exiled from both realms that might afford him identity and, as a consequence, ends up "outside of history," as the protagonist puts it, a denizen of the streets (424). The Invisible Man comes upon him in the no-man's-land of midtown Manhattan—affiliated with neither the power structures of downtown nor the black community of Harlem—where Clifton seems to assert that, in the face of an inability to form an acceptable self-image, either as a leader of the black community or in cooperation with whites, the only recourse is to the stereotypes that have been the mainstay of images of blacks in the U.S. context. For, when the protagonist discovers him, Tod Clifton is hawking paper dancing dolls, each of which is distinguished with a "black, mask-like face," and which Clifton refers to for his street-corner audience as "the . . . Sambo Boogie Woogie paper doll" (421).

If the tragedy of Tod Clifton consists in the fact that, estranged though he is from the Brotherhood, he continues to represent to the public the organization's apparent conception of blacks, then his redemption is based in the fact that, through his example, the protagonist comes to realize an alternative means of expression, one that he believes to be unimplicated in the program of the Brotherhood and of the white power structure. This new mode of aesthetic production is signaled by the protagonist's query to the reader, which ends the novel: "Who knows but that, on the lower frequencies, I speak for you?" (568). This speaking for others marks a shift in the protagonist's conception of his relationship to the black community, for if, as a leader, his task has been to speak *to* his followers in an effort to direct their activities—to impose his subjectivity on the mass—as one who speaks *for* the mass, he becomes rather the means through which the collective expresses its own subjectivity. He finds his individual subjectivity in that of the community of which he is a part, and he comes to this discovery through his examination of the example of Tod Clifton.

Soon after Clifton is discovered peddling his dolls, he is accosted by the police for his lack of a vendor's license. Upon being shoved—and, we surmise, made the object of a racial epithet—by an officer in the process of his arrest, Clifton strikes the policeman, which is quickly followed by the officer's shooting and killing the black man. Aside from precipitating almost all of the events detailed in the remainder of the narrative, Clifton's murder necessitates that there be a burial, and with it a ceremony, at which the Invisible Man, logically, is to deliver some type of eulogy. Facing the crowd that is gathered for his speech, however, he becomes aware of his inability any longer to *direct* the community, to *teach* its members anything, and he screams his exasperation at them: "What are you waiting for me to tell you?" (443). As they continue to await his words, however, he takes on his new function—not to hand down directives for political action, but to speak the "truth" of what has happened to one of their own; he resorts merely to stating the facts of Tod Clifton's life and death, and one of those facts seems to hold the key to the realization of black subjectivity. When Clifton was shot, the Invisible Man tells us, "[h]e fell in a heap like any man and his blood spilled out like any blood; *red* as any blood, wet as any blood and reflecting . . . your face if you'd looked into its dulling mirror" (445). This final confirmation of identity by means of the mirror—so long sought and yet thwarted in the novel—consists in the reflection of one black individual in the essence of another. This physical process is the analog of the new relation between protagonist and collective, for this final speech is the activity through which the Invisible Man seems to find his subjectivity by exercising that of the community. The result is the emergence of individual identity even in the context of the collective, heretofore the major threat to individual subjectivity: As the protagonist ends his speech, he looks out upon the audience to see, at last, "not a crowd but the set faces of individual men and women" (448).

This apparent resolution of the tension between individual and collective—a type of "depersonalization" in which the actual productive subject is not displaced but really multiplied, and this time in a substantive rather than monstrously illusory way—parallels that conventionally found in black American musical forms. It is analogous to the "true jazz moment" of which Ellison speaks, as opposed to the commercialization of oratorical effect operative in the Brotherhood. Houston Baker clarifies the matter when he speaks of the classic blues singers' signatory coda:

> "If anybody ask you who sang this song / Tell 'em X done been here and gone." The "signature" is a space already "X"(ed), a trace of the already "gone"—a fissure rejoined. Nevertheless, the "you" (audience) addressed is always free to invoke the X(ed) spot in the body's absence. For the signature comprises a scripted authentication of "your" feelings. Its mark is an invitation to energizing intersubjectivity. Its implied (in)junction reads: Here is my body meant for (a phylogenetically conceived) you. . . .
> The blues are a synthesis. . . . (*Blues, Ideology* . . . , 5)

And synthesis is what Ellison's protagonist himself has sought: Turning midway through the novel to music for a symbol of the psychic integration he desires, he complains, "If only all the contradictory voices shouting inside my head would calm down and sing a song in unison, whatever it was I wouldn't care as long as they sang without dissonance; yes, and avoided the uncertain extremes of the scale" (253). The Invisible Man achieves this harmony during his funeral speech, when he recognizes in the black collective the synthesis of active subjects rather than the destructive absorption of individual personality, and his final query to the reader—"Who knows but that . . . I speak for you?"—is his version of the signatory coda of the blues, an invitation to the "intersubjectivity" newly recognized as "energizing" and salutary.

Formal Popularization/Political Cooptation

Intersubjective African-American aesthetic forms are not, however, without their potential drawbacks. Having used such a form to authorize a space through which anyone might lay claim to the experiences of a given narrative, the originary subject is left open to subversion by external agents who might act to erode the very subjectivity that the aesthetic production is meant to affirm. The absence, the "already-gone"-ness, the *invisibility* of the "author" provides the exciting possibility of shared subjectivity, on the one hand, but on the other hand it paves the way for cooptation of the very subject position that it "authorizes." From his peculiar perspective, Ellison's protagonist gets a glimpse of both the hopefulness *and* the danger of invisible subjectivity.

Ironically, the personage in the novel who most succeeds in his invisibility is not the "Invisible Man" but really the anticharacter named Rinehart. The experience of Rinehart in the novel is the counterpoint to that of the protagonist in that, while the latter is actively present throughout the narrative, indeed *produces* the narrative, thus effecting his subjectivity despite his namelessness, Rinehart is manifested in name only, through the utterances of others, just as the elder Emerson exists only as verbal references made by his son. The *difference* between Emerson and Rinehart is that verbal allusion fixes the identity of the former character—firmly establishes him as a powerful industrialist—while each reference to Rinehart only complicates his persona, showing it up as a fundamentally unstable phenomenon.

Rinehart has many acquaintances within Harlem, acquaintances whom the Invisible Man has occasion to meet during his confrontation with the black nationalists, led by the redubbed Ras the Destroyer. The protagonist has donned dark glasses and a wide-brimmed hat to disguise himself from Ras's men, only to be repeatedly mistaken for Rinehart, whom he now resembles. But each person who addresses him as Rinehart has a unique conception of just who Rinehart is—a preacher, a gambler, a numbers runner, a ladies' man—to all of which the same proper name adheres. We are reminded of Oscar Wilde's play in which the instability of the signifier is thematized by the transferral of a single name between different men, who attempt to use it to their advantage. But the Importance of Being Rinehart, in Ellison's novel, consists in the fact that it is the *signified* entity, the man himself, who is seen to be unstable, liminal, uncircumscribed, like the protagonist himself is to become—a border dweller. Rinehart's achievement consists in his exploiting his invisibility, predicated on this liminal status, while the protagonist had conceived of his own invisibility as a liability—tracing his ineffectiveness in the Brotherhood to the fact that Jack and the others, as he says, "[didn't] even see me" (464). Rinehart seems to have taken the advice of the "insane" black veteran, who counseled the protagonist early on that "[y]ou're hidden right out in the open—that is, you would be if you only realized it. . . . [t]he world is possibility if only you'll discover it" (152; 154). The protagonist himself realizes that Rinehart *has* discovered this truth, remarking, "[H]is world was possibility and he knew it" (487); but it is the "possibility" of loss as well as gain that characterizes Rinehart's existence.

Rinehart's world, seemingly representative of boundless opportunity, is predicated upon an ironic dichotomy: synthetic unity on the level of signification, of naming—for Rinehart has only the one name—and simultaneous fragmentation of the "real" man into many different entities. A synthesis of expression (such as that achieved by the Invisible Man through his speech at Tod Clifton's funeral) seems attended, then, by profound fragmentation on the psychic level, and it is this site of fragmentation that seems open to the potential *danger* of intersubjectivity, given the political context in which it is founded. The protagonist himself represents that danger to Rinehart's order since, in the latter's absence, he unwittingly takes the "X(ed)" position scripted by Rinehart, and this instance of intersubjectivity seems to threaten rather than affirm black subjectivity. The danger is alluded to by one of the women who mistakes the protagonist's identity. Correcting her, the Invisible Man says, " 'I'm sorry. Who was it you mistook me for?' 'Rinehart,' " she replies, " 'and you'd better not let him catch you pretending to be him. . . . You git away from here before you get me in trouble' " (472). This threat of "trouble" belies the promise of intersubjectivity always to produce a benevolent, "energizing" effect, and though its local referent is the harm that will come to the protagonist should Rinehart "catch" him in his dissembling, it indicates, more profoundly, the greater danger faced by Rinehart himself.

What Rinehart has to lose, of course, is the income garnered through the different rackets he operates in Harlem. The variedness of the personae he deploys in order to maintain these "trades," while enabling him to increase his take, enables others, as well, to insinuate themselves into the multifaceted entity that is Rinehart, and this all the more easily since the signs that refer to the man—the name "Rinehart," the manner of dress—are simple, recognizable, and easily appropriated. Thus the very juxtaposition of a synthesized, unified system of signification and an essentially fragmented, disintegrated psychopolitical entity creates the possibility of the cooptation of the originary "author" of the signs themselves, in this case the con man Rinehart. When—as is the case in the contemporary cultural context—the authorizing force in question is the black community generally, or any given subset of the community, and the entity that insinuates itself into the operative signifying system is not an individual subject—already necessarily imperfect—but rather the machinery of capitalism with all its attendant raciopolitical factors, then the risk to black identity is great, indeed.

Black experience may itself manifest a profound fragmentation, hence the repeated breaking of mirrors—presented in the novel's early scenes with Mr. Norton as holding the key to psychic integrity and wholeness—throughout the riot scenes in the last part of the novel; or the fate of Ras the Destroyer, silenced by his own spear, which the protagonist gains possession of and lets fly, "watching it catch [Ras] as he turn[s] his head . . . , ripping through both cheeks" (547); or the final dream of the Invisible Man himself, in which he is castrated and watches his "blood-red parts" disseminate themselves from the apex of a bridge's arch (556–58). Such fragmentation may indeed characterize black experience, and it can certainly be considered (as I argue here) an effect of the dominant U.S. racial ideology, in the context of whose early manifestations it was a definite impairment. But within the political–economic context of the late-twentieth-century United States, it is not fragmentation *per se* that poses the primary threat to black identity; indeed, it may well represent the closest approximation we have to the "cognitive map" that Jameson proposes is necessary for the effective negotiation of the postmodern condition. Even Ellison's protagonist, in the end, sees nothing at all detrimental in the fact of fragmentation itself; on the contrary, he realizes "that all life is divided and that only in division is there true health" (563).[18] The danger arises when the fact of the essential dividedness, multiplicity, and, hence, *specificity* of black experience—evident in blacks' peculiar relation to the conventional processes of psychic definition—is dissembled beneath signs that suggest black culture's simpleness, and the consequent ease of its containment and assimilation. The evident role that the contemporary culture industry plays in perpetrating this ruse suggests the uniqueness of the phenomenon—call it the marketing of marginality—to the twentieth century, and points to mass media as the field onto which theorists of Afro-American culture might most fruitfully turn their critical eye.[19] In the meantime, for the purposes of this study, it remains to examine some postmodern literary representations of fragmented subjectivity in order not just to draw analogies between these and the incomplete subjectivities of social marginality but to consider a possible relation between the two. Our objective is, through our deepened understanding of the specific fragmented experiences of various "minority" constituencies in the U.S. context, to theorize more fully the nature of the postmodern condition itself.

POSTMODERN NARRATIVE /
BIOGRAPHICAL IMPERATIVE

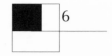

Identifying a Postmodernist "Canon"

The novels we have considered thus far depict personages whose social marginalization results in a range of symptomatic psychic effects:
the waywardness that distinguishes West's characters; the fragmentation that plagues Nin's and Barnes's women and Ellison's Invisible Man;
the consumerist logic that drives Brooks's Maud Martha. That these
same effects can be discerned in examples of postmodernism "proper"
suggests the need to examine these latter works for the potential implication within them of the politics of marginality, in order to determine
the extent to which they conceive such marginality as constitutive of
the psychosocial phenomena they represent. This undertaking may have
a tautological appearance, insofar as identifying these effects in the
works I am about to examine seems to entail merely enumerating precisely the qualities that constitute them as postmodernist, thus begging
the question of how we are to recognize postmodernist literary practice
in the first place. In fact, however, I derive my authority for claiming
these works as postmodernist from the extensive theorization of such
practice that has been undertaken by numerous commentators from
the 1970s through the mid-1980s. Indeed, many of these commentators themselves have—conveniently enough for my purposes here—
actually drafted lists of artists whose work they take to embody most
strongly a postmodernist impulse. My objective, then, is not to identify
various textual effects as postmodernist but rather to examine more
closely the effects that other observers have *already* identified as postmodernist in order to interrogate their relation to the aesthetics of marginality that I have traced in the foregoing chapters. And, as regards
selecting the works that we might examine toward this objective, it
seems to me that the aforementioned lists of postmodernist practitioners provide us with a good place to begin.

In his sweeping theoretical study of postmodernism (which we have already considered in chapter 1), Fredric Jameson enumerates exemplars of postmodernist practice across the various genres of artistic production: Andy Warhol, John Cage, Philip Glass, Terry Riley, William Burroughs, Thomas Pynchon, and Ishmael Reed.[1] Similarly, Ihab Hassan provides a list of artists promulgating a postmodernist aesthetic in literature and theater, giving particular attention to fiction writers: John Barth, William Burroughs, Thomas Pynchon, Donald Barthelme, Walter Abish, John Ashbery, David Antin, Sam Shepard, and Robert Wilson.[2] And John Barth, writing as a spokesman for contemporary literary culture, posits a veritable canon of postmodernist fiction writers, including himself, William Gass, John Hawkes, Donald Barthelme, Robert Coover, Stanley Elkin, Thomas Pynchon, and Kurt Vonnegut.[3]

Obviously, the compilation of such lists as I have cited above raises serious questions about the nature of canon formation, questions I hope to address at least implicitly in the present study. At the same time, though, given the frequency with which the names of certain authors are cited in considerations of postmodern aesthetics, it is clear that there has been achieved among critics some degree of consensus, however problematic, as to what constitutes postmodernist practice in prose fiction.[4] Consequently, it seems that a short review of works by some of the recognized practitioners of postmodern fiction can provide us with at least a minimal sense of how they elaborate the defining characteristics of that practice, and thus with an arena in which to investigate the implication within postmodernism of the politics of social marginality.

Limiting my inquiry for the sake of clarity, I explore here some of the principal characteristics of postmodern fiction through their manifestation in works by three different authors from the recognized roster of postmodernist fiction writers. That this roster—as exemplified in Barth's listing, for instance—seems to embody an overwhelmingly white, male constituency says something, obviously, about the nature of a great deal of the theorizing of postmodernism that went on through the mid-1980s. At the same time, this emphatic location of the postmodern condition within the normative subjectivity of the white male sets the stage for just the sort of correlation of postmodern subjectivity and social marginality that I want to undertake in this study. Consequently, we can hope for no better examples of postmodernist fiction to consider than works by Donald Barthelme, Robert Coover, and Thomas Pynchon.

Donald Barthelme's Unspeakable Subject

To the extent that we are concerned to investigate psychic fragmentation as a characteristic of the postmodern condition, we are concerned as well to consider the nature of and the limits to language as a constitutive factor in human subjectivity, a project consistently undertaken in the fictions of Donald Barthelme. The sentiment reflected in the oft-quoted statement by the narrator in the story "See the Moon?"—"[f]ragments are the only forms I trust"—is frequently taken as a gloss on Barthelme's own attitude toward his works, which derive their structural logic from the discursive characteristics of fracture and discontinuity, and thus suggest the inevitably fragmented nature of human subjectivity itself.[5] As Maurice Couturier and Régis Durand point out in their examination of the Barthelme story "Brain Damage," for instance, the construction of that piece as a disjointed series of first-person statements precludes the possibility of our conceiving of those statements as representing the consciousness of a single, coherent subject. Specifically, Couturier and Durand note that "[t]he absence of cross-references in these fragments makes it impossible to decide whether or not it is the same 'speaker' who is uttering all these 'I's and 'we's."[6] Thus the inherently disjunctive nature of language is played upon by Barthelme in such a way as to highlight the equally disjunctive condition of the human psyche—a technique that has been widely cited as characteristic of Barthelme's work.

Indeed, in her consideration of Barthelme's fiction, Lois Gordon asserts that

> most of his writing deals with . . . the word as an emblem of man in the universe, the way we separate ourselves from the universe in words, how we strive to define what we all think is that world out there, and ultimately how very feeble . . . we are in our efforts to do so.[7]

As Alan Wilde points out in his highly influential analysis of Barthelme's work, however, the world is not really "out there" in relation to human consciousness; indeed, Wilde suggests that one of the signal characteristics of Barthelme's fiction is that it "recognizes . . . that consciousness is implicated in the world."[8] Consequently (and as evidence of Wilde's claim), it is by the same "feeble" verbal mechanism that we use to define the objective world that we attempt, as well, to achieve our own subjectivity; as Gordon herself puts it, "the word . . .

is our means of realizing consciousness (as the modern Cartesian might say: 'I speak, therefore I am')" (31). Given the gaps, ruptures, and discontinuities that characterize discourse, however—and that serve as the raw material for much of Barthelme's work—Barthelme's fiction raises serious questions about the tenability—the "speakability," as it were—of a complete human subject. As John M. Ditsky put it in 1975, at what has turned out to be the midpoint of Barthelme's career, "[t]he Barthelme man is the prisoner of language," and the inadequacy of language to embody a coherent unitary significance accounts for what Ditsky sees as "that notable tone of melancholy that permeates [Barthelme's] work."[9]

At the same time, other critics have drawn a careful distinction between the absence of a unified human subject in Barthelme's work and the objective incoherency of his fictional compositions. As Jerome Klinkowitz puts it in his study of "reflexive fiction,"

> [t]he most typical Barthelme story . . . uses the principle of collage for all the elements of fiction, including narrative, plot, action, and character. Because each component remains itself even as it is combined into a new entity, the artist's reflexive act of creation is kept in mind. . . . [The] forward action of narrative makes [the unlike elements of Barthelme's fiction] interact; but in collage, each element retains its own material identity, so that like the head of George Washington pasted atop the body of Marilyn Monroe the artist's act of combination is always in the foreground, while the various parts of his composition keep their former identity [sic] as well.[10]

The fact that the disparate elements of Barthelme's fiction retain their individual identities even once they are assembled in collage indicates to Stanley Trachtenberg that they "are not . . . incomplete parts of an overall vision; they are themselves the objects at which the author invites the reader to look," and Trachtenberg therefore eschews as "mistaken" the conventional approach to Barthelme's stories "as a collection of fragments that reflect the dispersed quality that experience has come to have for the contemporary sensibility."[11] Nonetheless, even if each of the elements in Barthelme's fiction retains its individual integrity in the context of the narrative in which it appears, the consequent impossibility of organizing those disparate elements into an integrated whole has ramifications for our sense of the feasibility of effective human subjectivity. As Trachtenberg himself puts it, "It is not only the sequence of actions that is absent from Barthelme's fictions so that there are no plots, but also the connected series of individual gestures so that there are no persons as well" (25); and, a bit later: "The absence either of connected movement or even internal logic further conveys what might be taken as the lack of a subject" (28).

This awareness of the "lack of a subject" in Barthelme's work seems to inform (if only implicitly) most assessments of the fiction. For instance, in his study of "metafiction," Larry McCaffery identifies as Barthelme's primary interests

> the difficulties of expressing a total vision of oneself in a fragmenting universe, the failure of most of our social and linguistic systems, [and] the difficulties of making contact or sustaining relationships with others. But above all, Barthelme has been our society's most consistently brilliant critic of the language process itself and of the symbol-making activity of modern man.[12]

Later on in his study, McCaffery goes further to claim that "[a]s a result of his views about language, Barthelme often suggests that language itself may be responsible for the isolation of his characters, their inability to put the pieces of their lives together, and their inability to sustain personal relations" (109). These "views about language" that Barthelme holds obviously approximate the basic tenets of poststructuralist theory, which implicitly recognizes the fundamental interrelation of what McCaffery identifies as the discrete "interests" treated in Barthelme's fiction. However we arrive at an understanding of that interrelation, once we achieve it we can comprehend a bit better why, as McCaffery says, Barthelme's characters "never develop into psychologically convincing people so much as mere linguistic consciousnesses or collections of odd words" (115). Indeed, we may even come to consider that the psychological "roundedness" against which McCaffery contrasts the rather undeveloped nature of Barthelme's characters is itself a "mere" linguistic construct, which discovery is likely the "point" of Barthelme's fiction in the first place.

Couturier and Durand iterate this most clearly when they note that "the most striking feature of all [Barthelme's] stories . . . is the absence of the *subject,* of a stable, confident self. . . . Of course," they continue, "this sense of insecurity and precarious identity is tied up with discourse, with its discontinuities, hesitations and aporias" (33). In order to elucidate this point more fully, Couturier and Durand consider the story "Robert Kennedy Saved from Drowning" (*Unspeakable Practices,* 31–44) in which, they say, the title character's "reactions are difficult to predict and catalogue because he himself is unsure about them, about his own role(s) and his exact emotional states" (36). That uncertainty, they suggest, is a result of Barthelme's (and his characters') recognition of the fundamentally undecidable nature of the signs on which we base our emotional affects; this is the "great discovery" made by Joseph, the protagonist of Barthelme's "Me and Miss Mandible"— "that signs are signs, and that some of them are lies." [13] This indeterminacy of the characters' emotional dispositions—the "suspension" of affect, in which meaning is conventionally discerned—provides the necessary condition for Barthelme's characteristic "exploration of the distance that separates sign from meaning," according to Couturier and Durand. Such an exploration, they claim, is "characteristic of an allegorical stance and, beyond that, of a post-modernist aesthetic" (37). [14] This postmodernist aesthetic is in evidence throughout Barthelme's oeuvre, and exemplarily so in his second collection of stories, *Unspeakable Practices, Unnatural Acts,* in which both "See the Moon?" and "Robert Kennedy Saved from Drowning" appear. Indeed, that collection provides a good introduction to the variety of ways that Barthelme elaborates the imperfect linguistic constitution of human experience, so it is worthwhile to consider it in some detail.

There are two levels on which the pieces in *Unspeakable Practices, Unnatural Acts,* treat of the linguistic constitution of human experience. The first is what we might call the *thematic* level, which is signaled in the stories by relatively straightforward, even didactic, narrative declarations of the implication of language in daily experience. For instance, in the first story of the collection, "The Indian Uprising" (1–11) (which has been interpreted as an allegorical commentary on the repression of "natural" emotion and spontaneity in contemporary civilization [15]), the disjointed narrative is punctuated by a metanarrative commentary that declares, "Strings of language extend in every direction to bind the world into a rushing, ribald whole" (*Unspeakable Practices,* 10). That linguistic "binding" of the objective world is recapitulated with respect specifically to the human subject in "This Newspaper Here" (23–30). The protagonist and narrator of the story is an elderly man whose obsession with his daily newspaper is based on the fact that he sees in it "rare lies and photographs incorrectly captioned," which few other people can discern. As he says to the reader at one point in his discussion of the paper, "I would be pleased really quite if you could read it. But you can't. But some can" (26). And he goes on to relate a tale about his encounter with a California university professor whom he tries to introduce to the fascinating account that appears on page two of his paper:

> [T]he amusing story of the plain girl fair where the plain girls come
> to vend their wares but he said "on *my* page 2 this newspaper here
> talk about the EEC." Then I took it from his hand and showed him
> with my finger pointing the plain girl fair story. Then he commences
> to read aloud from under my finger there some singsong about the
> EEC. So I infer that he is one who can't. So I let the matter drop. (27)

Subsequently the narrator visits the "plain girl fair," where he procures
a young woman named Marie whom he treats to lobster dinner, dancing, and a flirtatious sojourn in "my hay," all of which activities are
qualified at the end of the paragraph in which he describes them, by a
summary comment that declares simply, "In my mind" (27).

It is clear, then, that the experiences of the protagonist, whether they
can be said to occur objectively or not, are conditioned by the narratives that he reads in his newspaper, whether they are "actually" printed
there or not. And once again, the narrative itself provides a didactic
gloss on this fact in the initial paragraph of the story, which has the
protagonist being visited by an eleven-year-old neighbor girl who tor-
ments him by poking him with a knitting needle as he sits in the chair
to which he is "theoretically" confined. When he implores her to stop,
asking her "what pleasure is there hearing me scream like this?" she
replies that

> "torment is the answer old pappy man it's torment that is the game's
> name that I'm learning about under laboratory conditions. Torment is
> the proper study of children of my age class and median income and
> *you* don't matter in any case you're through dirty old man can't even
> get out of rotten old chair." (25)

Musing on this assessment, the protagonist declares, "Summed me up
she did in those words which I would much rather not have heard so
prettily put as they were nevertheless" (25–26). The linguistic "summing up" that the character identifies here seems a parallel process to
the constitution of his experiential life by the stories he reads in "this
newspaper here," on which that "summing up" also seems to be an
implicit commentary.

The constitutive power of language as demonstrated in these excerpts is countered in at least one story in the collection that thematizes its more destructive capacities. "Report" (45–53) is narrated by a
member of an antiwar group who has been assigned to meet with military engineers in Cleveland in order to "persuade them not to do what
they are going to do" (47). He reports that while at the meeting,

Postmodern Narrative/Biographical Imperative

> I noticed many fractures among the engineers, bandages, traction. I
> noticed what appeared to be fracture of the carpal scaphoid in six
> examples. I noticed numerous fractures of the humeral shaft, of the
> os calcis, of the pelvic girdle. I noticed a high incidence of clay-
> shoveller's fracture. I could not account for these fractures. (47)

As the meeting progresses, he becomes aware of additional injuries
among the engineers: "I noticed then distributed about the room a
great many transverse fractures of the ulna. . . . I noticed about me
then a great number of metatarsal fractures in banjo splints" (50). Finally, an explanation for these fractures is revealed as the chief engineer lists the various new weapons that his research teams have developed, one of which is "a secret word that, if pronounced, produces
multiple fractures in all living things in an area the size of four football
fields" (51); the broken bones among the engineers themselves result
from the fact that, as the chief puts it, "[s]ome damned fool couldn't
keep his mouth shut" (52). The disintegrative effects of this linguistic
weapon complement the effects of two other strategies developed by
the engineers. As the chief explains, "We have hypodermic darts capable of piebalding the enemy's pigmentation. We have rots, blights,
and rusts capable of attacking his alphabet" (51). The juxtaposition of
these two weapons in the chief engineer's summary suggests the parallel—and therefore possibly linked—disintegrations of the enemy's
verbal capacity and of his physical person, at the same time as the
engineers' own secret word will itself wreak physical destruction upon
the enemy. Either case makes clear the degree to which physical integrity, in the realm of this story, is subordinated to discursive processes,
and further indicates Barthelme's preoccupation with the effective power
of linguistic forms.

In addition to these thematic treatments of the discursive constitution
of the human subject, *Unspeakable Practices, Unnatural Acts* contains
a number of stories that might be said to constitute such treatments at
the *stylistic* level. That is, rather than commenting didactically on the
implication of language in human experience, these stories are structured in such a way as to *effect* such an implication in the ontology
they represent. "Robert Kennedy Saved from Drowning" (31–44) presents a picture of the title character (designated as "K." in the manner
of Kafka) through a collection of short vignettes with titles such as "K.
at His Desk," "Attitude Toward His Work," "Childhood of K. as Re-
called by a Former Teacher," and so on. These vignettes consist variously of quotations from K. reflecting his thoughts on different matters,
quotations by other characters (K.'s former teacher, his secretaries, etc.)

summing up different aspects of his personality, and omniscient third-person descriptions of K.'s actions and demeanor. There is no continuous narrative thread that binds these vignettes together, so the portrait that emerges as the piece progresses is that of a profoundly disjunctive personality, our knowledge of which might be made more comprehensive through the accumulation of more discrete details about it, but is never able to achieve coherence through the discursive technique that characterizes the piece.

A similar effect is achieved with respect not merely to an individual personality but to an entire interpersonal relationship in the stories "Edward and Pia" (73–83) and "A Few Moments of Sleeping and Waking" (85–95). The stories catalog the adventures of a young couple, Edward and Pia, and a few of their friends and relatives as they make an apparently aimless sojourn through various European countries. The narrative progresses in a series of simple declarative sentences that by and large seem to bear no logical relation to one another. The opening of "Edward and Pia" provides a prime example:

> Edward looked at his red beard in the tableknife. Then Edward and Pia went to Sweden, to the farm. In the mailbox Pia found a check for Willie from the government of Sweden. It was for twenty-three hundred crowns and had a rained-on look. Pia put the check in the pocket of her brown coat. Pia was pregnant. (75)

"Edward and Pia" follows the two protagonists on their travels from the Swedish farm to Amsterdam, Berlin, France, and finally Copenhagen, with flashbacks to previous trips to London and the Soviet Union. Their rambling itinerary is regulated only through its punctuation by references to Pia's endless morning sickness, and Edward's equally endless (and mostly unsuccessful) attempts to get Pia to have sex with him. "A Few Moments of Sleeping and Waking" takes place mostly in Denmark, in Edward's and Pia's Copenhagen apartment, where a number of friends and relatives pay them pointless visits and the activity they engage in most regularly is to attempt Freudian interpretations of the dreams Pia is constantly having.

It is possible to characterize the unorganized events that make up the bulk of the Edward and Pia stories as representative of the "*dreck*" or "trash phenomenon" that Barthelme has famously identified as the primary constituent of contemporary life and—through his works, particularly the novel *Snow White*—as the paramount ingredient of contemporary literature.[16] If it is true that this material appears to be irrelevant to the "story" Barthelme is ostensibly presenting to his reader, then the relatively mundane events that I am claiming "punctuate" this waste material (Pia's illness, Edward's sexual advances) seem to serve the regulatory function of orienting the reader by providing a vague idea of what is really "going on" in the works. Indeed, a similar phenomenon can be observed in the stories "Can We Talk" (97–102) and, particularly, "Alice" (113–23). In the former, a first-person narrator chronicles his activities during a single day in New York City, which process—especially studded as it is with regular references to the narrator's transactions at his bank and to his lunch of artichoke hearts—actually provides a normalizing backdrop for his less comprehensible musings on his romantic relationship and the woman with whom he is involved. "Alice" consists of a series of sparsely punctuated paragraphs that present the stream-of-consciousness–type meditations of an unnamed male protagonist. The majority of these passages are incoherent and difficult to associate with referents in the objective world. Distributed throughout the piece, however, are paragraphs focused on the protagonist's desire to "fornicate with Alice," the wife of a friend. Unconventionally composed as they are, these ruminations on the possibility, pleasures, and ramifications of such fornication provide a sort of hermeneutical anchor by means of which readers can glean some sense of the story's narrative import, in the conventional sense, even as the structure of the piece generally defies the terms through which we generally define the concept.

What these structurally disjunctive pieces seem to do, then, is to demonstrate not Barthelme's disruption of a world or of a human experience that is fundamentally unified and coherent but rather the opposite—his positing of a fundamentally disjunctive and incoherent assortment of events and occurrences from which meaning can be extracted only by the imposition upon them of a system of nodal points intended to "fix," as it were, their significance. Thus, Barthelme's work might be said to be more about the specious *ordering* of human experience than about its unpredictable disruption, which we might gather Barthelme believes occurs all too seldom.

This notion is reinforced by the well-known story "The Balloon" (13–21), in which an anonymous protagonist inflates a huge balloon above some two hundred square blocks of Manhattan, as a symbol of his malaise over the absence of his lover. The city's inhabitants, however, have no knowledge of the balloon's intended significance (as, indeed, neither do we until the end of the story), so that, for the twenty-two days that the balloon covers the city, they find for it an altogether

Framing the Margins

different use as an antidote to the thoroughly regulated and rationalized nature of contemporary life:

> The balloon . . . offered the possibility, in its randomness, of mislocation of the self, in contradistinction to the grid of precise, rectangular pathways under our feet. The amount of specialized training currently needed, and the consequent desirability of long-term commitments, has been occasioned by the steadily growing importance of complex machinery, in virtually all kinds of operations; as this tendency increases, more and more people will turn, in bewildered inadequacy, to solutions for which the balloon may stand as a prototype, or "rough draft" (21).

Thus the "mislocation of the self" referenced here is actually a *salutary* phenomenon that, more importantly, derives not from a sense of the inherent disjunctiveness and incoherency of the subjective human self but rather from the self's engagement with an external phenomenon that jars it out of its normal position in the grid of daily significance. As Couturier and Durand put it in reference to what they identify as the "painful affects" Barthelme treats in his fiction—"fear, guilt, anxiety and disconnection"—

> . . . these affects seem, most of the time, to be floating—unrelated to a specific, particular situation. More like a permanent condition of the subject, they are not clearly induced by a psychological context; rather, they seem to be waiting for something to fasten on to, a situation they can take over and claim as their correspondent in the "real" world. (Couturier and Durand, 34)

As I have suggested above, the crucial issue at this point seems not to be whether the affects Barthelme treats are painful or meliorative; rather, what is crucial is that they appear to be abstract and ahistorical—not dependent on the subject's relation to a particular and specific set of conditions. The effect of such a conception of subjective displacement is to render it as a *general* phenomenon whose source is no more exact than the widely discernible depersonalization of twentieth-century life. While such a conception appears perfectly valid as far as it goes, it goes almost no distance toward specifying the various permutations of that displacement given the complexities of contemporary political and social life, and in this lack of particularity it falls short of effectively limning the significance of the postmodern condition.

There are other authors whose fictional approach to that condition differs somewhat from Barthelme's, but whose works, like his, are nonetheless generally considered to illuminate it for us effectively. An examination of a couple of those works in search of our newly established criterion of sociocultural specificity will help us discern whether, for all their technical difference from Barthelme's fiction, they actually share its limits as cultural analysis.

Robert Coover and Metafictional Baseball

It is widely recognized among critics that Robert Coover's 1968 novel, *The Universal Baseball Association, Inc., J. Henry Waugh, Prop.,* is an exemplary work of *metafiction.*[17] There is general agreement, as well, as to what metafiction is. William H. Gass's originary use of the term serves as the foundation for most other formulations; in his 1970 essay *Fiction and the Figures of Life,* Gass asserted that, in metafiction, "the forms of fiction serve as the material upon which further forms can be imposed."[18] About a decade later, in a study of the works of Gass, Coover, and Donald Barthelme, Larry McCaffery simultaneously appropriated and expanded this short definition, claiming that "metafictions [are] fictions which examine fictional systems, how they are created, and the way in which reality is transformed by and filtered through narrative assumptions and conventions."[19] And Patricia Waugh closely approximates this formulation in her general study of the topic, in which she defines metafiction as "fictional writing which self-consciously and systematically draws attention to its status as an artefact in order to pose questions about the relationship between fiction and reality."[20] To affirm the status of Coover's novel as a metafiction, then, entails discerning the degree to which, as Roy C. Caldwell, Jr., puts it, "[t]he true subject of Coover's novel is not the playing of baseball [as the title suggests it is] but the making of fiction."[21]

The easiest way to do this may well be to consider not the novel itself but rather the Coover short story on which it was based. "The Second Son" was published in the *Evergreen Review* in 1963;[22] and since, as Larry McCaffery points out, it presents essentially the same events that occur in chapter 2 of *The UBA*—which really constitutes the core of the novel's story line—McCaffery's summary of it will serve as a very useful indication of the novel's concerns. As McCaffery puts it, "The Second Son"

> tells a fairly conventional story of a fiftyish accountant who has become fanatically obsessed with a table-top baseball game which he

has rigged up with an elaborate system of dice and charts (real base-ball, he finds pretty boring). The complication arises when the hero, J. Henry Waugh, becomes so involved with the people and events of his game that he begins to believe in their literal existence. Specifi-cally he grows so attached to one of the imaginary players (Damon Rutherford, who has become a sort of "second son" for him) that when the game decrees that Damon must die—struck by a pitched ball—Henry at first becomes enraged and then collapses into uncon-trollable sobs. (McCaffery, 42)

Expanding the short story into novel form, Coover provides us with some preliminary indication of why Henry is so attached to Damon Rutherford (in chapter 1, the enigmatic rookie pitcher has just scored a perfect game, reinvigorating Henry's interest in his imaginary league) and a much more fully elaborated illustration of the extent of Henry's obsession (after Damon's death, Henry fixates on punishing Jock Casey, the player who pitched the fatal ball, and this fixation disrupts his ac-tivities in the "real" world until, finally, he rigs the game so that Casey too is killed, by a line drive, after which Henry disappears from the text, apparently insane, while his players live out the rest of their ca-reers pondering the nature and meaning of their existence). As much as these details contribute to the overall effect of Coover's novel, how-ever, the metafictional quality of the work is sufficiently illustrated in the second chapter/"Second Son" narrative. After all, what Roy Cald-well says about the novel as a whole generally holds about this short section as well:

> The Universal Baseball Association presents a structure of nested fic-tions. The first fictional frame, the outer diegesis, establishes the world of the protagonist Henry Waugh, an accountant who passes his time by playing a complex baseball game of his own invention [involving dice and tables of statistical probability by which he makes his ball games progress]. The second fiction, the inner diegesis, is the world of the game itself—the league, its players, its history. Three narratives coincide within the text: the story of Henry's life (his job, his friend-ships with Lou and Hettie, and so on); the story of the events within the Association (the games, the seasons, the players' lives); and, be-tween these two, the story of Henry's continuing transformation of the world he has created. (Caldwell, 163)

Applying Caldwell's idea of "nested fictions," it is easy to see how *The UBA* works as a metafiction, since the function of what Caldwell calls "[t]he first fictional frame, the outer diegesis"—the realm of everyday reality in the ontology of the novel—is to provide us with a means by which to observe the construction and workings of the *second* fiction, Caldwell's "inner diegesis." This examination of the fictional system constituted by Henry's baseball league is precisely the sort of operation that metafiction undertakes, according to the definitions we have reviewed. Yet there is also another facet to the function of metafiction, as McCaffery and Waugh describe it, that is not accounted for in Caldwell's summary of *The UBA,* and it is this facet that is of primary significance for the present study.

Both McCaffery and Waugh cite, as a consequential function of metafiction's examination of fictional systems, its inquiry into the effect of those systems on lived reality itself. McCaffery claims that metafiction considers "the way in which reality is transformed by and filtered through narrative assumptions and conventions," while Waugh argues that it "pose[s] questions about the relationship between fiction and reality." Caldwell, however, while granting that relationship with one hand—acknowledging "Henry's continuing transformation of the world he has created"—denies it with the other, for he asserts that the fictional world of Henry's baseball league is "hermetically sealed within a magic circle; ordered by its own time, space, rules, ends; undergoing changes dictated by internal forces . . ." (162). While it may be true that the UBA is ordered by a logic internal to itself, it is not the case that it is "hermetically sealed" against influence from the outside (as Caldwell himself admits when he cites Henry's "continuing transformation" of the UBA) or, conversely, itself prevented from affecting the external world. Indeed, the internal *operation* of the UBA's ordering principles does not imply their necessarily internal *origin*—we know that they originate with Henry, as they must if the book's interrogation into standard notions about the nature of God is to be intelligible; and while it is true that deliberate intentions on the part of that originator cannot be accommodated by the logic of his fictive world once it is set into motion (Henry's calculated execution of Jock Casey has a catastrophic effect on the entire UBA), that world is nonetheless affected by the vicissitudes in Henry's existence. Thus, the depression that Henry suffers after Damon Rutherford's death is reflected in the world of the UBA by the general disorientation that begins to characterize the life of the league. Not only, for instance, does Rutherford's team, the Pioneers, begin losing games to far inferior teams such as the Beaneaters but the matches between the remaining top two teams—the Pastimers and Jock Casey's Knickerbockers—deteriorate into ridiculously one-sided contests, with the Knicks sweeping all play according to the aleatory dictates of the dice (see *The UBA,* 148). And the UBA members themselves sense the disarray, with league chancellor Fennimore McCaffree "aware that his Association was undergoing a radical transformation," which he speculates on in densely philosophical language, while the elderly ex-chancellor Woodrow Winthrop understands only that "things were not going well in the Association[e]ver since that boy's death. Like the soul had gone out of it or something . . ." (145, 148).

Conversely, the events that occur in the UBA significantly affect Henry's life in the "real world" of the novel. To put it in McCaffery's terms, Henry's reality becomes "transformed by and filtered through" the occurrences in the league. Again, this is clear even from the scant evidence of the events of chapter 2. As McCaffery notes in his summary, when the dice dictate that Damon Rutherford must die, Henry responds with profound emotion, "first becom[ing] enraged and then collaps[ing] into uncontrollable sobs," a vivid indication of the degree to which the UBA is not a "hermetically sealed" fiction but rather profoundly implicated in the reality of Henry's everyday life. If Roy Caldwell doesn't see this, it is because he mistakes Henry's obsession with the league for an example of the standard "alienation" represented by a plethora of characters in modern fiction. Indeed, he says specifically that "[t]he protagonist's life—his increasing alienation from those around him—represents a rather conventional story and offers little interest to a discussion of the interplay of baseball and narrative" (163). While it is true that a full understanding of that interplay need not take into account Henry's disengagement from lived reality, a full understanding of the novel's postmodernism does depend upon realizing that Henry's condition is not one of "alienation" in the classic sense.

The defining characteristic of Henry's existence is that he, like Caldwell in his essay, is profoundly interested in the relation between baseball and narrative. What is particularly notable about Henry, though, is that he conceives of the essence of baseball as inhering not in the action that takes place on the field (as Larry McCaffery points out, Henry finds real baseball boring; see *The UBA,* 165–66) but rather in the statistics that derive from that action. As he says to his coworker, Lou Engel, the one time he tries to explain his fascination with the game,

> " . . . I would leave a [real baseball] game, elbowing out with all the others, and feel a kind of fear that I could so misuse my life; what was the matter with me, that I could spend unhappy hours at a ball park, leave, and yet come back again? Then, a couple days later, at home, I would pick up my scoreboard. Suddenly, what was dead

had life, what was wearisome became stirring, beautiful, unbelievably real . . .

    I found out the scorecards were enough. I didn't need the games." (166)

Thus Henry's primary interest is in numbers as a distillation of the events of baseball, so that, when he first sets up his own game, it is the *statistics* that he begins with and that define the action, rather than the other way around. Indeed, fascinated by the "complexity" of real baseball,

> [w]hen he'd finally decided to settle on his own baseball game, Henry had spent the better part of two months just working with the problem of odds and equilibrium points in an effort to approximate that complexity. Two dice had not done it. He'd tried three, each a different color, and the 216 different combinations had provided the complexity, all right, but he'd nearly gone blind trying to sort the colors on each throw. Finally, he'd compromised, keeping the three dice, but all white, reducing the total number of combinations to 56, though of course the odds were still based on 216. (19–20)

The primacy Henry gives to statistics accounts for the peculiar relation between numbers and narrative in the novel. As Caldwell concisely puts it in comparing Henry's game with real baseball, "Waugh's game, by contrast, produces not actions but numbers. From the abstract schema of box scores, Waugh works 'backward' to his fuller narratives" (164).[23] For the construction of "fuller narratives" is the secondary element in Henry's execution of his game. As Henry thinks to himself, "The dice and charts and other paraphernalia were only the mechanics of the drama, not the drama itself" (47). Representative of the verbal production that actually constitutes that drama, in Henry's estimation, are the names he assigns to his players:

> Names had to be chosen . . . that could bear the whole weight of perpetuity. . . . Now, it was funny about names. All right, you bring a player up from the minors, call him A. Player A, like his contemporaries, has, being a Rookie, certain specific advantages and disadvantages with the dice. But it's exactly the same for all Rookies. You roll, Player A gets a hit or he doesn't, gets his man out or he doesn't. Sounds simple. But call Player A "Sycamore Flynn" or "Melbourne Trench" and something starts to happen. (47)

So, as Arlen J. Hansen puts it, "The name's the thing; the statistics are simply the mechanics. . . . Names create and shape things not covered by number: the player's physical, psychological, and social character"[24]—the elements of narrative, in other words. In a different passage, Hansen summarizes more fully the narrativizing that Henry undertakes in the novel:

> Fleshing out the numbers registered by his dice, Henry tabulates and files box scores, writes songs and newspaper accounts, and creates imaginary characters to act out the events dictated by the dice. It is his focusing imagination that imposes the continuity, as well as the texture, upon the dice. (54)

It is Henry's intense interest in the construction and meaning of narrative that, to my mind, constitutes the uniqueness of his disengagement from "reality" and distinguishes it from the modernist alienation that Roy Caldwell invokes in his essay. If we recall from the previous chapter Georg Lukács's assertion that such alienation is manifested in the modernist presentation of "man as a solitary being, incapable of meaningful human relationships," and Jameson's elaboration that modernism is calculated to "'manage' historical and social . . . impulses," then, in order to identify Henry's condition as one of "alienation," we must recognize it as his disengagement not only from the other people in his world but also from the very processes by which an historical narrative is constructed in order to render that world ideologically intelligible. But Henry *does not* evidence a disengagement from those processes. On the contrary, he recognizes in his negotiation of the interplay between numbers and narrative regarding the UBA a version of the very activity that constitutes history in the "real world." As Richard Alan Schwartz points out, "[m]uch of *The Universal Baseball Association* is concerned with how we describe and record reality/history,"[25] a claim that is substantiated by a passage in the novel in which Henry reflects to Lou on the nature of history. Having pushed their way onto a crowded city bus after work one evening, the two men are standing in the packed aisle of the vehicle, water dripping

> from the brim [of Lou's hat] onto the evening paper of a man sitting next to them. The paper spoke blackly of bombs, births, wars, weddings, infiltrations, and social events. "You know, Lou," Henry said, "you can take history or leave it, but if you take it you have to accept certain assumptions or ground rules about what's left in and what's left out. . . .
>
> "History. Amazing, how we love it. And did you ever stop to think that without numbers or measurements, there probably wouldn't be any history?" He asked it that way for Lou's sake. Really, he was thinking the thoughts he always thought on buses and subways, drawing the old comparisons. . . . [H]e and the Association were

the same age, though of course their "years" were reckoned differently. He saw two time lines crossing in space at a point marked "56." Was it the vital moment? . . . "At 4:34 on a wet November afternoon, Lou Engel boarded a city bus and spilled water from his hat brim on a man's newspaper. Is that history? . . .

"Who's writing it down?" Henry demanded. (49–50)

The "comparisons" that Henry draws in this passage between the progression of the UBA and the history of the real world, along with his passionate inquiry about what constitutes that latter history, indicate that the construction of narrative in which he is engaged through his play with the UBA is not really a function of his "alienation" from the real world—a Walter Mitty–like fantasy by which he escapes from social and historical demands; rather, Henry's narrativizing represents his profound implication in and engagement with the very logic that shapes those demands. This phenomenon, whereby a subject's vexed relation to and apparent disengagement from the social sphere is demonstrated to be a function precisely of the logic of that sphere itself, seems to me to characterize exactly the postmodern condition, which is itself, it must be acknowledged, founded on a notion of modernist alienation to which it is nevertheless not identical.

The thematic manifestation of this postmodernism in Coover's novel consists in the subjective decentering and psychic fragmentation that Henry undergoes in the course of the story. If it looks as though Henry is suffering from "alienation," as Caldwell suggests, then this is because he has become absorbed by the narrative logic of "real-world" history only to apply it elsewhere, in the realm of his UBA; he is "decentered" to the extent that the focus of his concern now lies not in the world that his fellow human beings inhabit but in the baseball league that he has created. And the full realization of that imagined world depends upon Henry's own psychic fragmentation to the extent that the various elements that constitute the UBA—particularly the different members of the league—represent different facets of Henry's own psyche, all of which must necessarily become increasingly distinct and individuated as the UBA develops.

As Frank W. Shelton notes, from early on in the novel, Coover presents the different characters that inhabit the UBA as elements in Henry's psyche that are ready to emerge as needed whenever Henry finds himself in a stressful position.[26] When he has sex with Hettie, the neighborhood "B-girl," in chapter 1, for instance, he is the triumphantly virile Damon Rutherford, who's just pitched his perfect game; he is Damon again when he is confronted by Horace Zifferblatt, his boss at the accounting firm where he is employed, who asks what is interfering with his work, to which Henry condescendingly responds, "How's that, fella?" (42). He is Willie O'Leary when, out to dinner with Lou, he flirts with the buxom waitress, "lifting his right hand in a benediction upon that bosom, sa[ying]: 'When he stretched forth his hand, the mountains trembled' " (160). The effect is not unlike that evoked by narratives about multiple personalities, from *The Three Faces of Eve*, to *Sybil*, to *When Rabbit Howls*,[27] except that in Henry's case there is no recognition of his psychic dissociation—much less any progress toward the reintegration of the different psychic characteristics into one "personality"—but only the crystallization of that dissociation as Henry himself disappears from the text in the last chapters of the novel.

In the end, then, we have a fragmenting of the human psyche that looks remarkably like what we have seen in the earlier works discussed in the preceding chapters, particularly those by West, Ellison, and Nin. There is a difference, however, between the fragmented subjectivities depicted by those authors and that evident in Coover's "properly" postmodernist novel in that the earlier writers' characters are, as I have shown, fragmented due specifically to the socially marginalized status that they occupy as a result of their class, gender, and/or racial identifications; Coover's novel, on the other hand, explicitly signals Henry's psychic fragmentation as a function of a generalized social phenomenon that does not take into account division and stratification within the social ontology. Not only does the novel's title itself invoke the "universality" of the problematic that Coover explores but the correlation of Henry's construction of the UBA with a generalized "history" that is not thoroughly interrogated in the novel indicates the degree to which Coover's postmodernism fails to address the very questions on which it is based. After all, Henry's query to Lou about the status of their actions as history—"Who's writing it down?"—could represent more than the general metaphysical and epistemological inquiry that it clearly does in the context of the novel; it could represent a politically motivated examination of exactly whose interest conventionally received social narratives are meant to serve in the U.S. context. In that case, the answer to the question "Who's writing it down?" becomes clear: Robert Coover. And the task of the critic becomes clear as well— to determine who Robert Coover is in terms of his positioning as a social subject, and how that positioning enables him to write as a "universalist" in the face of overwhelming evidence as to the problems of such a conception. The answers could provide us with important

new ways of reading not only writers whose primary defining characteristic is all too often taken to be their difference from Robert Coover
but the difference in Robert Coover himself. That Coover neglects this
undertaking in his own work indicates that, for all the postmodernist
narrative technique that characterizes it, his fiction falls short of adequately interrogating the nature of the postmodern subject itself, and
thus is limited as a commentary on the sociopolitical context in which
it emerges.

Multiplicity and Uncertainty in Thomas Pynchon's
The Crying of Lot 49

The fate that befalls Coover's J. Henry Waugh comprises two constituent facets, each of which has been identified as an important characteristic of the general postmodern condition: Henry's disappearance
from the final chapters of Coover's novel signals the death of the human subject as a unified, integrated entity; and his psychic dispersal
into the various consciousnesses of his UBA players and administrators
identifies that death as predicated on the proliferation of a multitude
of different subject positions that any given individual might occupy,
even simultaneously.

Such multiplicity as is found in Coover's novel also serves as the
source of the large degree of epistemological uncertainty that characterizes the fiction of another major postmodernist author, Thomas Pynchon. While Pynchon's body of work includes the long-awaited 1990
novel *Vineland,* as well as the collection of his early short fiction, *Slow
Learner,* published in 1984, his reputation nonetheless rests on his three
major novels of the 1960s and early 1970s—the monumental and
complicated *V.* (1963) and *Gravity's Rainbow* (1973), and the much
sparer *Crying of Lot 49* (1966), which, despite its relatively narrower
narrative scope, nonetheless presents many of the same issues as the
two longer works that frame it in Pynchon's oeuvre. As Robert D.
Newman puts it in his useful study of Pynchon's work,

> . . . literary critics, at least those initially inclined to appreciate Pyn-
> chon, seem to welcome *The Crying of Lot 49* . . . as a compact,
> unified work that distills many of the issues encountered in the more
> diffuse and convoluted *V.* and *Gravity's Rainbow.* Numerous general
> essays on Pynchon choose to light upon *Lot 49* rather than the other
> novels in order to demonstrate their assertions, and instructors of

contemporary literature courses choose it as an introduction to the intricacies of Pynchon's works.[28]

Obviously, then, by positing *The Crying of Lot 49* as the distillation of Pynchon's concerns, I am replicating the efforts of a number of other critics who have already characterized it as an exemplary text. Additionally, however, I want to use the observations of previous commentators as a basis from which to draw some new insights about Pynchon's narrative strategy in *The Crying of Lot 49*, and thus to situate Pynchon's fiction in the larger context of commentary on the postmodern era. I want to demonstrate that in that context, Pynchon surpasses both Barthelme and Coover in indicating how best to interrogate the nature of the postmodern subject, though, like them, he falls short of performing that interrogation himself.

The plot of *The Crying of Lot 49* is widely familiar.[29] The protagonist, Oedipa Maas, is a young California housewife who is jarred out of her suburban existence when she becomes the executor of the estate of her late lover, the wealthy developer Pierce Inverarity. In order to undertake her duty with respect to Inverarity's will, she leaves her home in Kinneret-Among-the-Pines for the more southerly locale of San Narciso, where Inverarity had been based. Once she does this, she has a series of "revelations" that indicate to her the existence of—and Pierce's involvement in—an underground society known as the Tristero that communicates through an illicit postal system called W.A.S.T.E., whose mailboxes masquerade as garbage cans. Two initial clues key her in to the existence of the Tristero: One is a letter to her in San Narciso from her husband, Mucho, on the envelope of which appears the printed message, ostensibly from the post office, "REPORT ALL OBSCENE MAIL TO YOUR POTSMASTER" (the subtle subversion of official postal slogans turns out to be a signal activity of the Tristero); the other is a symbol she discovers on the wall of the women's restroom in a San Narciso bar called The Scope, which she later figures to be a drawing of a buglelike post horn with a mute in its bell. As she tries to untangle the intricacies of Pierce Inverarity's holdings, the clues proliferate— everywhere she sees the muted post horn, the initials W.A.S.T.E., references to Tristero or Trystero, until finally she learns that the very stamp collection over which Pierce had obsessed while he was alive is itself a relic of Tristero and the W.A.S.T.E. postal system. Unsure at last whether there really is a Tristero underground or she is only imagining it, whether the whole thing is a hoax perpetrated by Inverarity or she is insanely paranoid, Oedipa hopes to discover the truth by attending the auction at which the stamp collection is going to be sold off, where she waits to see who will bid on lot 49, which it constitutes. The novel ends on this note of anticipation, the only certainty being that the legacy Pierce Inverarity has left is coextensive with the intricacies of America itself, the secret of which Oedipa has actually, inadvertently, been seeking all along.

As at least one critic has suggested, it is evident that "the plotline of *The Crying of Lot 49* follows that of the detective story, wherein a heroine-sleuth attempts to solve a mystery through the logical assembling and interpretation of palpable evidence."[30] It is also true, as Lance Olsen further points out, that *Lot 49* "reverses" that conventional plotline: "The movement becomes one from certainty to uncertainty" (158). As Stefano Tani puts it, *Lot 49* "'deconstructs' conventional detective fiction," as it presents "a structural non-solution . . . a proliferation of clues which lead nowhere."[31] This situation of epistemological uncertainty holds true both for the reader—as Frank Palmeri notes, the novel "raises expectations of meaning that it satisfies partially or not at all"[32]—and for Oedipa herself—Olsen observes that "[a]lthough for Oedipa meaning always seems near . . . [,] it never materializes" (159). Indeed, at one point during her quest, Oedipa herself wonders whether "at the end of this . . . , she . . . might not be left with only compiled memories of clues, announcements, intimations, but never the central truth itself" (95); later, she considers whether "the gemlike 'clues' were only some kind of compensation. To make up for her having lost the direct, epileptic Word . . ." (118).

If the uncertainty that characterizes *The Crying of Lot 49* substantiates Lance Olsen's claim that Pynchon "revels in ultimate confusion and indeterminacy" (154), it is also true that it is based in a very specific theoretical notion about the nature of indeterminacy. Ever since the appearance of Anne Mangel's founding article on the subject in 1971, critics have discussed the import for *The Crying of Lot 49* of the concept of entropy—a concept that has dual significance in the fields of thermodynamics and information theory.[33] Deriving his formulation from a standard dictionary entry, Peter L. Abernethy actually offers the most concise explanation of the meaning of entropy in those two fields:

> Thermodynamics defines entropy as "the degradation of the matter and energy in the universe to an ultimate state of inert uniformity." In communications it is "a measure of the amount of information in a message that is based on the logarithm of the number of possible equivalent messages" (i.e., the more ambiguous the message, the more entropic it is).[34]

Robert Newman further specifies the significance of entropy in its different contexts: Because "[i]n thermodynamic theory entropy refers to . . . a uniform randomness that allows for no differentiation among the parts of a system . . .[,] maximum entropy yields a chaos of sameness." On the other hand, "[i]n information theory . . . disorganization increases the potential information that may be conveyed. Maximum entropy in this respect produces a chaos of multiplicity" (Newman, 73).

Overlaid onto social and cultural contexts, these two notions of entropy provide a workable metaphor for the development in the plot of Pynchon's novel. As Newman points out, "[a]t the beginning of the novel Oedipa's conventionality and the lifeless repetition the reader encounters in the traces of American culture suggest an entropic system in the thermodynamic sense" (73). And, indeed, such a system is indicated in Pynchon's description of Oedipa's life up until she is named executor of Inverarity's estate—"a fat deckful of days which seemed (wouldn't she be first to admit it?) more or less identical" (11), or in the appearance of San Narciso as Oedipa first approaches it in her car:

> Like many named places in California it was less an identifiable city than a grouping of concepts—census tracts, special purpose bond-issue districts, shopping nuclei, all overlaid with access roads to its own freeway. . . . if there was any vital difference between it and the rest of Southern California, it was invisible on first glance. (24)

As Newman further suggests, however, as the novel progresses Oedipa seems to enter into a system that is entropic in informational terms, since "the estate that Inverarity leaves Oedipa to sort out yields more and more information about that system . . . , to the point that its diversity becomes bewildering" (73–74), hence the unresolved nature of Oedipa's quest at the end of the novel. The defining characteristic of The Crying of Lot 49 (as with all of Pynchon's novels), however, is the degree to which not only the characters but the readers themselves are implicated in the uncertainty that the story manifests. As John Leland puts it,

> Pynchon's novel is not only about entropy but is itself entropic. . . .
>   The entropic nature of communication informs both Oedipa's quest to sort out the earthly effects of Inverarity and our attempts to sort out the "results" of Oedipa's experience—that is, to sort out the information Pynchon provides about his novel.[35]

Moreover, the uncertainty that we and Oedipa experience as Pynchon's plot unfolds is also thematized rhetorically in the narrative. It is a critical commonplace to say that Pynchon's syntactic structures in *The Crying of Lot 49* foster a profound semantic multiplicity;[36] what remains is to identify the specific ramifications of that multiplicity. A look at one of Pynchon's characteristic narrative techniques will shed some light on the exact import of his postmodernist strategy.

Richard Pearce has claimed that in *The Crying of Lot 49*, Pynchon "abandons the stable omniscient perspective [that characterizes *V.*] to focus on Oedipa Maas's developing consciousness; the narrator only knows what Oedipa knows at each step in her quest."[37] While it is true that the narrator of *Lot 49* is not at all omniscient in the standard manner, the imperfectness of his knowledge, which approximates Oedipa's own uncertainty, is much more disorienting than the latter. Relatively early in the book, we already can spot passages by which we can discern the non-omniscience of the narrator. In chapter 2, Oedipa, just arrived in San Narciso, is sharing wine and tequila with Metzger, the lawyer who drew up Pierce Inverarity's will, while the TV plays an old movie in which Metzger starred as the child actor Baby Igor. As they get increasingly tipsy, Metzger challenges Oedipa to place a bet on the outcome of the movie. Finally, she relents: " 'So,' she yelled, maybe a bit rattled, 'I bet a bottle of something. Tequila, all right? . . . ' " (34). Right after this, having realized by his response that Metzger is interested not in more alcohol but in sex, Oedipa "grew more and more angry, perhaps juiced, perhaps only impatient for the movie to come back on" (35). At another point in the novel, the narrator relates for us Oedipa's discovery of the "potsmaster" slogan on her letter from Mucho, and attempts to correlate it with her discovery of the post horn logo, noting that "[i]t may have been that same evening that they happened across The Scope," the bar in which Oedipa first sights the emblem (47). Finally, once Oedipa is fully embroiled in her quest for the meaning of the Tristero, she spends a delirious evening tracking clues throughout San Narciso, fighting sleep as she goes. As the narrator puts it, "What fragments of dreams came [to her] had to do with the post horn. Later, possibly, she would have trouble sorting the night into real and dreamed" (117).

A common characteristic of all of these passages is their use of adverbs of uncertainty—"maybe," "perhaps," "possibly"—adverbs that indicate the narrator's lack of sureness about the events being described. To a large degree, that lack of sureness can, as Richard Pearce claims, be read as a sign of the congruence of the narrator's knowledge with that of Oedipa. After all, the style of the passages in question can be identified as a form of "free indirect discourse," which is characterized by Tzvetan Todorov as

> a discourse that presents itself at first glance as an indirect style (that is, it includes marks of time and person corresponding to a discourse on the part of the author) but is penetrated, in its syntactic and semantic structure, by enunciative properties, thus by the discourse of the character.[38]

It is as an element in Oedipa's discourse, then, that we can identify the uncertainty in the passages under consideration: If Oedipa is presented as "*maybe* a bit rattled" when she wagers a bottle of tequila with Metzger, this could be because the passage in question represents her own uncertain reflection on her state of mind at the time of the bet rather than an indirect assessment by the novel's narrator; the same situation obtains in the description of Oedipa as "*perhaps* juiced, *perhaps* only impatient . . ."; the speculation that the night on which Oedipa first noticed the "potsmaster" reference "may have been" the same evening on which she discovered the post horn logo at The Scope can similarly be read as Oedipa's own attempt, after the fact, to settle the sequence of events in her mind; and, if we follow the logic of the preceding example, then the narrative reflection that "[l]ater, possibly, she would have trouble sorting the night into real and dreamed" would represent Oedipa's anticipatory musing about her psychic state in the future, after the disorienting night is over.

But there is not a true parallel between this "anticipatory" passage and the "retrospective" one that precedes it in my discussion. While it is true that all four of the passages under consideration are "penetrated . . . by the discourse of the character," Oedipa, even as they are presented as specifically narrative discourse, their significance as instances of free indirect style varies depending on the tense that characterizes them. The first two passages that I cite occur in the context of a simple-past-tense narrative, conventional in realist fictional discourse, with the effect that the cognition of the narrator seems merged in that of Oedipa at the moment that the described events are taking place. The perfect-past-tense construction of the third example functions similarly, with the narrator's cognition apparently subsumed in Oedipa's as she engages in a relatively realistic retrospection about her first evening at The Scope. The fourth, anticipatory passage, however, jars in the context of the pattern I have noted. It does this not because it is impossible to see the narrator's cognitive capacity absorbed in

Oedipa's as she anticipates what her memory of her peripatetic night will be; rather, it jars precisely because that absorption itself paradoxically reminds us of the radical distinction between narrator and character that normally obtains in conventional fictional discourse. Because it seems feasible to us that a character might be represented as unsure of her own state of mind at any given juncture, or as uncertain about the exact sequence of a set of events that happened in the past, then it is easy for us to read the first three passages I have cited as relatively conventional instances of free indirect discourse as I have described it above, with the narrator's customary omniscience yielding to the less reliable knowledge of the character for the sake of a particular realistic narrative effect. That effect—the sense of a character's cognitive fallibility—can only be achieved, however, in a narrative context in which the character might realistically be presented as effectively knowing in the first place. That condition does not obtain in the case of the anticipatory passage I have cited, since there is no way a character might realistically be presented as knowledgeable about what her state of mind will be at any given point in the future. The passage under consideration is unusual, then, not simply because, read as an instance of free indirect discourse, it presents the narrator as deferring to a character's imperfect knowledge about a given realm but because the realm in question—the fictional future engaged by the novel—is precisely the one regarding which the traditional narrator's omniscience is usually made manifest. Indeed, we might say that narrative itself depends upon a narrator's knowledge of what will happen next. Consequently, the uncertainty in the statement that "later, possibly, [Oedipa] would have trouble sorting the night into real and dreamed" jars us because it is posited in the context of a future about which we would never expect a character to have reliable knowledge anyway, and, further, because it represents the failure of the text to buttress the character's limited knowledge through recourse to the narratorial omniscience that conventionally governs the representation of the fictional future. Thus the uncertainty in this passage is much more unsettling than that in the more conventional instances of free indirect discourse, since rather than representing merely the subsumption of the narrator's cognition in that of the character, this passage represents the apparent *failure* of the narrator's cognitive ability in such a way that the whole ontology of the fictive world—which is conventionally expressed through, if not created by, the narrator—is rendered apparently unstable. The disorienting nature of Pynchon's novel, then, derives not merely from the subjective uncertainty represented in the single character of Oedipa but rather from the fact that indeterminacy appears to be an objective phenomenon that characterizes the whole world of the novel—a universal effect not traceable to the specific circumstances in which individual characters find themselves.

This is the effect that obtains, at any rate, if we consider the narrator's uncertainty in light of his relation to the fictive world that we take him to be shaping for us, as readers conditioned to suspend reasonable disbelief in order to accept the "realistic" quality of a conventional work of fiction. For, in relation to that world, the conventional third-person narrator—as the fictive stand-in for the author, however disparate those two personae might otherwise be—assumes the status of a primary ordering force that endows phenomena with their objective significance. Thus, the discovery of the narrator's imperfection suggests a similar and analogous lack of coherency in the organization of the "real" world that we inhabit, a lack of objective meaning in life that, while disorienting, is nonetheless familiar and recognizable, insofar as it constitutes the signal crisis of the modern age.

If, on the other hand, we consider the implications of narratorial uncertainty in light of the relation between the narrator and *ourselves,* the readers, then we might be inclined to take the matter much more personally and, thus, to find its implications rather more startling. For, in relation to the *reader,* as opposed to the world of the novel, the narrator represents not so much an objective organizational force as a mirror for our own subjective efforts to construct effective systems of meaning. From *this* perspective, then, the discovery of the narrator's imperfection suggests a similar and analogous lack of coherency in our own psychic subjectivity, and thus the introjection of the modern crisis of meaning into the human subject itself with the consequent emergence of a crisis of self-cognition that is specifically *post*modern.

In thus adumbrating the problematic coherency and questionable efficacy of individual psychic identities, Pynchon comes closer than either Barthelme or Coover in limning the intricacies of postmodern subjectivity through a postmodernist narrative technique. In order to appreciate fully the implication in such subjectivity of a complex politics of identity, however, it is necessary first to *personalize* the crisis of self-cognition in a way that Pynchon, along with both Barthelme and Coover, fails to do.[39] A brief look at how one contemporary author *does* effect this process of personalization will provide some idea both of the political import of the postmodern subject and of the function within it of social marginality.

Maxine Hong Kingston's Postmodern Life Story

We need not look very far into Maxine Hong Kingston's *Woman Warrior* before experiencing an epistemological uncertainty reminiscent of that effected by postmodernist fiction. Indeed, we need not actually look *into* Kingston's book at all; the very cover of the 1977 Vintage paperback edition of the work represents a site of cognitive dissonance that founds the uncertainty to which I refer.[40] The front cover announces the subtitle of Kingston's book: "Memoirs of a Girlhood Among Ghosts"; the back cover, on the other hand, identifies the genre or "subject category" of the book as "autobiography." The disjunctiveness of this presentation might not be clear to us until we consider that the autobiography, as a consciously constructed, linear narrative, actually contravenes the logic of the memoir, which is distinguished by the explicitly associative, *nonlinear* quality of its structure and presentation. In other words, while all memoirs are in some sense *autobiographical,* they tend not to be, technically speaking, *autobiography,* insofar as they violate the sense of narrative progression upon which our idea of that genre is founded.[41] And if the structure of Kingston's book belies the "autobiography" rubric under which the publisher has sought to fix it—it consists, after all, of five loosely related, meditative reminiscences rather than a single coherent narrative—even more do the topics it treats (and the nature of that treatment) militate against the presentation of a realistic life narrative that autobiography is thought to comprise. Simply put, Kingston's book represents not the relation and concomitant establishment of autobiographical fact but rather a considered working through of the various fictive elements that actually constitute autobiographical consciousness.

The first section of Kingston's book, titled "No Name Woman," centers on the story of the narrator's anonymous aunt, whose illegitimate pregnancy brought shame upon the family in their Chinese village before they immigrated to the United States. The usefulness of this account inheres not in its truth value, which is ultimately undecidable, but rather in its function as a warning to the young daughters of the family, to whom, the narrator says, her mother related the tale as "a story to grow up on," thus "test[ing] our strength to establish realities" (5). The second section, "White Tigers," which might be called the title chapter of the book, presents the narrator's vision of herself as an expert female warrior, after the legendary Fa Mu Lan, about whom her mother had "talked-story" when the narrator was a child. In this vision, the narrator uses her fifteen years' training in martial arts (gained under the tutelage of a wise old mountain couple) to avenge her family against a corrupt marauding army. "Shaman" actually takes the narrator's mother, Brave Orchid, as its protagonist, recounting the story of her medical education and subsequent medical practice in China, through which experiences she negotiates the complex interrelation of ancient ritual and modern science, the Chinese occult and Western medicine. "At the Western Palace" describes the relationship between Brave Orchid and her sister, Moon Orchid, who relocates from China to North America as an old woman, after many years' separation from her family. In particular, Moon Orchid has been separated from her husband, a physician quite a bit younger than she who arrived in California long before, took a younger wife, and commenced living a relatively westernized life without Moon Orchid. Brave Orchid's failed attempts to force this husband to acknowledge Moon Orchid and restore her to her rightful position underscore the difficulty—really the theme of the whole chapter—of reconciling the conflicting cultural demands of the Chinese-American condition. Moon Orchid's eventual loss of sanity and subsequent death stand as the tragic emblem of this conflict. Finally, "A Song for a Barbarian Reed Pipe" recounts the narrator's own struggles with cultural incongruency, chronicling her difficulties adjusting in American school, her tortured efforts to situate herself in the social hierarchy operative therein, and her childhood rebellion against a Chinese-identified home life—represented most potently by her mother—that she experiences as confusing and oppressive. That rebellion, to which I recur later, represents the narrator's triumph, insofar as it provides the condition for the emergence of her own subjectivity, constituted through a discourse that, while fragmented and incoherent, is nonetheless effective and productive.

Even these brief synopses of the various sections of Kingston's book suggest the degree to which the work diverges from the presentation of a coherent autobiographical narrative. Specifically, only one of the chapters—"A Song for a Barbarian Reed Pipe"—comprises a realistic account wherein the memoirist herself is the central subject. The rest either focus on other members of her family (the unnamed aunt in "No Name Woman," the mother Brave Orchid in "Shaman," the aunt Moon Orchid in "At the Western Palace") or, in the case of "White Tigers," present a fantastical narrative whereby autobiographical reflection is transmuted into an exemplum of magic realism. Furthermore, all of the first four sections, even when they seem grounded in the conventions of realist narrative, as is the case with "No Name Woman," "Shaman," and "At the Western Palace," nonetheless work counter to the

Postmodern Narrative/Biographical Imperative

conventions of direct autobiographical narration insofar as they are really metanarrative productions—the memoirist's reworkings of or elaborations on stories related to her by others, chiefly her mother. And even when these stories seem to yield hard facts about the memoirist's family history, almost simultaneously they also call into question the certainty of those facts. A central example in the book involves the two older siblings that the narrator remembers her mother having told her about. This sister and brother, we learn in the opening pages of the "Shaman" section, were supposedly born in China and died there before the family moved to North America and the narrator and her younger siblings were born (71). But when, as related later in the same section, the narrator directly questions her mother about these firstborn children, the mother denies their ever having existed. The passage begins with the mother saying,

> "I never do call you Oldest Daughter. Have you noticed that? I always tell people, 'This is my Biggest Daughter.'"
> "Is it true then that Oldest Daughter and Oldest Son died in China? Didn't you tell me when I was ten that she'd have been twenty; when I was twenty, she'd be thirty?" Is that why you've denied me my title?
> "No, you must have been dreaming. You must have been making up stories. You are all the children there are." (120)

Then, in a parenthetical aside, the narrator manifests her own epistemological uncertainty:

> (Who was that story about—the one where the parents are throwing money at the children, but the children don't pick it up because they're crying too hard? They're writhing on the floor covered with coins. Their parents are going out the door for America, hurling handfuls of change behind them.) (120–21)

The question of the existence of these two oldest children having thus seemingly been settled—and by their own putative mother, at that— we are startled to see them invoked again in the very next section, "At the Western Palace," when Moon Orchid is presented as ruminating on what strikes her as the strange melancholy of her sister's U.S.-born children: "None of Brave Orchid's children was happy like the two real Chinese babies who died. Maybe what was wrong was that they had no Oldest Son and no Oldest Daughter to guide them" (153). Thus, where Kingston's chapters overlap in their treatment of certain facets of her story, they also contradict each other, with the result that they raise more questions then they answer, in distinct contrast to what we normally expect from autobiographical narrative. Before we consider the effects of Kingston's narrative technique on the reader's ability to know the facts of her story, however, let us recall, regarding the passages cited above, that the narrator herself experiences a profound epistemological uncertainty in the familial and cultural contexts in which she is situated. It will be useful to trace the sources of the narrator's personal disorientation—her subjective decenteredness—for their specific social and political significance so that we can better understand the function of the disorientation that the narrator *effects* for the reader through the disjunctive presentation of her life story.

Through my characterization of her book as a largely metanarrative production, I have already indicated the degree to which Kingston is interested in exploring the processes and functions of storytelling. We might go further and say that she is particularly interested in the nature of discourse as constitutive of the individual human subject. Indeed, she offers a striking figure for this phenomenon in the "White Tigers" section of the book, when the Woman Warrior returns from her martial-arts training to wage war against the enemy army. Before she proceeds to battle, her parents help her prepare for her crusade by carving on her back the litany of wrongs that have been committed against their family. Having thus inscribed their "revenge" on her person in characters that look to her "like an army," "in red and black files" (41, 42), the warrior's mother announces to her, "Wherever you go, whatever happens to you, people will know our sacrifice. . . . And you'll never forget either." And the narrator further explicates: "She meant that even if I got killed, the people could use my dead body for a weapon . . ." (41). It is specifically the discursive inscription on the Woman Warrior's back that renders her very body as a "weapon," and thus bestows upon her her subjective function and her effectiveness as an avenging soldier. Moreover, the role of the parents in thus constituting the Woman Warrior's subjectivity parallels that of the narrator's own mother, who, in the descriptions provided of their everyday life, most strongly manifests the constitutive force of narrative discourse. As the narrator puts it at the beginning of "White Tigers," while she is reminiscing about the legends of brave heroines her mother used to relate to her, "At last I saw that I too had been in the presence of great power, my mother talking-story" (24). The commentary that the book provides about the stories she has related makes clear the "great power" that the mother's words have had over the development of her daughter's consciousness; it also makes clear, however, that that power, far from being stabilizing, has contributed to the narrator's development as a fundamentally incoherent subject. As the narrator her-self—in her status as autobiographical protagonist in "A Song for a Barbarian Reed Pipe"—says to her mother in a fit of resistance against the disorienting effect of the older woman's narratives, ". . . I don't want to listen to any more of your stories; they have no logic. They scramble me up" (235). The invocation of "scrambling" here has a specifically epistemological significance: The protagonist is referring to the effect of her mother's stories on her ability to know the truth, to distinguish truth from falsehood. Thus she accuses her mother: "You lie with stories. You won't tell me a story and then say, 'This is a true story,' or, 'This is just a story.' I can't tell the difference. . . . I can't tell what's real and what you make up" (235). We might note here that this same charge might reasonably be lodged against Kingston herself, with respect to *The Woman Warrior* and its complex presentation of intermingled fantasy, legend, and autobiographical reflection; I return to this point shortly. In the meantime, we should be aware that the significance of the protagonist's reference to her scrambled state ex-tends beyond the epistemological and into the ontological; it touches not merely on the question of what she knows but also on her sense of who she is.

That sense is conditioned to a large extent by the memoirist's expe-rience of traditional Chinese culture as sexist and misogynistic, detri-mental to women's self-realization. Her estimation of the culture's ef-fect on women is indicated in her commentary on the existence of "a Chinese word for the female I—which is 'slave.' Break the women with their own tongues!" (56). And yet, it is not merely the narrator's own tongue that betrays her but also, and primarily, those of her elders in the Chinese immigrant community in which she grows up. In the "White Tigers" section of the book, the narrator recounts the conventional wisdom of the "emigrant villagers" in the community that declared: "Feeding girls is feeding cowbirds"; "There's no profit in raising girls. Better to raise geese than girls"; and "When you raise girls, you're raising children for strangers" (54). This sense of girls' relatively val-ueless character is manifested in the narrator's own family, as well, notably by her great-uncle, "the ex-river pirate" who would call for the children to accompany him when he did the family shopping on Saturday mornings:

> . . . "Get your coats, whoever's coming."
> "I'm coming. I'm coming. Wait for me."
> When he heard girls' voices, he turned on us and roared, "No girls!" and left my sisters and me hanging our coats back up, not

looking at one another. The boys came back with candy and new toys. . . . At my great-uncle's funeral I secretly tested out feeling glad that he was dead—the six-foot bearish masculinity of him. (55–56)

And it is evinced, as well, by the narrator's parents, whose partiality she challenges when they mark the births of her brothers with elaborate celebration:

. . . "Did you roll an egg on *my* face like that when I was born?" "Did you have a full-month party for *me?*" "Did you turn on all the lights?" "Did you send *my* picture to Grandmother?" "Why not? Because I'm a girl? Is that why not?" . . . (55)

Recognizing the disparity in the treatments afforded boys and girls, the narrator responds with suitable ambivalence: When she rebels against being assigned the feminine task of dishwashing by cracking a few dishes, her mother yells at her, "Bad girl." "[S]ometimes that made me gloat. . . . ," she confesses. "Isn't a bad girl almost a boy?" (56). On the other hand, when she cries angrily in response to the emigrant villagers' denigration of girls and her mother threatens to hit her if she doesn't stop being a "bad girl," she only cries more, screaming, "I'm not a bad girl[,] I'm not a bad girl," and later reflecting, "I might as well have said, 'I'm not a girl'" (54–55). This reference to the intractability of her gender identity, which is thus made to appear as the root of her problems, indicates as well the narrator's inability discursively to counter the negative characterizations lodged by her Chinese elders, since her words have as much effect on their assessment of girls' worth as they do on the fact that she *is*, indeed, a girl. Moreover, the ultimate significance of these words of protest—"I'm not a bad girl"—is determined not by their speaker but by her mother, already identified in the book as the primary subject of discursive power: Talking-story about the narrator's childhood, she "reminds" the latter that "[w]hen you were little, all you had to say was 'I'm not a bad girl,' and you could make yourself cry" (55). Thus the mother not only elides the significance of misogynistic sentiment in her daughter's psychic development, she also, in casting the narrator as the agent of her own distress, refigures the latter's own role—"scrambles up" her ontological status—within that development, and this in a manner that the daughter cannot challenge, due to her apparent lack of facility with the conventions of talking-story.

This inability to negotiate the conventions of Chinese culture seems to promise practical consequences for the narrator's ability to relate successfully with other people and thus to make her way in the world. The difficulties begin, as usual, with the U.S.-born children's interactions with their Chinese-born elders. In "At the Western Palace," when the aunt Moon Orchid comes to North America to stay with her sister's family, she marvels at her nieces' and nephews' apparent lack of politeness:

> "They're so clever," Moon Orchid would exclaim. "They're so smart. . . ."
> "Thank you," the child said. When she complimented them, they agreed with her! Not once did she hear a child deny a compliment.
> "You're pretty," she said.
> "Thank you, Aunt," they answered. How vain. She marveled at their vanity.
> "You play the radio beautifully," she teased, and sure enough, they gave one another puzzled looks. She tried all kinds of compliments, and they never said, "On, no, you're too kind. I can't play it at all. I'm stupid. I'm ugly." They were capable children; they could do servant[']s work. But they were not modest. (155)

And this lack of manners translates, in the minds of the elders, into the children's general social ineptitude and undesirability: "I don't see how any of them could support themselves," Brave Orchid says to her sister about her own children. "I don't see how anybody could want to marry them" (153). The problem of marriage looms particularly large for the girls of the family:

> . . . The wealthiest villager wife came to the laundry one day. . . . "You better do something with this one," she told my mother. "She has an ugly voice. She quacks like a pressed duck." Then she looked at me unnecessarily hard; Chinese do not have to address children directly. "You have what we call a pressed-duck voice," she said. . . .
> "Improve that voice," she . . . instructed my mother, "or else you'll never marry her off. . . ." (223–24)

And the mother reiterates this assessment when the narrator protests, " 'I'm never getting married, never!' 'Who'd want to marry you anyway?' " her mother demands. " 'Noisy. Talking like a duck. Disobedient. Messy . . .' " (235). But, in the end, the narrator's sense of these negative judgments turns out merely to be the result of a problem in translation, of her lack of facility with the rhetorical conventions of the village Chinese. Rebutting her mother's criticisms of her, she asserts:

> "When I get to college it won't matter if I'm not charming. And it
> doesn't matter if a person is ugly; she can still do schoolwork."
>
> "I didn't say you were ugly."
>
> "You say that all the time."
>
> "That's what we're supposed to say. That's what Chinese say. We
> like to say the opposite." (237)

Thus, the narrator's incoherency—both epistemological and ontological—results specifically from her status as a doubly marginalized subject: a female constrained by the dictates of a sexist traditional culture that simultaneously demeans her and worries over her marriageability; and a member of a Chinese immigrant community from which she is nonetheless estranged as a result of her U.S. birth and socialization, which factors prevent her from successfully decoding the terms through which the immigrant community defines her.

As the narrator tells it, the initial effect on her of the elders' powerful and psychically disorienting discourse—and particularly her mother's—is to render her silent. This silence results partly from her mother's explicit injunctions not to repeat the stories that she is told (indeed, the book opens with the narrator's memory of her mother's warning: "You must not tell anyone . . . what I am about to tell you"—the story of the unnamed adulterous aunt).[42] But it is also an effect of the narrator's real uncertainty about the actual facts that underlie the cultural practices of the immigrant Chinese. She frequently complains that her family doesn't explain the Chinese traditions in which it furtively engages. At one point in "At the Western Palace," she recalls watching her mother's actions when Moon Orchid arrives at the house:

> . . . She opened the front door and mumbled something. She opened
> the back door and mumbled something.
>
> "What do you say when you open the door like that?" her children used to ask when they were younger.
>
> "Nothing. Nothing," she would answer.
>
> "Is it spirits, Mother?" Do you talk to spirits? Are you asking them
> in or asking them out?"
>
> "It's nothing," she said. She never explained anything that was
> really important. . . . (140–41)

Elsewhere she laments that ". . . we kids had to infer the holidays" from the behavior of their mother, who would sometimes lay out place settings for an invisible gathering:

> Mother would pour Seagram's 7 into the cups and after a while, pour
> it back into the bottle. Never explaining. How can Chinese keep any

traditions at all? They don't even make you pay attention, slipping in a ceremony and clearing the table before the children notice special-ness. The adults get mad, evasive, and shut you up if you ask. You get no warning that you shouldn't wear a white ribbon in your hair until they hit you and give you the sideways glare for the rest of the day. . . . I don't see how they kept up a continuous culture for five thousand years. Maybe they didn't; maybe everyone makes it up as they go along. If we had to depend on being told, we'd have no religion, no babies, no menstruation (sex, of course, unspeakable), no death. (215–16)

In the face of this, the narrator confesses, "sometimes I hated the se-crecy of the Chinese. 'Don't tell,' said my parents, though we couldn't tell if we wanted to because we didn't know" (213). It is her hatred of this secrecy, along with her desire to overcome the stifling silence that her ambiguous cultural heritage imposes upon her, that motivates the narrator's rebellion against her mother's doctrine of restraint, a rebel-lion that the book both thematically represents and itself enacts.

The conditions for this rebellion are first realized not in the context of the narrator's home, among her family, but (not surprisingly) at school, where she is able to draw comparisons between herself and people from outside Chinese tradition. In "A Song for a Barbarian Reed Pipe," she recalls, "I liked the Negro students . . . best because they laughed the loudest and talked to me as if I were a daring talker too" (192–93). The falseness of this latter assumption, and the protagonist's real inability to assert herself verbally, are suggested by her difficulty in pronouncing the English first-person-singular pronoun. Directed to read aloud in class, she fumbles, explaining as she recalls her hesitancy,

> I could not understand "I." The Chinese "I" has seven strokes, intri-cacies. How could the American "I," assuredly wearing a hat like the Chinese, have only three strokes, the middle so straight? . . . I stared at that middle line and waited so long for its black center to resolve into tight strokes and dots that I forgot to pronounce it. (193)

And when she and her sister do actually succeed in getting through a classroom recitation, it is in voices that are weak and unreliable. The narrator recalls listening to her sister recite a lesson in front of a class:

> She opened her mouth and a voice came out that wasn't a whisper, but it wasn't a proper voice either. . . . She sounded as if she were trying to sing though weeping and strangling. She did not pause or stop to end the embarrassment. She kept going until she said the last word, and then she sat down. When it was my turn, the same voice

came out, a crippled animal running on broken legs. You could hear
splinters in my voice, bones rubbing jagged against one another. . . .
(196)

The protagonist responds to her sense of shame at the inefficacy of her
own voice by transmuting it into a hatred that she projects outward
onto another Chinese girl whose inadequacy mirrors her own. Having
described her own "splintered" voice, she finds some compensation
for it in its volume: "I was loud, though. I was glad I didn't whisper.
There was one little girl who whispered" (196). She finds a further
distinction between herself and this girl in that "[M]ost of us eventually
found some voice, however faltering. We invented an American-feminine
speaking personality, except for that one girl who could not speak up
even in Chinese school" (200). And yet her comforting sense of difference from this girl is quickly mitigated by a recollection of their equally
striking similarities—the fact, for instance, that "[W]e were similar in
sports. We held the bat on our shoulders until we walked to first base.
. . . Sometimes the pitcher wouldn't bother to throw to us. 'Automatic
walk,' the other children would call, sending us on our way" (200–
201). It is these embarrassing similarities, obviously, that account for
the protagonist's deep antipathy for this girl, whom, she proclaims, "I
hated. . . . I hated her when she was the last chosen for her team and
I, the last chosen for my team. I hated her for her China doll hair cut.
I hated her at music time for the wheezes that came out of her plastic
flute" (201–2), wheezes that vividly recall the broken quality of the
protagonist's own voice. Consequently, the protagonist's first outburst
of rage against the silence she feels is her family's legacy takes the form
of a cruel torture that she inflicts upon this mute girl. Cornering the
latter in the girls' lavatory after school, she announces to her, "You're
going to talk" (204), and proceeds to berate, pinch, and pull at her to
make her speak, all to no avail, until the protagonist herself breaks
down in frustrated sobs, protesting, "If you don't talk, you can't have
a personality" (210).

This metaphorical story of self-opposition (which recalls Virginia
Woolf's killing of the "angel in the house") ends with the onset of a
mysterious illness that lays low the protagonist for eighteen months, a
sort of hibernation after which she seems ready to confront directly
what she believes to be the source of her stiflement. Her sense of her
mother's implication in her confused silence is made clear in the protagonist's ambivalent response to the fact that "the first thing my mother
did when she saw me was to cut my tongue":

> She pushed my tongue up and sliced the frenum. . . .
>
> "Why did you do that to me, Mother?"
>
> "I told you."
>
> "Tell me again."
>
> "I cut it so that you would not be tongue-tied. Your tongue would be able to move in any language. You'll be able to speak languages that are completely different from one another. You'll be able to pronounce anything. Your frenum looked too tight to do those things, so I cut it."
>
> "But isn't 'a ready tongue an evil'?"
>
> "Things are different in this ghost country." (190–91)

Despite her mother's explanation, the protagonist is ready to interpret the cutting of her tongue as an attempt to thwart her speech. For instance, having angrily muttered to herself at the misogyny displayed by her third grand-uncle, "What an asshole," she reflects, "Maybe my mother was afraid that I'd say things like that out loud and so had cut my tongue" (223). As both her daughter's silencer and the agent who enables her to speak, the mother assumes a complex function in the protagonist's transformative act of rebellion, serving simultaneously as the object of the girl's resistance and the source of her ability to enact it. At the same time, the circularity of the mother's role recapitulates the structure of the dilemma that her daughter seeks to resolve through an intricate strategy that, notably, she sees as rooted in her mother's primal act:

> Maybe because I was the one with the tongue cut loose, I had grown inside me a list of over two hundred things that I had to tell my mother so that she would know the true things about me and to stop the pain in my throat. When I first started counting, I had had only thirty-six items: how I had prayed for a white horse of my own— white, the bad, mournful color—and prayer bringing me to the attention of the god of the black-and-white nuns who gave us "holy cards" in the park. How I wanted the horse to start the movies in my mind coming true. How I had picked on a girl and made her cry. . . . Then there were my fights at Chinese school. And the nuns who kept stopping us in the park, which was across the street from Chinese school, to tell us that if we didn't get baptized we'd go to a hell like one of the nine Taoist hells forever. And the obscene caller that phoned us at home when the adults were at the laundry. And the Mexican and Filipino girls at school who went to "confession," and how I envied them their white dresses and their chance each Saturday to tell even thoughts that were sinful. If only I could let my mother know

the list, she—and the world—would become more like me, and I would never be alone again. (229–30)

To the extent that her mother is considered to be the cause of the protagonist's painful silence, then the strategy of confession outlined here as much constitutes the protagonist's radical break with her—the repudiation of her order—as it potentially effects the almost pre-Oedipal mergence with her for which the protagonist apparently longs. The paradox is concisely rendered in the reference to the Mexican and Filipino girls, for whose ability to confess the protagonist would have to confess her own envy—practically compelled to do so by her mother's "cutting loose" of her tongue—but which latter action itself would be taboo according to the order of silence that the protagonist feels her mother has imposed. Sure enough, it is an order of silence that greets the protagonist when she does begin to disclose her secrets. Wringing shirts over the starch tub at the family laundry, the mother is impassive at the confession of the prayer for the white horse: " 'Mm,' she said, nodded, and kept dipping and squeezing" (233). The girl tries to press on:

> "Mother," I whispered and quacked.
>   "I can't stand this whispering," she said looking right at me, stopping her squeezing. "Senseless gabbings every night. I wish you would stop. Go away and work. Whispering, whispering, making no sense. Madness. I don't feel like hearing your craziness."
>   So I had to stop. . . . (233)

Thus thwarted in her attempt to resolve her dilemma through tremulous private confession, it isn't until she experiences the familial order as impinging on her socialization with others that the protagonist finds the wherewithal to assail the constraints on her subjectivity. Convinced that her parents are conspiring to marry her off to a reputedly wealthy mentally retarded boy who loiters near their laundry, the protagonist explodes one night at the family dinner:

> I looked directly at my mother and at my father and screamed, "I want you to tell that hulk, that gorilla-ape, to go away and never bother us again. I know what you're up to. You're thinking he's rich, and we're poor. You think we're odd and not pretty and we're not bright. You think you can give us away to freaks. You better not do that, Mother. I don't want to see him or his dirty boxes here tomorrow. If I see him here one more time, I'm going away. I'm going away anyway. . . . I'm going to college. And I'm not going to Chinese

school anymore. I'm going to run for office at American school, and I'm going to join clubs. I'm going to get enough offices and clubs on my record to get into college. . . . Ha! You can't stop me from talking. You tried to cut off my tongue, but it didn't work." So I told the hardest ten or twelve things on my list all in one outburst. (233–35)

This outburst—the same one that I cite earlier, in which the protagonist complains that her mother's stories "scramble me up"—constitutes not just the daughter's rebellion against that process of disorientation (in a section of the passage excised from the above quotation, she extols the noninvoluted nature of "American school" logic, asserting that "[t]hings follow in lines at school. They take stories and teach us to turn them into essays" [234]) but also her own enactment of a similar scrambling—the misinterpretation of fact and the conflation of fact and fiction. In angry response to her reference to her mother's cutting of her tongue, the latter shouts,

"I cut it to make you talk more, not less, you dummy. You're still stupid. You can't listen right. I didn't say I was going to marry you off. Did I ever say that? Did I ever mention that? . . . Who would want you? Who said we could sell you? We can't sell people. Can't you take a joke? You can't even tell a joke from real life. . . ." (235)

Thus the protagonist's resistance against the potent "illogic" of her mother's talk-story rhetoric—which, as we have seen, contributes to the girl's psychic disorientation in both epistemological and ontological terms—actually opens into a similarly scrambled narrative logic that is nonetheless oppositional to that of the mother. Indeed, we can see a hint of the degree to which the latter experiences her daughter's narrative as alien to her own order of meaning when she complains that the girl's confessions "make no sense." Thus, out of one convoluted rhetorical practice—the mother's—emerges another, the daughter's, which is exemplified not only in the disjointed nature of her railings against her parents but also in the involuted quality of the text she produces. For as we have already noted, The Woman Warrior comprises a dense interrelation of autobiographical reflection, legend, and fantasy that functions to undercut the linear progression of standard autobiographical narrative. And the self-conscious nature of the text regarding this unorthodox construction is indicated at the very opening of "A Song for a Barbarian Reed Pipe," which is actually a gloss on the preceding section, "At the Western Palace." Having presented therein a dramatic and elaborately detailed third-person account of Moon Orchid's confrontation with her estranged husband and her attempts, at her sister's urging, to receive restitution from him, the narrator begins "A Song for a Barbarian Reed Pipe" with an extensive confession:

> What my brother actually said was, "I drove Mom and Second Aunt to Los Angeles to see Aunt's husband who's got the other wife."
>
> "Did she hit him? What did she say? What did he say?"
>
> "Nothing much. Mom did all the talking."
>
> "What did she say?"
>
> "She said he'd better take them to lunch at least."
>
> "Which wife did he sit next to? What did they eat?"
>
> "I didn't go. The other wife didn't either. He motioned us not to tell."
>
> "I would've told. If I was his wife, I would've told. I would've gone to lunch and kept my ears open."
>
> "Ah, you know they don't talk when they eat."
>
> "What else did Mom say?"
>
> "I don't remember. I pretended a pedestrian broke her leg so he would come."
>
> "There must have been more. Didn't Aunt get in one nasty word? She must've said something."
>
> "No, I don't think she said anything. I don't remember her saying one thing."
>
> In fact, it wasn't me my brother told about going to Los Angeles; one of my sisters told me what he'd told her. His version of the story may be better than mine because of its bareness, not twisted into designs. The hearer can carry it tucked away without it taking up much room. Long ago in China, knot-makers tied string into buttons and frogs, and rope into bell-pulls. There was one knot so complicated that it blinded the knot-maker. Finally an emperor outlawed this cruel knot, and the nobles could not order it anymore. If I had lived in China, I would have been an outlaw knot-maker. (189–90)

This final admission—along with the recognition of the possible compromise to her own subjectivity that the knot-maker faces, her potential blinding—serves as the narrator's testimony to her own postmodernist sensibility. The convoluted design of her story, in contrast to the direct account provided by her brother, approximates the decentered narrative characteristic of postmodernist fiction, but it derives specifically, as we have seen, from the biographical experience of disorientation that the protagonist is presented as having undergone as a result of her status as a female of Chinese descent in a North American context. The sociopolitical engagement that Kingston's work thereby manifests effectively sets it apart from the rather more canonized works of postmodern fiction with whom it nonetheless shares key narrative strategies, indicating not that Kingston's work is any the less postmodernist but rather that the criteria according to which certain works are recognized as exemplarily postmodern do not sufficiently engage the sociopolitical issues that are unavoidably implicated in the concept, and thus fall short of constituting its full theorization.

Coda

Categorical Collapse and the
Possibility of "Commitment"

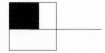

Read in light of the analysis that precedes it—and with a focus on the works by Barthelme, Coover, and Pynchon that it treats—the foregoing chapter functions as both reprise and culmination of my primary argument in the book as a whole: that the decenteredness of postmodern fiction closely approximates the subjective disorientation historically suffered by socially marginalized groups and thematized in the literature that engages their experiences. On the other hand, the assessment of Kingston's *Woman Warrior* provided in the latter portion of the chapter moves it beyond its recapitulatory function by both indicating the degree to which a contemporary literary production can actually accede to postmodernist status by virtue of its engagement with specific sociopolitical factors and providing us with a means for understanding the relation between "high" postmodernist literary practice and the fictions of marginality that seem to anticipate its effects.

The apparent dichotomy between the personalized specificity of Kingston's narrative and the generalized social problematic traced by such "high" postmodernists as Barthelme, Coover, and Pynchon suggests, at first glance, a sort of parallelism between the two modes such that we could identify them as two different types of literary postmodernism that exist alongside one another in the contemporary literary–historical context. A second consideration of the matter, however, in light of the complex nature of Kingston's accession to a postmodernist narrative strategy, suggests that the relation between the two brands of decentered narrative consists not so much in side-by-side juxtaposition as in profound involution and interimplication. A brief review of the context in which our apprehension of Kingston's narrative technique is conditioned will clarify this point.

Kingston's book represents her narrative technique as emerging in defensive response to the disorienting rhetorical strategies whereby her mother "talks-story" throughout the protagonist's formative years. In this sense, Kingston's technique may be considered as the endpoint of a progenitive, lineal trajectory: The protagonist's disorientation results in the narrator's contorted storytelling method. And yet, it is important to remember that the very nature of the book as memoir conduces to the reversal of that trajectory insofar as the narrative frame of the reminiscence defines the terms through which we understand the mother's rhetorical practice. That is, the memoir doesn't merely mimetically *re-produce* the mother's talking-story in order to demonstrate to us its powerful effect in the lived reality of the protagonist; rather, by assimilating it as an element in its own teleological exposition, the memoir actually *produces* the talk-story as a specifically narrativistic device and thus conditions our understanding of its function and significance. In this sense, then, the narrative structure of *The Woman Warrior* comprises not the end result of the logic of talking-story but rather the originating context for our conception of it.

This status of Kingston's postmodern narrative as simultaneously produced by and constitutive of another narrative logic, which it thematizes, may serve as a useful figure for the status of narratives of marginality—including Kingston's memoir and the works by West, Nin, Barnes, Brooks, and Ellison, discussed earlier—with respect to the postmodernist literary practice represented by Barthelme, Coover, and Pynchon. Not that either category of work "produces" the other, in the sense that I use the term above, but, just as the existence of the concept of postmodernist narrative allows us to frame Kingston's work within that conceptual context, so too might the subjective fragmentation that characterizes the narratives of marginality considered above actually found the terms through which we have come to understand the postmodern condition and the fictions that emblematize it.

This proposition would have ramifications not just for prose fiction, nor for literature alone. Indeed, as I have suggested near the end of chapter 5, the easy appropriability of the signifiers of certain forms of social marginality makes them prime commodities in the mass-cultural drive to market the effects of disfranchisement for the social cachet that can paradoxically attach to it. I have discussed elsewhere the effect of such marketing in the realm of popular music, where it seems particularly influential;[1] for the sake of the present discussion, however, it is actually more useful to discuss the phenomenon in light of recent commercial film, since the example I have in mind not only functions as both representation and enactment of the appropriative market dynamics to which I have referred but its manifestation of those dynamics also implicates a process of social–categorical collapse that I think largely characterizes postmodern culture and that we would do well to interrogate and check.

The story line of Alan Parker's film *The Commitments* (Twentieth Century Fox, 1991) is largely faithful to that of the novel on which it is based,[2] presenting a dozen mostly young Irish musicians who struggle to establish themselves as a viable band in the unpromising context of contemporary Dublin. The twist in the story consists in the type of music that they choose to perform—black soul music from the United States. In what is by far the most frequently quoted line from the movie— cited by countless reviewers as well as by me as providing the film's conceptual anchor—the band's manager and driving force, young Jimmy Rabbitte (Robert Arkins), lays out the logic of this choice to his skeptical crew: "The Irish are the blacks of Europe. And Dubliners are the blacks of Ireland. And the northside Dubliners are the blacks of Dublin. So say it once, say it loud, 'I'm black, and I'm proud!' "[3]

This speech is obviously destined to raise eyebrows, and various commentators have already noted the troubling logic of social and political identification that characterizes the lines. As Clarence Page puts it in response to Jimmy's declaration,

> Actually, blacks are the blacks of Europe. If Parker wanted to do a movie about prejudice, he could have turned his cameras on the blacks, Pakistanis and other non-whites who have run into growing discrimination in accordance with apprehension over their growing numbers in Britain, France and elsewhere. . . .[4]

At this point, however, I am less interested in the actual fact of Jimmy's specious identification of working-class Dubliners with U.S. blacks than I am in how that identification is effected in the world of the movie. And we can best understand that mechanism if we approach the film indirectly, through what strikes me as a critical overstatement of this identificatory move that characterizes Page's commentary.

By way of underscoring the necessity of his critique of *The Commitments* for the problematic parallels that it draws, Page emphasizes (in what is actually an Op-Ed column and not a movie review) that the young people whom the film depicts "decide not only to form an authentically black-sounding soul band but also to be something much more profound than that. They actually strive to *be* black, not physically, but spiritually." *Time* magazine reviewer Richard Corliss repeats this assessment when he exclaims, "How fervently these members of the Irish underclass wish to be black!"[5] In these commentators' perception of the matter, then, the Commitments—for that is the name of the band—go beyond mere *political* identification with African-Americans, itself already problematic, to evince a *psychic* identification by which they strive actually to remake their personae. The difficulty of this undertaking is clear since the musicians possess neither the biological characteristics popularly (and problematically) taken to ground racial identity ("They're physically as white as can be!" protests David Sterritt) nor the cultural–experiential background that largely constitutes it. And yet, I don't take this impulse toward psychic identification to represent the film's primary problem, since I don't think that it really constitutes the Commitments' central concern.

Indeed, while the metaphorical relation between blacks and poor Dubliners serves as the means by which Jimmy justifies to the band members his choice of material for them to play (they end up performing cover versions of songs originally recorded by the likes of Otis Redding, Wilson Pickett, and Aretha Franklin), because it does not (nor, I think, *can* it) actually function as the basis for their organizing in the first place, it is largely dropped as a thematic reference soon after the musicians accommodate themselves to the material. Significantly, the second—and final—reference to the black/north-side Dubliner relation occurs when saxophonist Dean Fay (Félim Gormley) caps his successful rehearsal of a soul riff by exclaiming to a cluster of young observers, "I'm black, and I'm proud!" much to the children's bemusement. Thus, the musician's accession to the musical style of soul *does* effect his identification with the blacks who originated it, but it also apparently *terminates* both that identification and the need for it, insofar as they are never again referenced in the film. From this point on, as a matter of fact, the movie concentrates on neither the musicians' psychic nor their political identification with blacks, but rather (and more conventionally) on the various practical problems and interpersonal difficulties that threaten the band's cohesion.

My characterization of the musicians' identification with blacks as evanescent and fleeting should not at all be taken to suggest that I think it is insignificant; on the contrary, I soon return to it in order to discuss exactly what I think it signifies about the political ramifications of postmodernity. First, however, I want to consider what appears to me as the Commitments' *organizational* principle, which attends their *motivational* one (as I think we can characterize the identificatory logic I have been discussing), and which I think is largely *displaced* by the latter both in the film and in discussions of it.

Framing the Margins

As I have already hinted, the basis for the Commitments' coming together in the first place—as it is conceived, once again, by Jimmy—consists not in their potential identification with African-Americans or African-American culture but rather in the class status of the young Irish themselves. At the same time, however, that latter status is quickly effaced in the film by the characters' developing interest in African-American soul music. In order to see how this is so, let us consider an early scene from the movie (one that precedes the comparison of Dublin north-siders to U.S. blacks) in which Jimmy first proposes his idea to the two original members of his troupe, guitarist Outspan Foster (Glen Hansard) and bassist Derek Scully (Kenneth McCluskey). Having pried the two musicians loose from the unaccomplished Wayne Newton–style vocalist with whom they constituted a trio that played at local weddings, Jimmy informs them that they are about to take a new musical direction. The two are eager for him to elaborate:

> DEREK: Well, what kind of music are we going to be playing, Jimmy?
> JIMMY: You're working-class, right?
> OUTSPAN: We would be if there was any work.
> JIMMY: So, your music should be about where you're from, and the sort of people you come from. It should speak the language of the streets. It should be about struggle and sex.
> . . .
> OUTSPAN: Jesus. What kind of music says all that?
> JIMMY: Soul.

This exchange, both despite and because of its extreme brevity, strikingly demonstrates the speed with which *The Commitments* first mobilizes working-class identity (through Jimmy's invocation of the life of "the streets") in order to establish solidarity among its young characters, and then transmutes that class identification into—and displaces it with—an identification between the Irish working class and African-Americans, effected through Jimmy's positing of "soul" as the appropriate type of music for the group to play. A sense of the practical inevitability of that displacement is suggested in Outspan's ironic assertion that the young people "would be [working-class] if there was any work." The disappearance of opportunities for employment constitutes a significant transformation in the conditions that ground the characters' working-class identity; consequently, there emerges for them an identificatory void that is immediately filled by an attachment to soul music that, while explained by Jimmy in (specious) political terms, and effected by means of a momentary psychic identification with blacks, as I have shown, is ultimately emptied of both psychic and political import to become a merely cultural phenomenon. Indeed, if we can discern any effort at all on the part of the band to "identify" with blacks once the group is finally assembled, it consists solely in their attempts to replicate precisely the sound of African-American soul performers in their own renditions of the work (in an early rehearsal, Jimmy reprimands the female backup vocalists for singing with their "own accents" as opposed to those showcased in the original recordings), and not in any further "theorizing" as to the parallels between their sociopolitical position and African-Americans', or in efforts to approximate African-Americans' psychic orientation. In other words, the Commitments don't really "strive to be black," as Clarence Page claims, but rather than saving the movie from embodying a problematic politics, this fact merely indicates in what direction the film's political problems lie.

It is important to recognize that not only does *The Commitments* displace its characters' class identification by their cultural attachment to black soul music, as I have suggested, but also that this displacement occurs according to a particular logic that has ramifications beyond the local case presented in the story. Specifically, it operates according to an analogical principle whereby it is justified by the perceived similarities between the situations of working-class Dubliners and African-Americans ("the Irish are the blacks of Europe"). This perception in turn founds the designation of soul music as the appropriate means by which to "express" the significance of the characters' working-class identification. At the same time, however, it is a fundamental effect of analogy, by emphasizing the similarities of the phenomena being compared, to elide the aspects of each of them that render them unique and thus divergent. In the case considered here, not only are the unique aspects of black and working-class Irish identities thus elided but so too is the specificity of racial and class categories *per se,* so that it becomes impossible critically to consider these latter categories either as effectively discrete phenomena or in their real and complex interrelation. Such elision both signals and constitutes what I will refer to as the "categorical collapse" that I think always potentially characterizes the postmodern era.

Such collapse seems to me to manifest in two significant ways, both of which can be extrapolated from the story line of *The Commitments.* Most obviously, and as I have made clear above, it manifests as the blurring into each other of categories comprising (usually relatively dis-

Framing the Margins

empowered) subsets of the social totality, such as blacks and the working class. This blurring accounts to some degree for the confusion and imprecision that characterize assessments of the parallels between such groups like that given by Jimmy in the movie. Such confusion is recapitulated off-screen in an interview with Bronagh Gallagher, who plays Bernie McGloughlin, one of the three female backup singers known as the "Commitment-ettes." Commenting on the degree to which the mostly inexperienced actors were able to identify with the characters they portray in the movie, Gallagher told the *Los Angeles Times,*

> "We're all working class, and we've all been in bands like the Commitments. . . . Soul music is appropriate, because it's working-class music. The great soul singers—Otis Redding, James Brown—music made them what they were. Look at the song titles: 'Working in the Coal Mine.' There's lots of oppression in Ireland."[6]

The swift, unexamined slippage from assertion of the actors' working-class identity to the role of soul music's working-class references in "making" the singers who performed it, to the song titles' apparent manifestation of those references, and, finally, to a generalized "oppression" that characterizes Ireland signals the careless blurring of the categories of racial and class identity that I think typifies popular considerations of them as parallel phenomena.

In addition to thus undermining the distinctions between different marginalized subgroups in the larger society, however, the categorical collapse to which I have referred often manifests as the discounting of the specificity of such groups' experiences by a "general public" that refers to those experiences for the means by which to "express" its own sense of dislocation. Indeed, in the case of *The Commitments,* it is possible to see this latter mode of categorical collapse as occurring behind the scenes, as it were, of the more evident former mode, and this in such a way as to actually found the conditions for the occurrence of the more evident mode.

This point will become clear if we recall my earlier reference to a sort of identificatory void that emerges for the Commitments as a consequence of the lack of employment opportunity with which they are confronted. The development of this lack constitutes, as I have suggested, a transformation in the conditions that ground the characters' working-class identity, and their *recognition* of it constitutes an instant of psychic groundlessness for them—a momentary inability to anchor their primary social identity in the material conditions amidst which they live. This inability corresponds exactly to what Jameson characterizes as the inability of the postmodern subject to orient itself in the face of a rapidly evolving postindustrial global capitalism, so that at the moment that the characters in *The Commitments* falter as specifically *working-class* subjects, they are effectively constituted as generalized *postmodern* subjects in search of a means of expressing the sense of dislocation that they now share with all other members of the "general public." For the Commitments, black soul music appears as a logical and convenient expression of that dislocation precisely because, by its inevitable connotation of the abiding problematic of racial difference, it fixedly emblematizes social disorientation no matter what the local referent in whose service it is mobilized in any given instance. At other sites in the field of postmodernism, other aspects of racially inflected cultures—or signs of other types of social marginality, such as those rooted in class, gender, or sexual orientation—will be deployed as seems appropriate to convey a sense of the general disorientation that is taken to characterize the postmodern condition. In such cases, the terms by which we understand that condition derive specifically from experiences of social marginality that approximate but are not identical to it.

Such appropriation of the cultural effects of socially marginalized constituencies obviously threatens to elide the specific significances of those effects in relation to their originary contexts in a way that militates against critical engagement with the political factors that found social marginality in the first place. This elision is a consequence of what Jameson calls the "superficial" nature of postmodernism, in that it issues from the apparent identicalness of the effects manifested by different social constituencies at the superstructural level, which dissembles and distracts our attention from the actual variedness of the conditions that found those constituencies' social orientation. This effect is thematized in what I have referred to as *The Commitments'* ultimate treatment of African-Americans' condition—and the relation of the working-class Irish to it—as a merely *cultural* phenomenon, disengaged from sociopolitical realities. And the film's assumption of such disengagement is underscored in what are (practically speaking) the closing lines of the story, spoken by Commitments trumpeter Joey "The Lips" Fagan (Johnny Murphy), in his mid-forties the band's oldest member and spiritual guide. Attempting to comfort Jimmy out of his disappointment at the band's failure (due to insuperable interpersonal tensions) to secure a recording contract and launch a successful career, Joey asserts,

> The success of the band was irrelevant! You raised their expectations
> of life, you lifted their horizons. Sure, we could have been famous
> and made albums and stuff, but that would've been predictable. This
> way it's poetry!

Joey's insistence that the band's dissolution represents an exalted "poetry" indicates the degree to which the movie focuses on abstracted
cultural effects rather than the hard social realities with which they are
associated, and indeed works to transmute those social realities into
mere disengaged cultural phenomena, according to the logic of superficiality that Jameson outlines.

The use to which the cultural realm is thus put in bracketing the
consideration of concrete sociopolitical conditions should have a mon-
itory effect in the context of my undertaking here, since I, too, have
concentrated on the cultural manifestations of social marginality in order to theorize its relation to the postmodern condition. Indeed, the
very circumstance that has allowed me, in this study, to consider as
allied the various types of social marginality that I treat—namely, their
common representation in literary culture in terms of subjective fragmentation—threatens to mitigate our awareness of their real specificity.
The consequent fault in our understanding of pertinent social conditions—an effect precisely of a postmodern logic that mandates and
emphasizes cultural massification and homogeneity—would preclude
our effective engagement in the sort of politically committed practice
that postmodernity demands.

At the same time, however, a full appreciation of the nature of contemporary "politics" must admit of the degree to which it is impinged
upon by specifically cultural phenomena, rendering crucial the type of
analysis that I provide here. For while it is obvious that this book addresses conventional cultural issues through the reconsideration of the
"literature of marginality" that it both advocates and enacts, that reconsideration itself will necessarily bear on sociopolitical discussion if
undertaken with an eye to its real objective: not merely the expansion
of a "canon" of postmodernist literature, the viability of which is already questionable, but rather the elaboration of postmodernism's full
sociocultural significance in order that we may better comprehend the
complex positioning of human subjectivities in the contemporary context. After all, only by understanding how such positioning works in
the first place can we embark on the process of altering the relative
positions of key social constituencies, thereby effecting the political
and cultural *change* in the name of which this book was conceived
and written.

NOTES

Chapter 1

1. bell hooks, "Postmodern Blackness," *Yearning: Race, Gender, and Cultural Politics*, 27.

I should note here that, in my commentary on the specifically *cultural* manifestations of postmodernism, I draw a distinction between the phenomena of "alienation," which hooks invokes, and "fragmentation"; indeed, in identifying the former with cultural *modernism*, I follow the lead of Fredric Jameson (see my discussion of his work in the succeeding text), and I further develop the significance of the distinction toward the end of this chapter and in my treatment of Robert Coover's fiction, in chapter 6.

2. Linda Hutcheon, *The Politics of Postmodernism*, 24. It is worth noting here that Hutcheon's assertions are made in the context of her argument against the conflation of the notions of postmodern*ism*, as a cultural and aesthetic mode, and postmoder*nity*, "as the designation of a social and philosophical period or 'condition' " (23). The import of the distinction, in Hutcheon's conception, has to do with her desire to claim for postmodernist art the ability to intervene critically in the socioeconomic order that grounds postmoder*nity* even while it is itself implicated in that order. If I do not maintain Hutcheon's recommended distinction in my discussion, it is because I am concerned less with the status of postmodernist art as motivated political critique than with its thematization of the status of the subject in the contemporary era, and thus with the continuity rather than the distinction between cultural mode and social–philosophical condition.

3. Jürgen Habermas, "Modernity—An Incomplete Project." All references are made to the 1983 edition of the article; see p. 9 for the current citation.

4. This is the theme sounded throughout Lyotard's book *The Postmodern Condition: A Report on Knowledge*. It is presented in its most condensed form in the appendix to the English-language edition of the book, comprising Lyotard's essay "Answering the Question: What Is Postmodernism," trans. Régis Durand, 71–82; see in particular pp. 81–82.

5. Fredric Jameson, "Postmodernism, or The Cultural Logic of Late Capitalism," 56, 57. An expanded version of this essay has since become the title

chapter in Jameson's book *Postmodernism, or, The Cultural Logic of Late Capitalism.*

6. Understandably, given the extent of his influence (which I am confident is discernible in my own work, despite my objections here), Jameson has been subject to critique by numerous writers in addition to myself. Perhaps most important to note at this point is the 1989 volume edited by Douglas Kellner, *Postmodernism/Jameson/Critique.* In particular, the essay in that book by R. Radhakrishnan identifies Jameson's elision of third-world subjectivity in a way that approximates my own criticism ("Poststructuralist Politics: Towards a Theory of Coalition," 301–32).

It is not the case that absolutely no work has been done to link postmodern subjectivity and the experience of social marginalization. Women's relation to postmodern praxis has received particular attention, from Craig Owens's "The Discourse of Others: Feminists and Postmodernism" (in Foster, 57–82) and Meaghan Morris's *The Pirate's Fiancée: Feminism, Reading, Postmodernism* to Linda Nicholson's compilation *Feminism/Postmodernism* and certain sections of Susan Rubin Suleiman's *Subversive Intent: Gender, Politics, and the Avant-Garde.* With respect to racial politics, before bell hooks Cornel West had already considered the relation between "Postmodernity and Afro-America" in his book *Prophetic Fragments,* 168–70, and in his 1989 essay, "Black Culture and Postmodernism." And the third and fourth volumes in the series, *Documentary Sources in Contemporary Art,* consider postmodern culture by presenting collections of materials that reflect "the heterogeneous nature of American culture, and . . . a multiplicity of voices," as series editor Marcia Tucker puts it in the foreword to volume 3 (*Discourses: Conversations in Postmodern Art and Culture,* edited by Russell Ferguson, William Olander, Marcia Tucker, and Karen Fiss, p.1 for the current citation; see also *Out There: Marginalization and Contemporary Cultures,* edited by Russell Ferguson, Martha Gever, Trinh T. Minh-ha, and Cornel West).

All of these works are of value in thinking about the relation between social identity and postmodern experience. What I offer in this study differs from these contributions, however, in that not only am I considering a range of various types of social marginality (unlike Owens, Morris, Nicholson, Suleiman, and West), in the context of a sustained analysis (such as cannot be provided by the anthologies), but, as becomes clear in the succeeding text, I am focusing very specifically on the particular phenomenon of subjective decenteredness and its literary manifestations. This focus allows me to work through my argument by means of extensive close reading, as opposed, for instance, to the more sketchy treatment of the texts given by Linda Hutcheon, the encyclopedic scope of whose work necessarily dictates such an approach.

7. Russell Ferguson, "Introduction: Invisible Center," *Out There;* 9–14; 9.

8. Marcia Tucker, "Director's Foreword," *Out There;* 7–8; 7.

9. Gerald Graff, "The Myth of the Postmodernist Breakthrough," 393.

10. Ihab Hassan, "Toward a Concept of Postmodernism," the 1982 postface

to *The Dismemberment of Orpheus: Toward a Postmodern Literature,* 259–71; 267–268.

11. Louis A. Renza, *"A White Heron" and the Question of Minor Literature,* xxviii–xxix.

12. Abdul R. JanMohamed and David Lloyd, "Introduction: Toward a Theory of Minority Discourse: What Is to Be Done?" *The Nature and Context of Minority Discourse,* 9.

Given JanMohamed's and Lloyd's title, it is worth my pointing out here that I do not use the term "minority" in this book other than in quotation marks, since it generally connotes specifically racial and/or ethnic identity in the U.S. context, and such identity is only one of the various social dispositions that I seek to consider under the more encompassing rubric of "social marginality."

13. Gilles Deleuze and Félix Guattari, *Kafka: Toward a Minor Literature,* 18.

14. M. H. Abrams, *A Glossary of Literary Terms,* 110.

15. Malcolm Bradbury and James McFarlane, "The Name and Nature of Modernism," *Modernism: 1890–1930,* 25.

16. Virginia Woolf, *Mrs. Dalloway,* 127.

Chapter 2

1. Throughout this chapter I quote from texts by the contemporary performance artist Laurie Anderson, whose work seems to address, in our own postmodern era, many of the issues that occupied West in the 1930s. All of the epigraphs are from Anderson's epic work, *United States.*

2. Jay Martin, *Nathanael West: The Art of His Life,* 399.

3. All references to West's novels are keyed to *The Complete Works of Nathanael West,* p. 9 for the present citation; brackets in the original.

4. David Galloway, "A Picaresque Apprenticeship: Nathanael West's *The Dream Life of Balso Snell* and *A Cool Million,*" 111.

5. Michel Foucault, *This Is Not a Pipe,* 20.

6. Guillaume Apollinaire, *Selected Writings,* 168–69.

7. In other words, class status, in West's novels, is a function of the amount of educational and/or cultural capital achieved by a given character. Thus, the type of social marginality that I am discussing in this chapter—though I find it useful to think of it in terms of class—is not necessarily a function of economic factors, which govern the category of class in the orthodox Marxist tradition. On cultural capital, see Pierre Bourdieu, *Distinction: A Social Critique of the Judgement of Taste.*

8. William Butler Yeats, "Among School Children," *The Collected Poems,* 249.

9. Of course, the reference to their self-sufficiency as specifically "egglike" underscores the fact that Faye's and Betty's marginality is also a function of their

status as women. I explore specific aspects of women's social marginality in chapter 3, on Anaïs Nin and Djuna Barnes, and chapter 4, on Gwendolyn Brooks.

10. It is this fact that Laurie Anderson comments upon when she muses on the design affixed on the Pioneer spacecraft sent into orbit by NASA in the late 1970s. It is a drawing of a man, arm extended outward and upward, away from his body. He is waving hello—or is it goodbye? It is impossible to say, for, "[i]n our country, Goodbye looks just like Hello." In another country, or on another planet, would the gesture mean anything at all? "Do you think that They will think his arm is permanently attached in this position? Or do you think They will read our signs?" (Laurie Anderson, "Say Hello").

11. I should emphasize that the tic can be considered as disassociated only from the *conscious* attempt at linguistic signification. Any involuntary gesture may certainly be psychoanalytically interpreted as referring to a repressed impulse in the *un*conscious, which, according to Lacan, is itself structured like a language. In this case, the tic would inevitably be implicated in a linguistic problematic and could never be conceived as "pure" motion. Given this perspective, we might identify repression itself as the means by which one system—signification—is made to appear distinct from another—movement, when in fact the two systems are intimately interrelated. The failure of language that I identify as the "window" between the two systems is thus no more than the mark of the occurrence of this repression. I am indebted to Carola M. Kaplan for suggesting that I consider this point.

At the same time, Oliver Sacks gives a very interesting account of how physical tics can be invested with a conscious *personal* significance for the "tic-queur" in his article "Tics." Sacks also provides an interpretive context in which we can understand the nature of Homer Simpson's tic. He quotes Friedrich Nietzsche's description, in *The Will to Power,* of "physiological states" manifested in "the artist," which seems a strikingly accurate characterization of Homer's performance. Nietzsche says that the "artistic personality" is characterized by an

> *extreme mobility,* that turns into an extreme urge to communicate . . . a need to get rid of oneself, as it were, through signs and gestures. . . . an *explosive* condition. One must think of this condition as a compulsion and urge to get rid of the exuberance of inner tension through muscular activity and movements of all kinds; then as an involuntary coordination between this movement and the processes within (images, thoughts, desires)—as a kind of automatism of the whole muscular system impelled by strong stimuli from within—; inability to prevent reaction; the system of inhibition suspended, as it were. (Quoted in Sacks, 41n)

In Homer's case, a few alterations might be made to Nietzsche's formulation, for it appears to be his "extreme urge to communicate," to express himself through signs, that "turns into" his "extreme mobility" or the attempt to "get rid of [himself] . . . through . . . gestures" that have no necessary significance for their observer.

12. Foucault, *Discipline and Punish,* 135.

13. Ephraim H. Mizruchi, *Regulating Society: Marginality and Social Control in Historical Perspective,* 1; my emphasis.

14. Paul Virilio, *Speed and Politics,* 3.

15. M. M. Liberman and Edward E. Foster, *A Modern Lexicon of Literary Terms,* 90.

16. For an analysis of *Balso Snell* and *A Cool Million* as examples of the picaresque, see Galloway. On the status of the Bergotte epigraph as a gloss on all of West's work, see Irving Malin, *Nathanael West's Novels,* 9; and Gerald Locklin, "The Dream Life of *Balso Snell*: Journey into the Microcosm," 24.

17. At this point we might amend the earlier reference to the "eccentricity" of West's characters. That term denotes deviation from a single, stationary point that serves as a normative center around which a given system is ordered. But insofar as the "decenteredness" of the characters in picaresque fiction inheres in their *waywardness,* in their divergence from an approved course of *motion,* then "eccentric" fails to characterize it accurately. To the extent that it denotes divergence from a prescribed trajectory rather than from a fixed point, then "digressive" might be the better way of describing West's characters. The distinction is important not because it makes a great difference in the way we conceive of those characters—they are still disordered—but because it clarifies for us the nature of the *system* whose ordering impulse they reject; that system is a prescription for regulated movement, whose importance for the smooth functioning of the social order we have already cited, and the characters' perversion of it represents their attempt to use the logic of circulation against the very system that mandates it.

18. Walter Benjamin, "The Work of Art in the Age of Mechanical Reproduction," *Illuminations,* 223. Indeed, that sense has increased, in the field of entertainment, more than Benjamin could ever have predicted. In its augmentation of the "sense of the universal equality of things" in "the field of perception," Benjamin compared the development of mechanical reproduction with "the increasing importance of statistics" in the theoretical sphere. In our own age, technological reproduction has itself come to be founded on the numbers that Benjamin saw as characteristic of theoretical statistics. In the field of electronics, there has lately been developed the "digital system . . . in which information of any kind . . . is stored, transmitted or processed in the form of electrical pulses representing numbers," specifically, either one or zero (Hans Fantel, "Digital VCR's Figure in the Future," 40). This sort of system stands at the forefront of developments in communications, and thus represents the future of the industry of reproducible culture. As Laurie Anderson puts it, it is "the language of the future. . . . And it is digital" (Laurie Anderson, "The Language of the Future," *United States,* pt.1).

19. Max Horkheimer and Theodor Adorno, "The Culture Industry: Enlightenment as Mass Deception," *Dialectic of Enlightenment,* 120, 121.

20. Duhamel's characterization comes from his *Scènes de la vie future,* a 1930 account of his travels in the United States. The book was translated into English in 1931 as *America the Menace: Scenes from the Life of the Future,* and

published by Houghton Mifflin. The chapter containing Duhamel's opinions of film is called "Cinematographic Interlude," and his guide for this part of his strikingly picaresque journey is named, suitably, Pitkin—Parker P. Pitkin.

21. This idea was suggested to me by Tzvetan Todorov's lecture "Heroic Narratives of the Warsaw Ghetto," given at Brandeis University, 13 October 1988.

22. Frederick Douglass, speech on West Indies Emancipation delivered at Canandaigua, New York, 4 August 1857, 437.

23. Foucault, "Intellectuals and Power," 216.

Chapter 3

1. Anaïs Nin, *Cities of the Interior* (comprising *Ladders to Fire* [1946], *Children of the Albatross* [1947], *The Four-Chambered Heart* [1950], *A Spy in the House of Love* [1954], and *Seduction of the Minotaur* [a 1961 enlargement of *Solar Barque,* 1958]), vii. All future references to this work appear in the text.

2. Laura Mulvey, "Visual Pleasure and Narrative Cinema," 11. I should point out that, since 1975, Mulvey has continually revised and refined her thinking on film spectatorship. See "Afterthoughts on 'Visual Pleasure and Narrative Cinema' Inspired by *Duel in the Sun,*" and "Changes." Other feminist film theorists—in particular Mary Ann Doane, Teresa de Lauretis, and E. Ann Kaplan—have attempted to rethink Mulvey's ideas in relation to the female film viewer. For a full bibliography and an overview of developments in this area, see *The Spectatrix,* a special issue of *Camera Obscura* edited by Janet Bergstrom and Mary Ann Doane. As important as these interventions are, it is not crucial for us to consider them here, as we are primarily concerned not with the techniques of cinematic narrative but rather with the gender relations that such narrative illuminates, which Mulvey's 1975 article theorizes quite well for our purposes.

It is important to note that, because "pleasure in looking," as Mulvey describes it, is split along gender lines, the power dynamic she observes is specific to a *heterosexual* context. Much could be said about the unique function of the male gaze in homosexual relations, where a relative balance of power produces a rather circular exchange of the active and passive roles: Being looked at actually empowers a man to look *back* at the perpetrator of the initial gaze, and so on in an exchange of spiraling intensity that often constitutes a kind of extended, nontactile foreplay in anonymous gay male encounters. Both Richard Dyer ("Male Gay Porn: Coming to Terms") and Tom Waugh ("Men's Pornography: Gay vs. Straight") touch a bit on the unique aspects of the homosexual male gaze in the March 1985 issue of *Jump Cut* (no. 30), but they have by no means exhausted the topic, which is ripe for consideration by theorists in gender and sexuality studies.

3. Eve Kosofsky Sedgwick, *Between Men: English Literature and Male Homosocial Desire.*

In *Vertigo,* this advantage is enjoyed both by Gavin Elster, who escapes prosecution for his wife's murder, and by Scottie, who is morally vindicated in the exposure of Judy's guilt and not legally culpable in her death.

4. Claude Lévi-Strauss, *The Elementary Structures of Kinship,* cited in Gayle Rubin, "The Traffic in Women: Notes on the 'Political Economy' of Sex," 174.

5. Radicalesbians, "The Woman-Identified Woman" (1970), and the Gay Revolution Party Women's Caucus, "Realesbians and Politicalesbians" (originally published as "Realesbians, Politicalesbians and the Women's Liberation Movement" in *Ecstasy,* June 1971), both reprinted in *Out of the Closets: Voices of Gay Liberation,* edited by Karla Jay and Allen Young.

6. See, for instance, Ann Japenga, "The Separatist Revival," and *For Lesbians Only: A Separatist Anthology,* edited by Sarah Lucia Hoagland and Julia Penelope.

7. *The Diary of Anaïs Nin,* 4: 125–27. All subsequent references to this work appear in the text.

8. On the discontinuity of male homoeroticism and homosocial structures of patriarchy, see Sedgwick, 1–5.

9. If we follow Nin's own cue and try to trace her failure to conceive a distinction between homoeroticism and homosocial bonds through psychoanalytic theory, we might say that her fundamental problem is a misunderstanding of the Freudian concept of identification. In *Group Psychology and the Analysis of the Ego,* Freud distinguishes three types of identification:

> First, identification is the original form of emotional tie with an object; secondly, in a regressive way it becomes a substitute for a libidinal object-tie, as it were by means of introjection of the object into the ego; and thirdly, it may arise with any new perception of a common quality shared with some other person who is not an object of the sexual instinct. (39–40)

We can leave aside the first mode of identification, as it is, in Freud's conception, nothing more than the necessary precondition for and originary element in the properly constituted Oedipus complex. The second mode, however, is used by Freud to explicate a possible genesis of (male) homosexuality, whereby a young man's Oedipus complex is resolved not through his exchange of his mother for another sexual object but rather through his identification with her, and his consequent search for a suitable (male) object upon which he can bestow the affection he has received from her. The possible function of this explication as the basis for such homophobic attitudes as Nin manifests is clear, especially in Freud's designation of such "introjective" identification as "regressive," an idea that no doubt founds Nin's own conception of the male homosexual as "childlike." Unfortunately, Nin's fixation on this second mode of identification blinds her to the ramifications of the third, based on the subject's perception of a shared quality with another person. Freud himself says that "we already begin to divine that the mutual tie between members of a group is in the nature of an identification of this kind, based upon an important emotional common quality; and we may suspect that this common quality lies in the nature of the tie with the leader" (40). This is as far as he goes, but we can already see by this observation that this mechanism of group identification can provide the basis for homosocial bonds that might constitute patriarchy, feminist resistance to it, or both. Indeed, Freud's speculation on the implication of this third mode of identification in a subject's tie to a group leader itself suggests the potential political ramifications of such identification, however much we might want to question the efficacy of the traditional leadership function in contemporary democratic struggles. Nin's recognition of this third mode of identification and the political strategies it implies—while it would not in itself necessarily defuse her homophobia—would at least allow her to distinguish the homosexual from the homosocial, and thus to develop an effective gender-political analysis of women's psychic fragmentation.

10. Shari Benstock, while emphasizing the "feminist viewpoint" from which Barnes considered social formations, nonetheless confirms the fact that "[s]he eschewed group causes and refused to become part of a 'sisterhood,' probably from fear of jeopardizing her individuality." See Benstock, *Women of the Left Bank: Paris, 1900–1940*, 238.

11. Djuna Barnes, *Nightwood*. All future references to the book appear in the text.

12. For an explication of the relationship between modernism and naturalism, see Georg Lukács, "The Ideology of Modernism," *The Meaning of Contemporary Realism*.

13. Benstock claims that of the Left Bank women, only Janet Flanner and, especially, Natalie Barney saw in lesbianism and in women's community a political response to the oppressive forces of patriarchy. See p. 115 in Benstock and her chapter 8, on Natalie Barney, 268–307.

14. Andrew Field, *Djuna: The Life and Times of Djuna Barnes*, 37.

Barnes's ambivalence about her lesbianism seems to resonate with the attitudes of Anaïs Nin, who reflected on the nature of her passionate attachment to June Miller in her diary of 1931. While that relationship apparently never encompassed genital sexuality, its intensity induced Nin to consider the possibilities of lesbian associations, which she envisioned as patterned on conventional heterosexual relationships: "I have imagined that a freer life would be possible to me as a lesbian because I would choose a woman, protect her, work for her, love her for her beauty while she could love me as one loves a man, for his talent, his achievements, his character" (*Henry and June*, entries from the unexpurgated diary of Anaïs Nin, 133). Encumbered though this vision of lesbianism is by its conception in terms of heterosexual role-playing, its positing of a "freer life" for women at least suggests the possible political ramifications of lesbianism in a homosocially constituted feminist strategy. We have already seen, however, that Nin never develops this line of thinking, and her failure to do so results in the rather limited conception of gender politics that characterizes her novels.

15. The textual "management" of political concerns—especially as it occurs in literary modernism—is the subject matter of Fredric Jameson's *The Political*

Unconscious: Narrative as a Socially Symbolic Act. I explore the phenomenon more fully in chapter 5 of this study, on Ralph Ellison's *Invisible Man.*

There are certainly other "irruptions" of the political into the existential problematic of Barnes's text. Even more striking than the reflections on Nora's and Robin's relationship are the references in the novel to Dr. O'Connor's transvestism and feelings of transsexualism. When Nora, in chapter 5 ("Watchman, What of the Night?") comes to the Doctor's rooms to confer with him, she surprises him in his bed, "in a woman's flannel nightgown," his face rouged and his eyes painted, a wig of blond curls on his head. Neglecting to remark on his dress, Nora says, "Doctor, I have come to ask you to tell me everything you know about the night." The Doctor, in apparent reference to the full exposure of his self to Nora, replies, "You see that you can ask me anything." But this invitation to engage issues of gender and sexual identification is ignored by Nora, who only thinks silently to herself—"Is not the gown the natural raiment of extremity? . . . why should not the doctor, in the grave dilemma of his alchemy, wear his dress?" (79–80)—and proceeds with her originally intended line of questioning. The doctor makes a few subsequent references to his peculiar existence—he professes an intimate and loving knowledge of "[his] Sodomites" (93), and confesses to Nora: "[N]o matter what I may be doing, in my heart is the wish for children and knitting. God, I never asked better than to boil some good man's potatoes and toss up a child for him every nine months by the calendar" (91); later, he complains to her, "I'm the other woman that God forgot" (143). But none of these confessions meets with a response, and thus they suggest the suppressed nature of the gender-political import of the novel, which nonetheless underpins the action of the story. Moreover, because these scenes are symptomatically less central to the plot of the novel than the relationship between Robin and Nora, they are paradoxically less useful for explicating the mechanism by which the text's gender-political commentary is suppressed.

16. The phenomenon of the severed body part as the offspring that bodes death for the body is replayed, as Stacy Carson Hubbard deftly shows, in the poems of Sylvia Plath, in which dissociated hands threaten death to their owners, and severed fingertips promise to run away with the lifeblood of the bodies from which they come. Hubbard fully explicates this trope in her book manuscript in progress, "Slender Accents: American Women Poets and the Feminine Vernacular."

17. The novel's thematization of a spatial logic is not the same as its manifestation of what Joseph Frank calls "spatial form" in his classic discussion of *Nightwood* (see Frank, "Spatial Form in Modern Literature." It would be interesting, however—though beyond the scope of my project here—to see how extensively Barnes's development of spatial logic is imbricated with the pattern of "reflexive reference" that Frank sees as grounding *Nightwood*'s spatial form.

18. For an account of how the experience of time and space has influenced the conception of the human subject in twentieth-century culture, see Stephen Kern, *The Culture of Time and Space 1880–1918.*

19. For a complete study of the role of duality in Barnes's work, see Louis F. Kannenstine, *The Art of Djuna Barnes: Duality and Damnation*.

20. The inadequacy of these spatially oriented modes to correct Robin's temporal alienation is suggested in her vague assertion upon first meeting Nora— "I don't want to be here"—and her simultaneous inability to conceive of an alternative to "here," for, as the narrator affirms, "it was all she said; she did not explain where she wished to be" (55).

21. It is worth noting not only that T. S. Eliot wrote the introduction to the volume but that he was in fact responsible for its publication by Faber and Faber in 1936, after heavily editing it of its more explicit lesbian references and social commentary. See Benstock, 427–28.

Along these same lines, Benstock argues at some length that conventional references to the "difficulty" of Barnes's work (and Gertrude Stein's) indicate commentators' inability to read texts that thematize the politics of gender difference or the specificity of lesbian experience. See chapters 5 and 7 in *Women of the Left Bank*.

Chapter 4

1. Rubin, "The Traffic in Women."

2. This concept of the "subject position" as characteristic of a discursively constituted social structure derives from the work of Foucault, particularly *The Archaeology of Knowledge and The Discourse on Language*. It has been widely utilized as an analytical tool in contemporary social theory and cultural criticism.

3. Jean Baker Miller, M.D., "The Construction of Anger in Women and Men," the proceedings of a colloquium published in the *Works in Progress* series; p. 1 for this quotation. All other page references appear in the text.

4. Maria K. Mootry, " 'Down the Whirlwind of Good Rage': An Introduction to Gwendolyn Brooks," 4.

5. Houston A. Baker, Jr., "The Achievement of Gwendolyn Brooks," 21.

6. I try to address some of the issues associated with the question of "essential blackness" in work in which I am currently engaged. Henry Louis Gates, Jr., has treated the topic extensively, particularly in his essays "Preface to Blackness: Text and Pretext," and "Writing 'Race' and the Difference it Makes."

7. Baker, *The Journey Back: Issues in Black Literature and Criticism*, 108. See also the "Biographical Chronology" in Mootry and Smith, 284.

8. Indeed, an indication of Brooks's turn toward black economic and cultural nationalism can be seen in her very choice of a publisher for her autobiography. Through 1968, Brooks published her work through the "mainstream" New York house of Harper & Brothers (later Harper & Row). In 1969, however, she committed herself to working with black-owned and -operated concerns, publishing the volume *Riot* through the Broadside Press, of De-

troit. *Report from Part One* was published by Broadside in 1972. Since 1980, Brooks's work has been published by the Brooks and Third World Presses of Chicago.

A sense of the Black Arts Movement's nationalist agenda can be gotten from such early 1970s works as *The Black Aesthetic*, edited by Addison Gayle, and Stephen Henderson's *Understanding the New Black Poetry: Black Speech and Black Music as Poetic References*. In chapter 5 of *The Journey Back*, Houston Baker offers some retrospective reflection on the movement as one who was heavily influenced by it. Elsewhere, writing largely in response to Gates's criticisms of the Black Aesthetic in his "Preface to Blackness" essay, Baker provides a comprehensive review and critique of the movement and its relation to twentieth-century African-American literary-critical history generally. See his essay "Generational Shifts and the Recent Criticism of Afro-American Literature." A revised and expanded version of this essay was printed as chapter 2, "Discovering America: Generational Shifts, Afro-American Literary Criticism, and the Study of Expressive Culture," in Baker, *Blues, Ideology, and Afro-American Literature: A Vernacular Theory*, 64–112.

9. For a full account of the case, see Stephen J. Whitfield, *A Death in the Delta: The Story of Emmett Till*.

10. Gwendolyn Brooks, "A Bronzeville Mother Loiters in Mississippi. Meanwhile, a Mississippi Mother Burns Bacon."

11. Mootry, " 'Tell It Slant': Disguise and Discovery as Revisionist Poetic Discourse in *The Bean Eaters*," 184. All other page references are given in the text.

12. Chantal Mouffe, "Hegemony and New Political Subjects: Toward a New Concept of Democracy," 98.

13. In the interest of clarity, I take all my citations from Mouffe's 1988 article "Hegemony and New Political Subjects." In order to achieve a full understanding of the development of Mouffe's ideas, however, it is necessary to review her earlier essay, "Hegemony and Ideology in Gramsci," and, especially, the book she co-wrote with Ernesto Laclau, *Hegemony and Socialist Strategy: Towards a Radical Democratic Politics*. From 1979 to 1985 ("Hegemony and New Political Subjects," though published in 1988, originated as a conference paper delivered in 1983), Mouffe drastically alters her analysis from a traditional Marxist one to a poststructuralist-informed post-Marxist one: In "Hegemony and Ideology," for instance, she not only proposes that there is a limited number of "hegemonic classes" but asserts that "only the working class . . . can be capable of successfully bringing about an expansive hegemony" (p. 183); with Laclau in *Hegemony and Socialist Strategy*, however, Mouffe accepts a poststructuralist account of social formations as constituted through "discursive discontinuity" (191), necessitating the renunciation of the "discourse of the universal and its implicit assumption of a privileged point of access to 'the truth' . . . " (191–92), represented in classical Marxism by the consciousness of the working class. Finally, therefore, Laclau and Mouffe declare that

> [t]he rejection of privileged points of rupture and the confluence of struggles
> into a unified political space, and the acceptance, on the contrary, of the plu-
> rality and indeterminacy of the social, seem to us the two fundamental bases
> from which a new political imaginary can be constructed, radically libertarian
> and infinitely more ambitious in its objectives than that of the classic left. (152)

14. Ferdinand de Saussure, *Course in General Linguistics*, 70.

It is on the basis of this principle that Foucault is able to disarm the "double trap" of the Apollinairean calligram, as I have discussed in chapter 2, on Nathanael West. See "The Unravelled Calligram," chapter 2 in Foucault, *This Is Not a Pipe*.

15. It is worth noting that Brooks's use here of the term "Other Woman"—with its connotations of adultery—indicates the highly overdetermined nature of the black woman's relation to white domesticity, as her mythic hypersexuality (so often cited as an excuse for her rape by white men) has been figured as a threat to the white family since the days of slavery. The nature of that threat is transfigured in Brooks's poem, but the association between the black woman and illicit sexuality remains a salient reference point for interpretation of it.

16. Brooks, "The Last Quatrain of the Ballad of Emmett Till," lines 3–6.

17. I hope it is clear that to deny, as I do here, that Brooks's characters achieve an effective alliance in her poem is not at all to deny either the logicality or the possibility of such an alliance. To do so would be to deny the feasibility of any progressive politics—a position that strikes me as completely untenable.

18. Mary Helen Washington, " 'Taming all that anger down': rage and silence in Gwendolyn Brooks's *Maud Martha*," 258.

This essay is groundbreaking precisely because it calls for the establishment of this relationship. Other recent commentary on the work is much less concerned to see the novel as reflecting a political reality. Harry B. Shaw ("*Maud Martha*: The War with Beauty"; and the chapter on *Maud Martha* in *Gwendolyn Brooks*) renders all the political struggle represented in the novel as constitutive of Maud Martha's private and trivialized "aesthetic war" regarding the terms of women's beauty, all the while ignoring the underlying political factors in the nature of aesthetic judgments. Barbara Christian ("Nuance and the Novella: A Study of Gwendolyn Brooks's *Maud Martha*," and *Black Women Novelists*, 68–71) focuses her concern on the poetic nuance that characterizes the novel rather than on the political struggles that inform it. Patricia Lattin and Vernon E. Lattin see Maud Martha's achievement in living with "grace" as a way of avoiding the political realities of racism and sexism rather than as an engagement with them ("Dual Vision in Gwendolyn Brooks's *Maud Martha*"). Hortense J. Spillers provides a rigorous and challenging account of Brooks's rendering of a "feminine order" in " 'An Order of Constancy': Notes on Brooks and the Feminine" but while she is clearly engaged in a discussion of the politics of Brooks's novel, Spillers does not verge on a consideration of how Maud Martha's experiences situate her in relation to a political collectivity, as Washington suggests must be done. Washington's own views, as presented in her essay in Gates, are more tentatively formulated in "Plain, Black, and Decently Wild: The Heroic Possibilities of *Maud Martha*."

19. Gwendolyn Brooks, *Maud Martha*. All citations are from the 1974 edition; p. 85 for the current citation.

20. Louise Mitchell, "Slave Markets Typify Exploitation of Domestics," 230.

21. Ella Baker and Marvel Cooke, "The Bronx Slave Market," 270.

22. We should note that Brooks's commentary on the ironic status of the Santa figure in African-American communities is part of a long tradition of such analysis by black artists. In particular, Brooks's treatment serves as a prelude to a rich "vernacular" tradition of Santa critiques undertaken in black music from the late 1950s through the early 1970s. Rock historian Ed Ward has discussed this musical tradition on the National Public Radio program *Fresh Air*, 19 December 1989.

Among European traditions, the conflicted relationship between Santa Claus and people of African descent is probably best depicted in legends from central and northern Europe that pair the Saint Nicholas figure with a black sidekick who either carries and helps distributes Christmas gifts or, in a more demonic incarnation, threatens retribution to those children who misbehave. In a 1957 book on *Christmas and Its Customs,* Christina Hole gives a summation of these legends. More recently, Bruce Curtis has reviewed some of the implicit politics of representations of the Santa figure in his paper "Myth and Gender Role Conditioning: St. Nicholas/Santa Claus in European and American Graphic Illustrations."

23. Given this, Santa Claus's failure to respond to Paulette suggests the degree to which different aspects of capital will develop at unequal rates in the face of shifting systemic demands. While the viability of capital as a total system clearly depends upon the eventual assimilation of the black woman into the market economy as a consumer, that assimilation nonetheless constitutes a profound crisis at the local level, where a host of social and political factors seem to mandate the black woman's continued exclusion from the system.

Chapter 5

1. For a discussion of a literary "critique" of the notion of blackness as a negative essence, see Henry Louis Gates, Jr., "The Blackness of Blackness: A Critique of the Sign and the Signifying Monkey."

2. Throughout this chapter I cite from the 1982 thirtieth Anniversary paperback edition of Ralph Ellison's *Invisible Man*, p. 15 for the present passage. All subsequent page references appear in the text.

3. Gates suggests that, contrary to appearances, Ellison's Invisible Man effects his substantiality and creates his own identity through the constitutive power of his language (Gates, 293–94). This is true, I think, up to the point where social and political forces limit the protagonist's verbal facility. Such factors, which constitute the very "marginality" that concerns me in this study, compli-

cate any theory of textuality, such as that Gates posits, for black cultural production.

4. Jacques Lacan, "The Mirror Stage as Formative of the Function of the I," *Écrits: A Selection*, 2.

5. Karl Marx, *Capital*, 1: 163–77.

Georg Lukács, "Reification and the Consciousness of the Proletariat."

6. Lauren Berlant, in a discussion of Alice Walker's *The Color Purple*, similarly notes the

> fragmented relation to identity suffered by subjects of a culture who have learned the message of their negation before they had a chance to imagine otherwise. This process of part-identification is different from that of the subject described by post-structuralism, who shuttles between the ruse of self-presence and its dissolution. ("Race, Gender, and Nation in *The Color Purple*," 845)

The poststructuralist subject mentioned here corresponds to the white businessman of *Invisible Man*, who is politically enabled to achieve the Lacanian "ruse of self-presence." I would also emphasize that postmodernism's popularization of the notion of the poststructuralist subject has the effect of defusing the political resonances of marginalized subjects' particular predicament with respect to fragmentation.

7. Thus, in addition to Dr. Bledsoe's donning of his mask for Mr. Norton, we witness the recounting by the sharecropper, Jim Trueblood, of his incestuous encounter with his daughter. Mr. Norton pays the black man to relate this story so that he might undergo a surrogate experience for his desired but never realized union with his own daughter, now dead; the much more "appropriate" enactment of incest by disenfranchised blacks is worth the $100 Norton pays Trueblood, for it reorients his status according to the "correct" racial order, which is, after all, the function of the minstrel show. Similarly, the coins scattered on the electrified carpet after the battle royal at novel's beginning represent payment to the black boys for appropriately humiliating themselves before the whites gathered at the smoker. There seems always to be an economic factor in the production of black affect, and control of that economics is itself determined according to a racial politics.

I am indebted to Houston A. Baker, Jr., for help in formulating these observations on the minstrel show. His own analysis can be found in his essay, "'To Move without Moving': Creativity and Commerce in Ralph Ellison's Trueblood Episode."

8. For a discussion of the effects of rationalization on the human subject, see Lukács, "Reification . . . ," especially part 1, "The Phenomenon of Reification," section 1, pp. 83–92.

9. Lukács, "The Ideology of Modernism" 24.

10. Fredric Jameson, *The Political Unconscious*, 266.

11. Booker T. Washington, *Up from Slavery*.

12. Saussure, *Course in General Linguistics*, 65–67.

13. For a more detailed discussion of signification in Afro-American culture, see Gates, "The Blackness of Blackness."

14. Ellison, "The Charlie Christian Story," 234; my emphasis.

15. Baker, *Blues, Ideology, and Afro-American Literature*, 112.

16. T. S. Eliot, "Tradition and the Individual Talent," 49.

17. Ellison, "Living with Music," 189.

18. For a most cogent and pertinent account of the salutary nature of divided experience, see Barbara Johnson, "Metaphor, Metonymy and Voice in *Their Eyes Were Watching God*."

19. A preliminary such exploration is presented in the Coda of this book, and in other of my own critical work that is referenced therein.

Chapter 6

1. Jameson, "Postmodernism, or The Cultural Logic of Late Capitalism," 54.

2. Ihab Hassan, "Toward a Concept of Postmodernism," 260.

3. John Barth, "The Literature of Replenishment: Postmodernist Fiction," 194–95.

4. For a useful compendium of titles that treat of the defining characteristics of postmodernist literature, see the bibliography in Hutcheon's *The Politics of Postmodernism*.

5. Donald Barthelme, "See the Moon?" *Unspeakable Practices, Unnatural Acts*, 149–65; 153. Citations for all further references to stories in this collection are provided in the text.

6. Maurice Couturier and Régis Durand, *Donald Barthelme*, 15.

7. Lois Gordon, *Donald Barthelme*, 30–31.

8. Alan Wilde, *Horizons of Assent: Modernism, Postmodernism, and the Ironic Imagination*, 141.

9. John M. Ditsky, " 'With Ingenuity and Hard Work, Distracted': The Narrative Style of Donald Barthelme," 398.

10. Jerome Klinkowitz, *The Self-Apparent Word*, 73–74. Klinkowitz has since published a book-length study of Barthelme's oeuvre: *Donald Barthelme: An Exhibition*.

11. Stanley Trachtenberg, *Understanding Donald Barthelme*, 30.

12. Larry McCaffery, *The Metafictional Muse: The Works of Robert Coover, Donald Barthelme, and William H. Gass*, 100.

13. Barthelme, "Me and Miss Mandible," 109.

14. Couturier and Durand derive their understanding of the relation between allegory and the postmodern aesthetic from Craig Owens's two-part essay, "The Allegorical Impulse: Toward a Theory of Postmodernism."

15. See Walter Evans, "Comanches and Civilization in Donald Barthelme's 'The Indian Uprising.' "

16. See Barthelme, *Snow White*. For critical commentary on Barthelme's

"aesthetics of trash," see McCaffery, especially pp. 116–19; and Couturier and Durand, 26–27.

17. Robert Coover, *The Universal Baseball Association, Inc., J. Henry Waugh, Prop.* Hereafter, all citations appear in the main text, and the novel is referred to as *The UBA.*

18. William H. Gass, *Fiction and the Figures of Life,* 25.

19. McCaffery, *The Metafictional Muse,* 5.

20. Patricia Waugh, *Metafiction: The Theory and Practice of Self-Conscious Fiction,* 2.

21. Roy C. Caldwell, Jr., "Of Hobby-Horses, Baseball, and Narrative: Coover's *Universal Baseball Association,*" 162.

22. Coover, "The Second Son," *Evergreen Review* 31 (October/November 1963): 72–88.

23. This aspect of Henry's game calls to mind the status of Oscar Wilde's work as a harbinger of the issues engaged in postmodern culture. A similar "backward" progression from statistics to the lived reality with which they are associated characterizes the logic of the character Lady Bracknell, in *The Importance of Being Earnest.* Upon learning first of her daughter Gwendolen's plan to marry the apparently unconnected Jack Worthing, and then of her nephew Algernon's intention of marrying the young Cecily Cardew, Lady Bracknell remarks,

> "I do not know whether there is anything peculiarly exciting in the air of this particular part of Hertfordshire, but the number of engagements that go on seems to me considerably above the proper average that statistics have laid down for our guidance." (Wilde, *The Importance of Being Earnest,* Act III, 46)

The notion presented here that statistics should "guide" rather than reflect human behavior governs Henry's generation of the narratives that flesh out the action in his imaginary baseball league.

24. Arlen J. Hansen, "The Dice of God: Einstein, Heisenberg, and Robert Coover," 55.

25. Richard Alan Schwartz, "Postmodernist Baseball," 146.

26. Frank W. Shelton, "Humor and Balance in Coover's *The Universal Baseball Association, Inc.,*" 84–85.

27. Corbett Thigpen and Hervey M. Cleckley, *The Three Faces of Eve.*
Flora Rheta Schreiber, *Sybil.*
Truddi Chase, *When Rabbit Howls.*

28. Robert D. Newman, *Understanding Thomas Pynchon,* 67–68.

29. All citations of *The Crying of Lot 49* appear in the text.

30. Lance Olsen, "Pynchon's New Nature: The Uncertainty Principle and Indeterminacy in *The Crying of Lot 49,*" 157.

31. Stefano Tani, "The Dismemberment of the Detective," 29–30.

32. Frank Palmeri, "Neither Literally Nor as Metaphor: Pynchon's *The Crying of Lot 49* and the Structure of Scientific Revolutions," 985.

33. See Anne Mangel, "Maxwell's Demon, Entropy, Information: *The Crying of Lot 49.*"

34. Peter L. Abernethy, "Entropy in Pynchon's *The Crying of Lot 49*," 20.

35. John P. Leland, "Pynchon's Linguistic Demon: *The Crying of Lot 49*," 46–47.

36. Two of the earliest essays to insist on the polysemous nature of Pynchon's language are by Annette Kolodny and Daniel James Peters ("Pynchon's *The Crying of Lot 49*: The Novel as Subversive Experience"), and Maureen Quilligan ("Thomas Pynchon and the Language of Allegory").

37. Richard Pearce, "Where're They At, Where're They Going? Thomas Pynchon and the American Novel in Motion," 220.

38. Tzvetan Todorov, on "Style," in Oswald Ducrot and Todorov, *Encyclopedic Dictionary of the Sciences of Language,* 303.

39. To argue, as I do in this chapter, that Barthelme, Coover, and Pynchon fail to engage crucial issues of identity politics is not to say that their work manifests no political engagement at all. In his recent study, Paul Maltby has classed these same three authors as "dissident postmodernists" who, through their highly self-conscious linguistic strategies, "explore the political and ideological implications of the fictionality of meaning," and thus carve out an "adversarial" position with respect to institutionalized power. (Paul Maltby, *Dissident Postmodernists: Barthelme, Coover, Pynchon,* 39, 22). Still, the degree to which these authors' explorations tend to thematize such power as a generalized phenomenon disengaged from differentials of subject position is precisely the degree to which they fail to address the specifically *socio*political questions that I am claiming characterize the postmodern moment.

40. Maxine Hong Kingston, *The Woman Warrior: Memoirs of a Girlhood Among Ghosts.* All page references to this work appear in the main text.

41. This fact is extensively treated by Samuel R. Delany in the introduction to his own memoir, *The Motion of Light in Water: Sex and Science Fiction Writing in the East Village, 1957–1965.* Delany's book is designated as "nonfiction" on its back cover.

42. King-Kok Cheung analyzes the narrative import of this injunction in her article, " 'Don't Tell': Imposed Silences in *The Color Purple* and *The Woman Warrior.*"

Coda

1. See my essay "Synesthesia, 'Crossover,' and Blacks in Popular Music."
Along these same lines, it is interesting to note that, while I was writing this final section of the book, there appeared next to each other in the Arts section of the *New York Times* two stories about just the sort of appeal by whites to African-American culture as I discuss in my *Social Text* article. One of the articles was a review of the film *Zebrahead* (directed by Anthony Drazan), whose

young white hero Zach (Michael Rapaport) identifies fully with blacks and with African-American culture (Janet Maslin, "A Racial Chameleon in a Hidebound World"). The other was about Roger Clinton, younger half-brother of then-Presidential candidate Bill Clinton, and his job as a production assistant for the CBS television sitcoms "Designing Women," "Evening Shade," and "Hearts Afire," entailing warming up studio audiences by performing rhythm-and-blues songs prior to live taping of the shows (Bernard Weinraub, "A TV Gofer Named Clinton with a Famous Brother"). The article relates how Clinton was hired by producers Linda Bloodworth-Thomason and Harry Thomason, friends of Bill and Hillary Clinton, after Thomason's own brother heard him perform at the 1980 Arkansas gubernatorial inauguration. Roger Clinton recalls laughingly that Danny Thomason "came up to me backstage and told me I was the blackest sounding white boy he had ever heard, which is the highest compliment that could be paid" (C17). This joking reference to the complimentary nature of Thomason's remark indicates precisely my point about the cachet that continues to attach to the cultural effects of marginalized populations in putatively "mainstream" U.S. social circles.

2. Roddy Doyle, *The Commitments*.

3. Over a third of the more than four dozen newspaper and magazine articles on *The Commitments* that I surveyed explicitly comment on this statement of Jimmy's. The value of listing them all here would be minimal, so I refrain, but the interested reader can find extensive commentary on the film in the pages of local newspapers and national periodicals published during and around August and September 1991, when the movie was first released, and around May 1992, when it became available on videotape.

4. Clarence Page, "A noble attempt by Irish kids to become 'black.' "
See also David Sterritt, "Singing Soul in Dublin"; and Dave Kehr, "Irish Soul: The Kids Put on a Show in 'Commitments.' "

5. Richard Corliss, review of *The Commitments*, 63.

6. Quoted in David Gritten, "Irish Soul," 78.

BIBLIOGRAPHY

Abernethy, Peter L. "Entropy in Pynchon's *The Crying of Lot 49.*" *Critique: Studies in Modern Fiction* 14:2 (1972): 18–33.

Abrams, M. H. *A Glossary of Literary Terms.* 5th ed. New York: Holt, Rinehart and Winston, Inc., 1988.

Anderson, Laurie. *United States.* Text published in New York: Harper & Row, 1984; audio recording produced by Warner Records, 25192–1, 1984.

Apollinaire, Guillaume. *Selected Writings.* Translated by Roger Shattuck. New York: New Directions, 1950.

Baker, Ella, and Marvel Cooke. "The Bronx Slave Market." 1935. In *Afro-American History: Primary Sources,* edited by Thomas R. Frazier. Chicago: The Dorsey Press, 1988. 265–71.

Baker, Houston A., Jr. "The Achievement of Gwendolyn Brooks." In Mootry and Smith, 21–29.

———. *Blues, Ideology, and Afro-American Literature: A Vernacular Theory.* Chicago: University of Chicago Press, 1984.

———. "Generational Shifts and the Recent Criticism of Afro-American Literature." *Black American Literature Forum* 15:1 (Spring 1981): 3–21.

———. *The Journey Back: Issues in Black Literature and Criticism.* Chicago: University of Chicago Press, 1980.

———. " 'To Move without Moving': Creativity and Commerce in Ralph Ellison's Trueblood Episode." In Gates, *Black Literature and Literary Theory,* 221–48.

Barnes, Djuna. *Nightwood.* 1937. New York: New Directions, 1961.

Barth, John. "The Literature of Replenishment: Postmodernist Fiction." 1980. *The Friday Book.* New York: Putnam, 1984. 193–206.

Barthelme, Donald. "Me and Miss Mandible," In *Come Back, Dr. Caligari.* Boston: Little, Brown, 1964. 95–111.

———. *Snow White.* New York: Atheneum, 1967.

———. *Unspeakable Practices, Unnatural Acts.* 1968. New York: Bantam, 1969.

Benjamin, Walter. "The Work of Art in the Age of Mechanical Reproduction." In *Illuminations,* edited by Hannah Arendt; translated by Harry Zohn. New York: Schocken, 1969. 217–51.

Benstock, Shari. *Women of the Left Bank: Paris, 1900–1940.* Austin: University of Texas Press, 1986.

Bergstrom, Janet, and Mary Ann Doane, eds. *The Spectatrix. Camera Obscura* 20–21 (May–September 1989).

Berlant, Lauren. "Race, Gender, and Nation in *The Color Purple.*" *Critical Inquiry* 14:4 (Summer 1988): 831–59.

Bourdieu, Pierre. *Distinction: A Social Critique of the Judgement of Taste,* translated by Richard Nice. Cambridge: Harvard University Press, 1984.

Bradbury, Malcolm, and James McFarlane, eds. "The Name and Nature of Modernism." In *Modernism: 1890–1930,* Pelican Guides to European Literature. Harmondsworth: Penguin, 1976. 19–55.

Brooks, Gwendolyn. "A Bronzeville Mother Loiters in Mississippi. Meanwhile, a Mississippi Mother Burns Bacon." *The Bean Eaters.* New York: Harper & Brothers, 1960. 19–25.

———. "The Last Quatrain of the Ballad of Emmett Till." *The Bean Eaters,* 26.

———. *Maud Martha.* 1953. New York: AMS Press, 1974.

———. *Report from Part One.* Detroit: Broadside Press, 1972.

Caldwell, Roy C., Jr. "Of Hobby-Horses, Baseball, and Narrative: Coover's *Universal Baseball Association.*" *Modern Fiction Studies* 33:1 (Spring 1987): 161–71.

Chase, Truddi. *When Rabbit Howls.* New York: Dutton, 1987.

Cheung, King-Kok. " 'Don't Tell': Imposed Silences in *The Color Purple* and *The Woman Warrior.*" *PMLA* 103:2 (March 1988): 162–74.

Christian, Barbara. *Black Women Novelists: the Development of a Tradition, 1892–1976.* Westport, Conn. Greenwood Press, 1980.

———. "Nuance and the Novella: A Study of Gwendolyn Brooks's *Maud Martha.*" In Mootry and Smith, 239–53.

The Commitments. Directed by Alan Parker. Twentieth Century Fox, 1991.

Coover, Robert. "The Second Son." *Evergreen Review* 31 (October/November 1963): 72–88.

———. *The Universal Baseball Association, Inc., J. Henry Waugh, Prop.* 1968. New York: New American Library/Plume, 1971.

Corliss, Richard. Review of *The Commitments* by Alan Parker. *Time,* 26 August 1991, 63.

Couturier, Maurice, and Régis Durand. *Donald Barthelme.* London and New York: Methuen, 1982.

Curtis, Bruce. "Myth and Gender Role Conditioning: St. Nicholas/Santa Claus in European and American Graphic Illustrations." Session on Gender Issues in Popular Culture, American Studies Association/Canadian Association for American Studies International Convention. Toronto, Canada, 3 November 1989.

Delany, Samuel R. *The Motion of Light in Water: Sex and Science Fiction Writing in the East Village, 1957–1965.* 1988. New York: Plume, 1989.

Deleuze, Gilles, and Félix Guattari. *Kafka: Toward a Minor Literature,* translated by Dana Polan. *Theory and History of Literature,* no. 30. general editors,

Wlad Godzich and Jochen Schulte-Sasse. Minneapolis: University of Minnesota Press, 1986.

Ditsky, John M. " 'With Ingenuity and Hard Work, Distracted': The Narrative Style of Donald Barthelme." *Style* 9:3 (Summer 1975): 388–400.

Douglass, Frederick. Speech on West Indies Emancipation delivered at Canandaigua, N.Y., 4 August 1857. In *The Life and Writings,* edited by Philip S. Foner. 5 vols. New York: International Publishers, 1950–75. 2:426–439.

Doyle, Roddy. *The Commitments.* 1987. New York: Vintage, 1989.

Duhamel, Georges. *America the Menace: Scenes from the Life of the Future.* Translated by Charles Miner Thompson. Boston: Houghton Mifflin, 1931.

Dyer, Richard. "Male Gay Porn: Coming to Terms." *Jump Cut* 30 (March 1985). 27–29.

Eliot, T. S. "Tradition and the Individual Talent." In *The Sacred Wood: Essays on Poetry and Criticism.* 1920. London: Methuen, 1928. 47–59.

Ellison, Ralph. "The Charlie Christian Story." In *Shadow and Act.* 1964. New York: Vintage, 1972. 233–240.

———. *Invisible Man.* 1952. New York: Vintage, 1972; 1982.

———. "Living with Music." In *Shadow and Act,* 187–98.

Evans, Walter. "Comanches and Civilization in Donald Barthelme's 'The Indian Uprising.' " *Arizona Quarterly* 42:1 (Spring 1986): 45–52.

Fantel, Hans. "Digital VCR's Figure in the Future." *New York Times,* 7 September 1986, sect. 2: 40.

Ferguson, Russell. "Introduction: Invisible Center." In Ferguson, Gever, Trinh, and West, 9–14.

Ferguson, Russell, William Olander, Marcia Tucker, and Karen Fiss, eds. *Discourses: Conversations in Postmodern Art and Culture.* Documentary Sources in Contemporary Art, vol. 3, general editor, Marcia Tucker. New York: The New Museum of Contemporary Art; Cambridge: The MIT Press, 1990.

Ferguson, Russell, Martha Gever, Trinh T. Minh-ha, and Cornel West, eds. *Out There: Marginalization and Contemporary Cultures.* Documentary Sources in Contemporary Art, vol. 4, general editor, Marcia Tucker. New York: The New Museum of Contemporary Art; Cambridge: The MIT Press, 1990.

Field, Andrew. *Djuna: The Life and Times of Djuna Barnes.* New York: Putnam, 1983.

Foster, Hal, ed. *The Anti-Aesthetic: Essays on Postmodern Culture.* Port Townsend, Wash.: Bay Press, 1983.

Foucault, Michel. *The Archaeology of Knowledge and The Discourse on Language.* Translated by A. M. Sheridan Smith. New York: Pantheon, 1972.

———. *Discipline and Punish.* Translated by Alan Sheridan. New York: Vintage, 1979.

———. "Intellectuals and Power." (A conversation with Gilles Deleuze.) In *Language, Counter-Memory, Practice: Selected Essays and Interviews,* edited by Donald F. Bouchard; translated by Donald F. Bouchard and Sherry Simon. Ithaca, N.Y.: Cornell University Press, 1977. 205–217.

————. *This Is Not a Pipe.* Edited and translated by James Harkness. Berkeley and Los Angeles: University of California Press, 1983.

Frank, Joseph. "Spatial Form in Modern Literature." 1945. *The Idea of Spatial Form.* New Brunswick and London: Rutgers University Press, 1991. 3–66.

Fresh Air. Report by Ed Ward. National Public Radio, WHYY, Philadelphia, 19 December 1989.

Freud, Sigmund. *Group Psychology and the Analysis of the Ego.* Translated by and edited by James Strachey. 1922. New York and London: Norton, 1959.

Galloway, David. "A Picaresque Apprenticeship: Nathanael West's *The Dream Life of Balso Snell* and *A Cool Million.*" *Wisconsin Studies in Contemporary Literature* 5:2 (Summer 1964): 110–26.

Gass, William H. *Fiction and the Figures of Life.* New York: Knopf, 1970.

Gates, Henry Louis, Jr., ed. *Black Literature and Literary Theory.* New York: Methuen, 1984.

————. "The Blackness of Blackness: A Critique of the Sign and the Signifying Monkey." In *Black Literature and Literary Theory,* 285–321.

————. "Preface to Blackness: Text and Pretext." In *Afro-American Literature: The Reconstruction of Instruction,* edited by Dexter Fisher and Robert B. Stepto. New York: MLA of America, 1979. 44–69.

————. "Writing 'Race' and the Difference it Makes." In *"Race," Writing, and Difference,* edited by Gates. Chicago: University of Chicago Press, 1986. 1–20.

Gay Revolution Party Women's Caucus. "Realesbians and Politicalesbians." In Jay and Young, 177–81.

Gayle, Addison, Jr., ed. *The Black Aesthetic.* Garden City, N.Y.: Doubleday, 1971.

Gordon, Lois. *Donald Barthelme.* Boston: Twayne, 1981.

Graff, Gerald. "The Myth of the Postmodernist Breakthrough." *TriQuarterly* 26 (Winter 1973): 383–417.

Gritten, David. "Irish Soul." *Los Angeles Times,* Calendar, 11 August 1991, 3, 67, 78.

Habermas, Jürgen. "Modernity versus Postmodernity." Translated by Seyla Ben-Habib. *New German Critique* 22 (Winter 1981): 3–14.

————. "Modernity—An Incomplete Project." In Foster, 3–15.

Hansen, Arlen J. "The Dice of God: Einstein, Heisenberg, and Robert Coover." *Novel: A Forum on Fiction* 10:1 (Fall 1976): 49–58.

Harper, Phillip Brian. "Synesthesia, 'Crossover,' and Blacks in Popular Music." *Social Text* 23 (Fall/Winter 1989; vol. 8, no. 2): 102–21.

Hassan, Ihab. *The Dismemberment of Orpheus: Toward a Postmodern Literature.* 2d ed. Madison: University of Wisconsin Press, 1982.

Henderson, Stephen. *Understanding the New Black Poetry: Black Speech and Black Music as Poetic References.* New York: William Morrow & Company, 1973.

Hoagland, Sarah Lucia, and Julia Penelope. *For Lesbians Only: A Separatist Anthology.* London: Onlywomen Press, 1988.

Hole, Christina. *Christmas and Its Customs.* 1957. New York: M. Barrows and Company, Inc., 1958.

hooks, bell. "Postmodern Blackness." In *Yearning: Race, Gender, and Cultural Politics.* Boston: South End Press, 1990. 23–31.

Horkheimer, Max, and Theodor Adorno. "The Culture Industry: Enlightenment as Mass Deception." In *Dialectic of Enlightenment,* translated by John Cumming. New York: Herder and Herder, 1972. 120–167.

Hubbard, Stacy Carson. "Slender Accents: American Women Poets and the Feminine Vernacular." Unpublished book manuscript.

Hutcheon, Linda. *The Politics of Postmodernism,* New Accents series, general editor, Terence Hawkes. London and New York: Routledge, 1989.

Jameson, Fredric. "Foreword." In Lyotard, vii–xxi.

––––––. *The Political Unconscious: Narrative as a Socially Symbolic Act.* Ithaca, N.Y.: Cornell University Press, 1981.

––––––. "Postmodernism, or The Cultural Logic of Late Capitalism." *New Left Review* 146 (July–August 1984): 53–92.

––––––. *Postmodernism, or, The Cultural Logic of Late Capitalism.* Durham, N.C.: Duke University Press, 1991.

JanMohamed, Abdul R., and David Lloyd, eds. "Introduction: Toward a Theory of Minority Discourse: What Is to Be Done?" In *The Nature and Context of Minority Discourse.* New York: Oxford University Press, 1990. 1–16.

Japenga, Ann. "The Separatist Revival." *Out/Look: National Lesbian & Gay Quarterly* 8 (Spring 1990): 78–83.

Jay, Karla, and Allen Young, eds. *Out of the Closets: Voices of Gay Liberation.* 2d ed. New York: Harcourt Brace Jovanovich, 1977.

Johnson, Barbara. "Metaphor, Metonymy and Voice in *Their Eyes Were Watching God.*" In Gates, *Black Literature and Literary Theory,* 205–19.

Kannenstine, Louis F. *The Art of Djuna Barnes: Duality and Damnation.* New York: New York University Press, 1977.

Kehr, Dave. "Irish Soul: The Kids Put on a Show in 'Commitments.' " *Chicago Tribune,* 16 August 1991, sec. 7, p. C (29).

Kellner, Douglas, ed. *Postmodernism/Jameson/Critique, PostModernPositions,* vol. 4, general editor, Robert Merrill. Washington, D.C.: Institute for Advanced Cultural Studies/Maisonneuve Press, 1989.

Kern, Stephen. *The Culture of Time and Space 1880–1918.* Cambridge: Harvard University Press, 1983.

Kingston, Maxine Hong. *The Woman Warrior: Memoirs of a Girlhood Among Ghosts.* 1976. New York: Vintage/Random House, 1977.

Klinkowitz, Jerome. *Donald Barthelme: An Exhibition.* Durham: Duke University Press, 1991.

––––––. *The Self-Apparent Word: Fiction as Language/Language as Fiction.* Carbondale: Southern Illinois University Press, 1984.

Kolodny, Annette, and Daniel James Peters. "Pynchon's *The Crying of Lot 49*: The Novel as Subversive Experience." *Modern Fiction Studies* 19:1 (Spring 1973): 79–87.

Lacan, Jacques. "The Mirror Stage as Formative of the Function of the I." In *Écrits: A Selection,* translated by Alan Sheridan. New York: Norton, 1977. 1–7.

Laclau, Ernesto, and Chantal Mouffe. *Hegemony and Socialist Strategy: Towards a Radical Democratic Politics.* London: Verso, 1985.

Lattin, Patricia, and Vernon E. Lattin. "Dual Vision in Gwendolyn Brooks's *Maud Martha.*" *Critique: Studies in Modern Fiction* 25:4 (Summer 1984): 180–88.

Leland, John P. "Pynchon's Linguistic Demon: *The Crying of Lot 49.*" *Critique: Studies in Modern Fiction* 16:2 (1974): 45–53.

Liberman, M. M., and Edward E. Foster. *A Modern Lexicon of Literary Terms.* Glenview, Ill.: Scott, Foresman, & Co., 1968.

Locklin, Gerald. "*The Dream Life of Balso Snell*: Journey into the Microcosm." In *Nathanael West: The Cheaters and the Cheated,* edited by David Madden. Deland, Fla.: Everett/Edwards, Inc., 1973. 23–56.

Lukács, Georg. "The Ideology of Modernism." In *The Meaning of Contemporary Realism,* translated by John and Necke Mander. London: Merlin, 1963. 17–46.

———. "Reification and the Consciousness of the Proletariat." In *History and Class Consciousness: Studies in Marxist Dialectics,* translated by Rodney Livingstone. Cambridge: MIT Press, 1971. 83–222.

Lyotard, Jean-François. *The Postmodern Condition: A Report on Knowledge,* translated by Geoff Bennington and Brian Massumi. *Theory and History of Literature,* vol. 10, general editors, Wlad Godzich and Jochen Schulte-Sasse. Minneapolis: University of Minnesota Press, 1984.

Malin, Irving. *Nathanael West's Novels.* Carbondale: Southern Illinois University Press, 1972.

Maltby, Paul. *Dissident Postmodernists: Barthelme, Coover, Pynchon.* Philadelphia: University of Pennsylvania Press, 1991.

Mangel, Anne. "Maxwell's Demon, Entropy, Information: *The Crying of Lot 49.*" *TriQuarterly* 20 (Winter 1971): 194–208.

Martin, Jay. *Nathanael West: The Art of His Life.* New York: Farrar, Straus and Giroux, 1970.

Marx, Karl. *Capital,* vol. 1. Translated by Ben Fowkes. New York: Vintage, 1977.

Maslin, Janet. "A Racial Chameleon in a Hidebound World." *New York Times,* 8 October 1992, C17, 21.

McCaffery, Larry. *The Metafictional Muse: The Works of Robert Coover, Donald Barthelme, and William H. Gass.* Pittsburgh: University of Pittsburgh Press, 1982.

Miller, Jean Baker, M.D. "The Construction of Anger in Women.and Men." *Works in Progress,* Stone Center for Developmental Services and Studies, Wellesley College, 1983.

Mitchell, Louise. "Slave Markets Typify Exploitation of Domestics." 1940. In *Black Women in White America: A Documentary History,* edited by Gerda Lerner. 1972. New York: Vintage, 1973. 229–231.

Mizruchi, Ephraim H. *Regulating Society: Marginality and Social Control in Historical Perspective.* New York: The Free Press/Macmillan, 1983.

Mootry, Maria K. " 'Down the Whirlwind of Good Rage': An Introduction to Gwendolyn Brooks." In Mootry and Smith 1–17.

———. " 'Tell It Slant': Disguise and Discovery as Revisionist Poetic Discourse in *The Bean Eaters*." In Mootry and Smith, 177–92.

Mootry, Maria K., and Gary Smith, eds. *A Life Distilled: Gwendolyn Brooks, Her Poetry and Fiction.* Urbana and Chicago: University of Illinois Press, 1987.

Morris, Meaghan. *The Pirate's Fiancée: Feminism, Reading, Postmodernism.* London and New York: Verso, 1988.

Mouffe, Chantal, ed. "Hegemony and Ideology in Gramsci." Translated by Denise Derôme. In *Gramsci and Marxist Theory.* Edited by Mouffe. London: Routledge & Kegan Paul, 1979. 168–204.

———. "Hegemony and New Political Subjects: Toward a New Concept of Democracy." Translated by Stanley Gray; In *Marxism and the Interpretation of Culture.* Edited by Cary Nelson and Lawrence Grossberg. Urbana and Chicago: University of Illinois Press, 1988. 89–104.

Mulvey, Laura. "Afterthoughts on 'Visual Pleasure and Narrative Cinema' Inspired by *Duel in the Sun*." *Framework* 15–17 (1981): 12–15.

———. "Changes." *Discourse* 7 (1985): 11–30.

———. "Visual Pleasure and Narrative Cinema." *Screen* 16:3 (Autumn 1975): 6–18.

Newman, Robert D. *Understanding Thomas Pynchon.* Columbia: University of South Carolina Press, 1986.

Nicholson, Linda, ed. *Feminism/Postmodernism.* New York: Routledge, 1990.

Nin, Anaïs. *Cities of the Interior.* 1961. Chicago: The Swallow Press, 1974.

———. *The Diary of Anaïs Nin.* Edited by Gunther Stuhlmann. 7 vols. New York: Harcourt Brace Jovanovich, 1966–1980.

———. *Henry and June.* San Diego: Harcourt Brace Jovanovich, 1986.

Olsen, Lance. "Pynchon's New Nature: The Uncertainty Principle and Indeterminacy in *The Crying of Lot 49*." *Canadian Review of American Studies* 14:2 (Summer 1983): 153–63.

Owens, Craig. "The Allegorical Impulse: Toward a Theory of Postmodernism." *October* 12 (Spring 1980): 67–86, and 13 (Summer 1980): 59–80.

———. "The Discourse of Others: Feminists and Postmodernism." Foster, 57–82.

Page, Clarence. "A noble attempt by Irish kids to become 'black.' " *Chicago Tribune,* 18 September 1991, sec. 1, p. 17.

Palmeri, Frank. "Neither Literally Nor as Metaphor: Pynchon's *The Crying of Lot 49* and the Structure of Scientific Revolutions." *ELH* 54:4 (Winter 1987): 979–99.

Pearce, Richard, ed. *Critical Eassays on Thomas Pynchon.* Boston: G. K. Hall & Company, 1981.

———. "Where're They At, Where're They Going? Thomas Pynchon and the

American Novel in Motion." 1980. In *Critical Essays on Thomas Pynchon*, 213–229.

Pynchon, Thomas. *The Crying of Lot 49*. 1966. New York: Harper & Row/ Perennial, 1990.

Quilligan, Maureen. "Thomas Pynchon and the Language of Allegory." 1979. In Pearce, *Critical Essays on Thomas Pynchon*, 187–212.

Radhakrishnan, R. "Poststructuralist Politics: Towards a Theory of Coalition." In Kellner, 301–32.

Radicalesbians. "The Woman-Identified Woman." In Jay and Young, 172–77.

Renza, Louis A. *"A White Heron" and the Question of Minor Literature*. Madison: University of Wisconsin Press, 1984.

Rubin, Gayle. "The Traffic in Women: Notes on the 'Political Economy' of Sex." In *Toward an Anthropology of Women*, edited by Rayna R. Reiter. New York: Monthly Review Press, 1975. 157–210.

Sacks, Oliver. "Tics." *New York Review of Books*, 29 January 1987, 37–41.

Saussure, Ferdinand de. *Course in General Linguistics*. Edited by Charles Bally and Albert Sechehaye, with Albert Riedlinger; translated by Wade Baskin. 1959. New York: McGraw-Hill, 1966.

Schreiber, Flora Rheta. *Sybil*. Chicago: Henry Regnery Company, 1973.

Schwartz, Richard Alan. "Postmodernist Baseball." *Modern Fiction Studies* 33:1 (Spring 1987): 135–149.

Sedgwick, Eve Kosofsky. *Between Men: English Literature and Male Homosocial Desire*. New York: Columbia University Press, 1985.

Shaw, Harry B. *Gwendolyn Brooks*. Boston: Twayne Publishing, 1980.

———. "*Maud Martha*: The War with Beauty." In Mootry and Smith, 254–70.

Shelton, Frank W. "Humor and Balance in Coover's *The Universal Baseball Association, Inc.*" *Critique: Studies in Modern Fiction*. 17:1: 78–90.

Spillers, Hortense J. " 'An Order of Constancy': Notes on Brooks and the Feminine." *The Centennial Review* 29:2 (Spring 1985): 223–48.

Sterritt, David. "Singing Soul in Dublin." *Christian Science Monitor*, 9 September 1991; 13.

Suleiman, Susan Rubin. *Subversive Intent: Gender, Politics, and the Avant-Garde*. Cambridge: Harvard University Press, 1990.

Tani, Stefano. "The Dismemberment of the Detective." *Diogenes* 120 (Winter 1982): 22–41.

Thigpen, Corbett H., and Hervey M. Cleckley. *The Three Faces of Eve*. New York: McGraw-Hill, 1957.

Todorov, Tzvetan. "Heroic Narratives of the Warsaw Ghetto." Lecture delivered at Brandeis University, 13 October 1988.

———. "Style." In Oswald Ducrot and Tzvetan Todorov, *Encyclopedic Dictionary of the Sciences of Language*, translated by Catherine Porter. Baltimore: The Johns Hopkins University Press, 1979. 300–304.

Trachtenberg, Stanley. *Understanding Donald Barthelme*. Columbia: University of South Carolina Press, 1990.

Tucker, Marcia. "Director's Foreword." In Ferguson, Gever, Trinh, and West, 7–8.

Vertigo. Directed by Alfred Hitchcock. Paramount, 1958.

Virilio, Paul. *Speed and Politics.* Translated by Mark Polizzotti. New York: Semiotext(e), 1986.

Washington, Booker T. *Up from Slavery.* Garden City, NY: Doubleday, Page, and Company, 1901.

Washington, Mary Helen. "Plain, Black, and Decently Wild: The Heroic Possibilities of *Maud Martha.*" In *The Voyage In: Fictions of Female Development,* edited by Elizabeth Abel, Marianne Hirsch, and Elizabeth Langland. Hanover, N.H.: University Press of New England for Dartmouth College, 1983. 270–286.

———. " 'Taming all that anger down': Rage and Silence in Gwendolyn Brooks's *Maud Martha.*" In Gates, *Black Literature and Literary Theory,* 249–62.

Waugh, Patricia. *Metafiction: The Theory and Practice of Self-Conscious Fiction.* New Accents series, general editor Terence Hawkes. London and New York: Routledge, 1984.

Waugh, Tom. "Men's Pornography: Gay vs. Straight." *Jump Cut* 30 (March 1985). 30–35.

Weinraub, Bernard. "A TV Gofer Named Clinton with a Famous Brother." *New York Times,* 8 October 1992, C17, 22.

West, Cornel. "Black Culture and Postmodernism." In *Remaking History,* edited by Barbara Kruger and Phil Mariani. Dia Art Fountation, Discussions in Contemporary Culture, No. 4. Seattle, Wash: Bay Press, 1989. 87–96.

———. "Postmodernity and Afro-America." *Prophetic Fragments.* Grand Rapids, Mich.: Eerdmans; Trenton, N.J.: Africa World Press, 1988. 168–170.

West, Nathanael. *The Complete Works of Nathanael West.* New York: Farrar, Straus and Cudahy, 1957.

Whitfield, Stephen J. *A Death in the Delta: The Story of Emmett Till.* New York: The Free Press, 1988.

Wilde, Alan. *Horizons of Assent: Modernism, Postmodernism, and the Ironic Imagination.* 1981. Philadelphia: University of Pennsylvania Press, 1987.

Wilde, Oscar. *The Importance of Being Earnest.* 1899. New York: Dover, 1990.

Woolf, Virginia. *Mrs. Dalloway.* 1925. San Diego: Harvest/Harcourt Brace Jovanovich, 1990.

Yeats, William Butler. "Among School Children." In *The Collected Poems.* New York: Macmillan, 1933. 249–251.

Zebrahead. Directed by Anthony Drazan. Sony/Triumph, 1992.

INDEX

Abernethy, Peter L., on *The Crying of Lot 49*, 166
Abrams, M.H., on postmodernism, 19
Adorno, Theodor. *See* Horkheimer, Max, and Theodor Adorno
Aestheticism, modernist, 20–21, 23, 137
African-American culture
  in *The Commitments* (Parker), 189–94
  and postmodernism, 4, 213 n.1
African-American musical form, 140
  blues, 136–37, 140
  commercialization of, 136–37
  individual/collective tension in, 135–37
  jazz, 135–36
Anderson, Laurie, 30, 31, 42, 49, 51
  on the ambiguity of signs, 200 n.10
  on digital electronics, 201 n.18
  and West's novels, 199 n.1
Apollinaire, Guillaume
  and the calligram, 34
  "L'Oeillet," 36–37
Apollinairean calligram
  Foucault on, 34, 36–37
  in *Miss Lonelyhearts*, 34–36
Avant-garde, the, 5–7

Baker, Ella, and Marvel Cooke, on domestic slave markets, 109–10
Baker, Houston
  on blues, 136–37, 140
  on Brooks, 93–95

Barnes, Djuna. *See also Nightwood*
  and feminism, 204 n.10
  lesbianism of, 78, 88, 204 n.14
  Nin on, 73–74
Barth, John, on postmodernism, 146
Barthelme, Donald, 27–28, 146, 187–88
  work of
    "dreck" in, 153–54
    human subjectivity in, 148–49, 155
    indeterminacy of signs in, 150
    and the linguistic problematic, 147–53
    postmodernity in, 155–56
    postmodern subjectivity in, 165, 171
    structural disjuncture in, 152–54
    subjective fragmentation in, 147, 149
  specific works:
    "Alice," 154
    "Balloon, The," 154–55
    "Brain Damage," 147
    "Can We Talk?," 154
    "Edward and Pia," 153–54
    "Few Moments of Sleeping and Waking, A," 153–54
    "Indian Uprising, The," 150
    "Me and Miss Mandible," 150
    "Report," 151–52
    "Robert Kennedy Saved from Drowning," 149–50, 152–53
    "See the Moon?," 147

free indirect discourse in, 169–70
ontological instability in, 170–71
postmodernism of, 168, 171
semantic multiplicity in, 168
subjective incoherency in, 171
summarized, 165–66
Curtis, Bruce, on Santa Claus, 209 n.22

Deleuze, Gilles, and Félix Guattari, on minor literature, 17–19
Derridean deferral, 37
Digital electronics, 201 n.18
Disciplinary power
Foucault on, 43–44
and social order, 43–46, 201 n.17
Ditsky, John M., on Barthelme, 148
Douglass, Frederick, on resistance to power, 53
Doyle, Roddy. See The Commitments
Duhamel, Georges, on film, 51
Durand, Régis. See Couturier, Maurice, and Régis Durand

Eliot, T. S.
and Nightwood, 206 n.21
"Tradition and the Individual Talent," 136–37
Ellison, Ralph. See also Invisible Man
on jazz, 135–37, 140

Feminism
and Barnes, 204 n.10
and lesbianism, 70, 204 n.13
in Nightwood, 25, 74–75, 78–81, 83, 88–89
in Nin's work, 25, 60–61, 65, 70–73, 88–89
and universalism, 91–92
Ferguson, Russell, on social marginality, 12–13
Field, Andrew, on Barnes, 78
Film
Benjamin on, 50–51
in The Day of the Locust, 50
Duhamel on, 51
Horkheimer and Adorno on, 50
as mechanism of social control, 49, 51, 53
and social marginality, 188

Film industry, in The Day of the Locust, 49, 51–53
Foucault, Michel
on the Apollinairean calligram, 34, 36–37
on disciplinary power, 43–44
on René Magritte, 36
on resistance to power, 53–54
on "subject position," 206 n.2
Frank, Joseph, on Nightwood, 205 n.17
Free indirect discourse, in The Crying of Lot 49, 169–70
Freud, Sigmund, on identification, 203–4 n.9

Gallagher, Bronagh, on The Commitments (Parker), 193
Galloway, David, on West, 33
Gass, William H., on metafiction, 156
Gates, Henry Louis, Jr., on Invisible Man, 209–10 n.3
Gaze, male
in Cities of the Interior, 62–63
and female subjectivity, 65, 67–69
in homosexual encounters, 202 n.2
theorized, 66–67
in Vertigo, 68–69
Gordon, Lois, on Barthelme, 147
Graff, Gerald, on postmodernism, 15
Gramsci, Antonio, on hegemony, 99
Guattari, Félix. See Deleuze, Gilles, and Félix Guattari

Habermas, Jürgen, 4
on modernity, 5
on the postmodern, 5, 8–9
Hansen, Arlen J., on The UBA, 160–61
Hassan, Ihab
on postmodernism, 15, 26, 146
Hegemony
in Brooks's poetry, 98–99, 102–3
Gramsci on, 99
Laclau and Mouffe on, 99, 207–8 n.13
Mouffe on, 99, 207–8 n.13
Heroism, sacrificial, in West's novels, 53–54
Hitchcock, Alfred. See Vertigo

Hole, Christina, on Santa Claus, 209
n.22
Hollywood. *See* film industry
Homophobia, in Nin's work, 25, 71–
73, 203–4 n.9
Homosexuality
and homosociality, 25, 70–74, 78,
88, 203–4 n.9
in *Invisible Man,* 121
and the male gaze, 202 n.2
Nin on, 71–72
Homosociality. *See* homosexuality
hooks, bell
on African-American experience and
postmodernism, 4
on postmodern "alienation," 197 n.1
Horkheimer, Max, and Theodor Adorno
on film, 50
on mass culture, 50–51
Hubbard, Stacy Carson, on Plath, 205
n.16
Humanism, 48–49, 56
Hutcheon, Linda, 4
on postmodernism vs. postmodernity,
197 n.2

Identification, Freud on, 203–4 n.9
Invisible Man (Ellison), 188
art/politics dichotomy in, 127, 130–
31, 135, 137–38
black accommodationism in, 123–24
black subjectivity in, 116, 126–28,
137–43, 163
color politics in, 122–25
community identification in, 128–29,
133, 135, 139–40
homosexuality in, 121
identity formation in, 26–27, 116–
22, 124–28, 131–33, 135, 138–
42, 209–10 n.3
individual/collective tension in, 127–
33, 135, 137–40
leadership function in, 129–30, 132,
139
minstrel show in, 120, 131, 210 n.7
modernism of, 122, 137
oratory in, 126–27, 129–32, 139–40
race relations in, 117–22, 124–28,
143

"signification" in, 125–26, 141–43
women in, 133–35

Jameson, Fredric, 4, 21
on "alienation" vs. "fragmentation,"
8, 197 n.1
on cognitive mapping, 8–9, 143
on Lyotard, 7
on modernism, 122, 161
on postmodernism, 7–11, 26, 146,
193–95
JanMohamed, Abdul, and David Lloyd
on minor literature, 17
use of "minority" by, 199 n.12
Jazz. *See* African-American musical
form
Jewish identity, and the biography of
West, 39–41

Kantian sublime
Lyotard on, 6
Jameson on, 8
Kingston, Maxine Hong. *See The
Woman Warrior*
Klinkowitz, Jerome, on Barthelme, 148

Lacan, Jacques
on the "mirror stage," 117
on the unconscious, 200 n.11
Laclau, Ernesto, and Chantal Mouffe, on
hegemony, 99, 207–8 n.13
Leland, John, on *The Crying of Lot 49,*
167
Lerner, Gerda, 111–12
Lesbianism
of Barnes, 78, 88, 204 n.14
and feminism, 70, 204 n.13
in *Nightwood,* 25, 74, 77–78, 88,
206 n.21
Nin on, 73, 204 n.14
Lévi-Strauss, Claude, 69–70
Lloyd, David. *See* JanMohamed, Abdul,
and David Lloyd
Lukács, Georg
on modernism, 122, 136
on modernist alienation, 161
on rationalization, 122
on reification, 118